D0907031

DOWN HOME

HOME

ORIGINS OF THE

AFRO-AMERICAN

SHORT STORY

ROBERT BONE

COLUMBIA UNIVERSITY PRESS

NEW YORK

COLUMBIA UNIVERSITY PRESS   MORNINGSIDE EDITION   1988
COLUMBIA UNIVERSITY PRESS
New York   Guildford, Surrey

Copyright © 1975 by Robert Bone
Preface to the Morningside Edition copyright © 1988
COLUMBIA UNIVERSITY PRESS

LIBRARY OF CONGRESS CATALOGING-IN-PUBLICATION DATA

Bone, Robert.
Down home : origins of the Afro-American short story /
Robert Bone, — Morningside ed.
p. cm.
Reprint, with new pref. Originally published: New York : Putnam, 1975.
Originally published in series: New perspectives on Black America.
Bibliography: p.
Includes index.
ISBN 0-231-06858-1.   ISBN 0-231-06859-X (Pbk.)
1. Short stories, American—Afro-American authors—History and
criticism.   2. Pastoral fiction, American—Afro-American authors—
History and criticism.   3. Southern States in literature.   4. Afro-
Americans in literature.   5. Folklore in literature.   I. Title.
PS153.N5B59 1988
813′.01′09896073—dc19   88-25841
CIP

Printed in the United States of America

For my daughters:

une espèce de réparation

All sorrows can be borne if you
put them into a story.

—ISAK DINESEN

Contents

Preface to the
Morningside Edition

THE early seventies, when *Down Home* was being written, were more an aftermath than a time of new beginnings. By the mid-sixties, a new generation of black intellectuals had emerged, and the voice of revolutionary nationalism was heard across the land. Its chief spokesman was LeRoi Jones, whose poems and plays, stories and essays marked a radical transformation of Afro-American writing. Key books in shaping the new consciousness, in addition to those of Jones, were Frantz Fanon, *The Wretched of the Earth* (1963), Alex Haley, *The Autobiography of Malcolm X* (1965), and Addison Gayle, *The Black Aesthetic* (1971). Black empowerment was in the air, and if white critics stood in the way of "decolonization," so much the worse for them.

Proponents of a Black Aesthetic were quick to pronounce their turf off-limits to marauding whites. And that made matters awkward for those of us who, despite a lifelong devotion to the field, were now to be debarred, on racial grounds, from attempting to understand, much less evaluate, the cultural expression of black America. I had published a pioneering study entitled *The Negro Novel in America* (1958; revised edition, 1965), and I wanted to move on to the short story form. But how to function in a hostile climate where black militants were declaring me ineligible to suit up for the game? That was my quandary, as I contemplated a book on the origins of the Afro-American short story.

Being of a stubborn and cantankerous New England temperament, I decided simply to proceed. The best way, it seemed to me, to deal with a philosophy that denied me access, as a critic, to Afro-American material, was to write another useful book. At the same time, I was very strongly drawn to an aesthetic theory emerging in the work of two black authors of an older generation: Ralph Ellison and Albert Murray. Their conceptual model, which is best described as a blues aesthetic, was older by three decades than the Black Aesthetic currently in vogue, emanating in fact from the Tuskegee campus in the mid-1930s, when LeRoi Jones was a child of two. In the body of this essay, I shall attempt to reconstruct this theory of the blues, as it impinged on my own sensibility, and the act of composition in which I was engaged.

Tuskegee

Ralph Ellison arrived at Chehaw Station in the late summer of 1933, having traveled from his native Oklahoma City to Macon County, Alabama, by empty boxcar.[1] He had to vamp it, as ole Gravel-Voice would say, on a sidedoor Pullman car. Albert Murray, a home-boy from Magazine Point, Alabama, on the outskirts of Mobile, made the campus scene two years later by Greyhound bus. Ellison, who was a music major, had come to study under the black composer William Dawson, while Murray was an education major, and after graduation in 1939 stayed on for several years to teach at his alma mater. Since Ellison left Tuskegee for New York at the end of his junior year, the two men were both on campus only during Murray's freshman year (1935–36), but that was long enough to establish an enduring friendship, and lay the groundwork for a theory of the blues.

Both men brought a rich knowledge of the blues tradition to their undergraduate years at Tuskegee. A trumpet player from the age of eight, Ellison had spent many a summer afternoon practicing the hard-driving blues of Clara Smith,

Ida Cox, and Ma Rainey, who made regular appearances in his hometown. Growing up in Oklahoma City, he had a deep respect for the work of such bluesmen as Jimmy Rushing and Charlie Christian, and for the tradition of southwestern jazz that culminated in the Basie band. Murray was not an instrumentalist, but an aficionado of the country blues from his preschool days. By his early manhood, he had developed an all-consuming passion for the blues-based compositions of Count Basie, Duke Ellington, and Earl Hines.

Their musical exposure at Tuskegee was intense. Ellison, who had a strong background in classical music as well as jazz, continued his formal studies under William Dawson, while at the same time, he was blowing trumpet in the marching band, and enjoying an extra-curricular immersion in the blues. Murray, in the after-curfew darkness of the Sage Hall lounge, was picking up the Duke, Cab Calloway, and Chick Webb on the Harlem networks, and Earl Hines from the Grand Terrace in Chicago. Such pursuits, as Murray recalls in *South to a Very Old Place,* were among the indispensable dimensions of Tuskegee-ness.

Still more intense was their discovery of the literary world, in part a result of independent reading, and in part an initiation rite, presided over by Morteza Sprague, head of Tuskegee's English department. Both Murray and Ellison have expressed their deep affection for this gifted teacher, who played a crucial role in their intellectual development. An excellent collection of modern authors was at hand, to be sure, in the Hollis Burke Frissell Library, and both were avid readers. But it was Mort Sprague who guided these questing undergraduates through the strange landscapes of literary modernism. And in so doing, he helped them to reorient their hopes and dreams, awakened their ambitions to become serious writers, and encouraged them to aim high, to play the literary game in the major leagues.

It was this young black professor, trained at Hamilton, Howard, and Columbia, who led them toward the alpine regions of the Western epic, as exemplified in the Greek tragedies, the plays of Shakespeare, and such contemporary novels as *Ulysses, The Magic Mountain,* and *Absalom, Absalom!* He invited them to contemplate the possibilities of brown-skin heroism, and to consider the relevance of the pica-resque novel, with its outlaw heroes, to American Negro life. Immersed as they were in the blues idiom, they began to make connections between the musical and literary spheres. Their undergraduate explorations did not amount as yet to a blues aesthetic, but the crucial ingredients were all in place. In the course of a close friendship lasting over several de-cades, these two aspiring authors, transplanted from the South and Southwest to New York, hammered out between them a poetics of the blues.

For ten years or so their paths diverged, Ellison moving to New York while Murray stayed on at Tuskegee; Ellison serv-ing in the Merchant Marine and Murray in the Air Force; the two men meeting only on rare occasions during the war. But in 1947–48, when Ellison was already well into the composition of *Invisible Man,* Murray came up to Gotham to study for his master's degree at NYU. It was then that their mature collaboration may be said to begin. After 1948 they corresponded often, sharing news of work-in-progress, dis-covering shared perspectives, and renewing personal ties as circumstances would allow. These contacts, sustained across the years, were deepened and extended after 1962, when Murray retired from the Air Force and settled in New York.[2]

Ellison's Blues

Ellison was the first to enter print on the subject of the blues. In the summer of 1945, with the writing of *Invisible Man* barely under way, he published an essay in the *Antioch Review* called "Richard Wright's Blues." Ostensibly a review of *Black Boy,* the piece was in actuality an effort to expound the philosophical foundations of the blues. Ellison goes straight to the essentials: to the lyricism of the form; to the blues lyric as a poetic confrontation with reality. As such, the blues offer no solutions to the problems they engage; rather, through their tragicomic vision of the world, they foster a toughness of spirit, a resiliency among those who cultivate them as an art. Stressing the transcendence of the blues, their potential as a mode of triumph over pain, Ellison establishes a basic metaphor that compares the blues singer or instrumentalist to a wounded quail.

In retrospect, we can see that this early essay is an announcement of his own intentions in *Invisible Man.* For everywhere in this monumental novel we hear the music of the blues. Chapter 9, for example, which attempts to define a blues sensibility, begins and ends with a down home blues. The episode of the pushcart man, singing so strangely of his love in the streets of Harlem, is dominated by the color blue. The mocking pile of blueprints that he hauls in his cart is emblematic of the white society that puts its faith in Plans, while his song confronts the ambiguities to which the human species is in fact exposed. Not certainty, but ambiguity, is the essence of man's fate, and his best means of coping is not through advance planning, as in scored music, but improvisation, which is the essence of the blues.[3]

Still more crucial to the novel's structure is the figure of Trueblood, the black sharecropper who, after impregnating both wife and daughter, sings some blues "ain't never been sang before." (I think of them as the Incest Blues.) Here is a blues hero of truly oedipal proportions! Trueblood is in fact an incarnation of Ellison's wounded quail, for he suffers an unhealing ax-wound at the hands of his outraged wife. And subtly, almost imperceptibly, by virtue of Ellison's artful juxtapositions (a trick he learned from T. S. Eliot), this unhealing wound fuses at the symbolic level with the festering foot of Philoctetes, and we move within the orbit not only of Sophocles' play, but of Edmund Wilson's theory of art set forth in *The Wound and the Bow.*

In the *Saturday Review* of July 28, 1962, Ellison published an essay that adds a significant dimension to his theory of the blues. Featuring the music of Charlie Parker, and entitled "On Bird, Bird-Watching, and Jazz," this piece offers yet another metamorphosis of the wounded quail: "For the postwar jazznik, Parker was Bird, a suffering, psychically wounded, law-breaking, life-affirming hero." Expanding his root metaphor, Ellison compares Parker to the mockingbird, *Mimus polyglottos,* who "takes off on the songs of other birds, inflating, inverting, and turning them wrong side out." What Ellison is analogizing here is the bluesman's tendency to "riff" on other people's tunes, as Duke Ellington takes off, in "Black and Tan Fantasy," from Chopin's B-flat piano concerto. Or as Ellison himself, by his evocation of a mockingbird, is riffing on Walt Whitman's "Out of the Cradle Endlessly Rocking."

The musical language of the riff, as understood by Ellison and Murray, explains the relationship of black writers to Western literary forms. Always somewhat mocking, as in the dance form of the cakewalk, the riff style can lend itself to burlesque and parody, but being sly, ironical, and frequently ambiguous, like a Louis Armstrong blues, it can also function as a sort of grudging compliment. Failing to appreciate these subtleties, the Black Aestheticians would sever all connections with Western literature, mistaking these bold appropriations and transformations for the servile imitation of "Eurocentric" models. For an antidote to such cultural myopia, Ellison would prescribe a closer look at the mockingbird, whose indisputable virtuosity and originality are in no way impaired by his habit of riffing on someone else's tunes.

Murray's Blues

When Major Albert Murray retired from the United States Air Force in 1962, he was an energetic man of forty-six. Having secured his supply lines and established his defense perimeters, he was free at last to write. Some twenty-five years and six books later, he can look back with satisfaction on an impressive, if late-blooming career. His first three books, which were published while I was writing *Down Home*, clarified many thorny problems, and helped this Connecticut Yankee to find his way around the briar patch of Southern Negro life.

The Omni-Americans (1970) is primarily a sharp attack on "social science fiction," which Murray accuses of projecting false images of brownskin reality. To the survey methods and pathological biases of contemporary social science he counterposes an epistemology of the blues. Unlike the discipline of sociology, with its rigid Cartesian categories, the blues idiom, which is at bottom an artistic mode, offers a more flexible response to the rich textures of Afro-American life. Based on rhythm-oriented and dance-oriented improvisations, "swinging the blues," for those bred to the style, is a way of ritualizing experience, and thus of rendering it meaningful. Hence Duke Ellington's famous dictum, "It don't mean a thing if it ain't got that swing!"

From these epistemological beginnings, Murray constructs a theory of American culture. As a mode of knowledge, the blues style is exploratory, impromptu, pragmatic. It is thus uniquely suited to a nation of pioneering stock, whose national character Murray traces to the frontier humor, irreverent wisdom, sudden changes, and adroit adaptations of the Andrew Jackson era. Nor is the blues style any less relevant to the American future than the American past. A nation that routinely confronts the discontinuities of technological change, and aspires to the exploration of outer space, is closely attuned to the extemporizing spirit of the blues. It is this affinity that causes Murray to speak of the blues as an Omni-American music, appropriate not only to the ever-shifting circumstances of American life, but to the universal predicament of contemporary man.

South to a Very Old Place (1971) serves to root the blues idiom in its southern context. For the blues were born when stars fell on Alabama; they are not indigenous to Africa or anywhere else. This book is a celebration of the author's southern identity, and a tribute to his southern ancestors: musical, educational, journalistic, and literary. Most are black, but many are white, since he believes that your real ancestors are those in whose footsteps you elect to walk. The regional dimension of Murray's writing sets him apart from such northern blacks as James Baldwin and LeRoi Jones, even as his southern heritage leads him to claim kinship with such white authors as Robert Penn Warren, William Faulkner, and Walker Percy.

In *The Hero and the Blues* (1973), Murray develops the concept of an epic hero adequate to the challenges of the modern world. His literary exemplar is Joseph, hero of Thomas Mann's tetralogy, *Joseph and His Brothers*, who is sold into bondage, but rises above his condition of servitude to become Pharoah's chief amanuensis. Murray sees Joseph, moreover, as a *blues* hero, since the blues style, in its spiritual essence, has always been a technique for making the best of a bad situation. Indeed, Murray's doctrine of "antagonistic cooperation" holds that there can be no heroes without dragons, no transcendence without adversity. And in the land of the Ku Klux Klan, dragons have never been in short supply. The result has been, in Afro-American folklore, a succession of such blues heroes as Brer Rabbit, John Henry, and Stagolee.

Note well that the blues hero, as Murray conceives him, is not an exclusive ethnic property, belonging to Afro-Americans alone. Rather he has many incarnations, appearing as the picaresque hero of the Joseph novels, the *nada*-confrontation hero of Hemingway's fiction, the Chaplinesque hero of slapstick and farce, or the detective-story hero who walks these mean streets. It is enough that he has the courage to confront chaos, and the requisite qualities of nimbleness, improvisation, and adaptability to succeed in his quest. No ethnic group, in short, has a corner on this brand of heroism, nor is debarred from producing pathfinders and trailblazers of its own. None of which is to subtract one percentile from Murray's ethnicity quotient, which is so conspicuously high, but rather to appreciate the paradox that the more James Joyce was exposed to cosmopolitan values, the more Irish he became.

Down Home

I have traced the development of a blues aesthetic through the early work of Ellison and Murray in part to set the record straight. For a prominent scholar in the field, intent on ideologizing the blues, has done less than justice to the past. In a recent book called *Blues, Ideology, and Afro-American Literature* (1984), Houston Baker has advanced the claim that the Black Aesthetic generation was the first to develop a literary theory of the blues.[4] But that is to bestow an accolade on the Black Arts Movement of the 1960s that rightfully belongs to Ellison and Murray. It amounts to badmouthing one's ancestors in order to affirm one's generational identity.

This false attribution is all the more unjust because the antipathy of Murray and Ellison toward the Black Arts Movement is well known. Murray makes a scathing attack in *South to a Very Old Place,* and follows up with some heavy body blows in *The Hero and the Blues.* As for Ellison, one has only to read his review of LeRoi Jones' *Blues People* to grasp his distinction between an aesthetic and a sociology of the blues.[5] Folk music can be approached, to be sure, from many points of view, including the political or ideological. What makes the Murray / Ellison approach unique, however, is its focus on the blues as an art form, as a source of inspiration to a writer as he approaches the problems of his craft.

In this essay, I have sought primarily to honor Ellison and Murray for their pioneering work, and incidentally to shed light on the genesis of *Down Home.* What, after all, are the essential features of the blues? First, an unpleasant reality to face, a dragon to be slain. And second, a constructive action, by which the blues hero rises above his difficulties. In 1969, when I began *Down Home,* I had no problem finding a dragon. Certain black intellectuals were challenging on a priori grounds my right to do the work that I had trained to do. And while I would lay no claim to epic stature, I did resolve to take constructive action by writing a book whose partial aim would be to demonstrate that certain racist theories were in error.

Ellison and Murray pointed the way, by focusing on the *interaction* between the vernacular and high literary traditions. In *Down Home,* I would stress the vernacular dimension in my treatment of Afro-American folklore: of Brer Rabbit, the animal fables in which he appears, the conjure stories, and ghost tales. At the same time, I would not ignore or undervalue the Western literary forms appropriated by black short story writers and adapted to their own ends. In particular, I would feature the modes of pastoral and anti-pastoral that seemed to dominate the first half century of the Afro-American short story. Such were my intentions at the outset of this project. To what extent they have been realized, you now must be the judge.

Postscript

If *Down Home* were being written today, two important changes in the data base would be necessary. First, the Black Periodical Fiction Project, under the direction of Professor Henry Louis Gates, has turned up an estimated 26,000 items of fiction that appeared in newspapers and periodicals between 1827 and 1940. That is an awesome figure, and it calls into question my strategy of focusing on short story *collections* as an index to achievement in the form. Second, our notion of Eric Walrond's output as a short story writer needs to be enlarged. Due largely to the research of his grandson, Mr. Frank Stewart, some twenty uncollected stories should be added to the titles in my bibliography. This oversight, which understates Walrond's importance as an author of the

Harlem Renaissance, will be put to rights in my forthcoming study of Eric Walrond.

NOTES

1. My sources for this section include the "Tuskegee" chapter of Murray's *South to a Very Old Place,* and various essays and interviews in Ellison's *Shadow and Act.*

2. My source for this account of the Ellison-Murray relationship, after their Tuskegee years, was a series of telephone interviews with Albert Murray in May of 1988.

3. I am indebted for certain readings of *Invisible Man* to Edith Schor's unpublished doctoral dissertation, "The Early Fiction of Ralph Ellison: the Genesis of *Invisible Man,*" Teachers College, Columbia University, 1973.

4. See Baker, *Blues, Ideology, and Afro-American Literature,* p. 112.

5. See *The New York Review of Books,* February 6, 1964.

WORKS CITED

HOUSTON BAKER: *Blues, Ideology, and Afro-American Literature.* Chicago and London: University of Chicago Press, 1984.

RALPH ELLISON: *Invisible Man.* New York: Random House, 1952.

——   *Shadow and Act.* New York: Random House, 1964.

ALBERT MURRAY: *The Omni-Americans.* New York: Outerbridge and Dienstfrey, 1970.

——   *South to a Very Old Place.* New York: McGraw-Hill, 1971.

——   *The Hero and the Blues.* Columbia, Missouri: University of Missouri Press, 1973.

Acknowledgments

To Herbert Hill, for conversations in the fall of 1968 which prompted me to undertake this study;

To Lawrence Graver of Williams College, for reading portions of the manuscript;

To Trygve Tholfsen of Teachers College, Columbia University, for his grasp of the human limitations and practical realities of authorship;

To the Faculty Research Fund of Teachers College, for a grant facilitating the initial purchase of books and materials;

To the Center for Twentieth Century Studies of the University of Wisconsin at Milwaukee, for its generous support during the fall of 1973;

To Mrs. Marjorie Content Toomer, for permission to quote from the Jean Toomer papers housed at Fisk University;

To my wife, Dorothea, who subsidized the enterprise in many ways;

To Jennifer Crewe of the Columbia University Press, for giving *Down Home* a second life.

Introduction

IN *The Lonely Voice*, Frank O'Connor develops a theory of the short story based on the concept of submerged population groups. These submerged populations may be ethnic, like Joyce's Dubliners or Babel's Jews; social-economic, like Maupassant's prostitutes or Turgenev's serfs; or even psychological, like Sherwood Anderson's grotesques or J. F. Powers' spoiled priests. The crucial factor is their marginality, their spiritual isolation from the dominant society. Out of this estrangement arises the storyteller's lonely voice, with its insistent moral claim that "These, too, are your brothers."

The best storytellers, according to O'Connor, are concerned with the theme of human loneliness. Moving beyond the obvious forms of social alienation, they universalize their theme by so depicting a submerged population that its circumstances come to represent the fate of modern man. Social marginality, in other words, functions as a metaphor: "Somewhere the tragedy ceases to be entirely one of justice and injustice, of society and its submerged population, and becomes a tragedy of human loneliness. At once the whole conception of the submerged population becomes enlarged and enriched."[1]

Some such process as O'Connor has described is surely at work in the short fiction of black Americans. From Charles Chesnutt's anguished slaves to Jean Toomer's deracinated intellectuals, from Langston Hughes' cooks and janitors and hoboes to Richard Wright's Mississippi sharecroppers, from

James Baldwin's storefront saints to James McPherson's troubled adolescents, black storytellers have designated various submerged populations and striven to give voice to their mute sufferings. And their best stories are precisely those in which social marginality acquires the force of myth.

In one respect, however, O'Connor's theory is flawed. He fails to discriminate sufficiently between *kinds* of submerged populations, stressing only their common feature: marginality. This leads to a serious distortion where ethnic populations are concerned. For marginality as such does not explain the remarkable vitality of Irish, Yiddish, or Afro-American short fiction. Rather we must look to the oral literatures created by these ethnic populations. Their jokes and proverbs, anecdotes and fables, legends and folktales are the cultural foundations on which their preeminence as storytellers rests.

O'Connor places, in short, too negative a value on ethnicity. Prostitutes and Irishmen may share a common marginality, but hookers do not possess a folk tradition that nourishes the art of storytelling. Dublin barflies, on the other hand, tell stories with the same natural grace as French Canadians play hockey. Fearing, perhaps, to be thought provincial, O'Connor has devised an ingenious theory that accords with the canons of literary modernism. But obfuscation is the chief result. For the simple truth remains that the Irish have a special gift for short fiction, nurtured by centuries of oral storytelling.

If O'Connor makes too little of his folk tradition, there are some who make too much. In the context of Afro-American writing, for example, critics of the nationalist school seek to foster the impression that black folklore is the primary source of black fiction. In point of fact, books by white authors are a far more important influence. These critics, eager to dissociate themselves from Western literary forms, have turned to black folklore as a cultural alternative. In folk forms they hope to discover the basis of a black esthetic. But they place a greater burden on their folk tradition than it can reasonably bear.

A folk tradition can enrich, but not supplant the written word. Black writers are not, after all, folk artists, nor can they repudiate their complex vision of the world. And insofar as they are *writers* as opposed to *raconteurs*, they become involved with Western literary forms. Cultural nationalists tend to minimize the difference between folk expression and a more self-conscious art. But Frank O'Connor is surely right to differentiate the public and communal art of the folktale from the private and individualistic art of the short story. A quantum leap occurs when the story enters print, and the storyteller moves from a supporting and assenting to a skeptical and critical audience.[2]

In any case, it is not so easy to secede from one's literary culture. The short story is an Occidental form; it was not invented by Asians, Africans, or Hopi Indians. If an author chooses to employ it, he becomes a part of the literary history of the West. To write short stories, moreover, it is necessary first to read a few, in order to acquire some notion of the possibilities inherent in the form. As it happens, most of the short fiction now in the world's libraries was written by white men. Serious short-story writers who are black must avail themselves of these models if they hope to become masters of the art.

"American Negro literature," according to Saunders Redding, "cannot be lopped off from the main body of American literary expression without doing grave harm to both. . . ."[3] The history of the Afro-American short story speaks for itself in this regard. The short fiction of Charles Chesnutt cannot be understood apart from that of Joel Chandler Harris and George Washington Cable. Similarly with Paul Laurence Dunbar and Thomas Nelson Page; Jean Toomer and Waldo Frank; Eric Walrond and Lafcadio Hearn. Even in the case of LeRoi Jones, a book like *Tales* cannot be approached without reference to the fiction of the Beat Generation.

The Afro-American short story is a child of mixed ancestry. Two cultural heritages meet and blend in its pages: the one

Euro-American, literary, cosmopolitan; the other African-derived, oral in expressive mode, rooted in the folk community. But as a child may be said to "favor" one or the other of his parents, so the Afro-American short story has more in common with its white counterpart than with the black folktale. To alter the figure, Afro-American writing is a variation on a theme. The theme is American; the variation black.

So much for the theoretical assumptions of the present work. I shall strive to give ethnicity its due, and to avoid O'Connor's specious "universalism." At the same time, I shall insist on the indebtedness of black short-story writers to Western literary forms. In particular, I hope to demonstrate that the alternating rhythms of the Afro-American short story are derived from the employment of two traditional literary modes: pastoral and antipastoral. Some preliminary definitions will therefore be required, before proceeding to the main argument.

The pastoral tradition stems in poetry from the *Idyls* of Theocritus and the *Eclogues* of Virgil; in prose, from the *Daphnis and Chloe* of Longus. In English literature, pastoral becomes a dominant form in the Elizabethan age, where it may be found not only in poetry, but drama and prose fiction. Edmund Spenser's *The Shepherd's Calendar* (poetry), John Fletcher's *The Faithful Shepherdess* (verse drama), and Sir Philip Sidney's *The Countess of Pembroke's Arcadia* (fiction) are the masterpieces of the form. In American letters, the pastoral mode has flourished more in prose than poetry, the major figures being Thoreau, Twain, Hemingway, and Robert Frost.

The major pastoral conventions, according to a recent critic, include "(1) people of a low socio-economic class, (2) living in simplicity and harmony, (3) against a background of rural nature. In the classical pattern, this subject emerges as (1) Corydon, Lycidas, and Amaryllis, (2) tending their flocks, weaving garlands, and singing songs, (3) out among the fields, caves, and brooks of Arcady. In the Christian-Judaic pattern, it is Adam and Eve, spinning and gardening in Eden."[4] The underlying assumption of the pastoral tradition is the superiority of simple, peasant life to that of the sophisticated, urbanized, or courtly upper class.

At first glance, the pastoral attitude would seem to be at fundamental odds with the black experience. Yet it is a fact that the pastoral impulse dominates the first half century or so of sustained black writing (roughly 1885 to 1935). Why this should be so is a complicated question that will be explored at length. Suffice it to observe for the moment that black American writing was a regional before it was an ethnic literature. Pastoral has always been the favored literary mode of the American South, whose agrarian values, classical ideals, and hierarchical social forms found in pastoral their natural vehicle.

The concept of antipastoral is perhaps better illustrated than defined.[5] Here are the opening stanzas of Christopher Marlowe's pastoral, "The Passionate Shepherd to His Love:"

> Come live with me and be my love,
> And we will all the pleasures prove
> That hills and valleys, dale and field,
> And all the craggy mountains yield.
>
> There will we sit upon the rocks
> And see the shepherds feed their flocks,
> By shallow rivers, to whose falls
> Melodious birds sing madrigals.

And here are the first two stanzas of Sir Walter Raleigh's antipastoral reply:

> If all the world and love were young
> And truth in every shepherd's tongue,

These pretty pleasures might me move
To live with thee and be thy love.

But time drives flocks from field to fold,
When rivers rage and rocks grow cold;
And Philomel becometh dumb;
The rest complains of cares to come.

Or consider a similar pairing from the eighteenth century. Here are the opening lines of Oliver Goldsmith's pastoral, "The Deserted Village":

Sweet Auburn! loveliest village of the plain,
Where health and plenty cheer'd the laboring swain,
Where smiling spring its earliest visit paid,
And parting summer's lingering blooms delay'd;
Dear lovely bowers of innocence and ease,
Seats of my youth, when every sport could please,
How often have I loiter'd on thy green,
Where humble happiness endear'd each scene!

And here are several lines from the opening section of George Crabbe's antipastoral, "The Village":

Yes, thus the Muses sing of happy swains,
Because the Muses never knew their pains:
They boast their peasants' pipes, but peasants now
Resign their pipes and plod beside the plough.
                    *   *   *
. . . I paint the Cot
As Truth will paint it, and as Bards will not.
                    *   *   *
Can poets soothe you, when you pine for bread,
By winding myrtles round your ruined shed?[6]

Just as the epic mode swells until it bursts into mock-epic, so the pastoral mode becomes more and more impossibly idyllic until it spills over into antipastoral. Thus we have genre and countergenre, the latter emerging as the traditional form exhausts itself. Antipastoral, it should be noted, has no autonomous existence. It is antithetical in nature, and always exists in tension with its opposite. Raleigh's poem is a satirical response to Marlowe's pastoral; Crabbe's is a "realistic" refutation of Goldsmith's overly idealized version of English peasant life.

Antipastoral, which is not a genre but a countergenre, may assume a variety of modes. We have already encountered two: satire in the case of Raleigh, and realism in that of Crabbe. To these must be added the picaresque, which Claudio Guillén designates as the chief alternative to pastoral.[7] But whatever its precise mode, the spirit of antipastoral is much the same. It reflects an ironic, rather than idyllic posture toward experience. Pastoral and antipastoral incorporate the rival claims of the ideal and the actual. Both claims have their place in literature, no less than life.

With the aid of these conceptual tools, the history of the Afro-American short story begins to manifest a recognizable design. Pastoralists like Paul Dunbar and Jean Toomer emerge in opposition to antipastoralists like Charles Chesnutt and Langston Hughes. Writers of the Harlem Renaissance, who for the most part adopt the pastoral mode, are set off against their successors of the Wright generation, who are inclined toward the picaresque. Pastoral or antipastoral never achieve exclusive dominion in the work of an individual or generation, but one or the other tendency is likely to gain the upper hand.

Pastoral and antipastoral are the "deep structures" of Afro-American short fiction. These literary forms spring from three primary sources, all intertwined, and all reflective of the black American's historical experience. First, his deep attachment to the Protestant tradition, and especially the Bible, whose pages are saturated, both in the Old and New

Testaments, with the rhetoric of pastoral. Second, his deep affection for the rural South, despite the terror and brutality which all too often were visited upon him within its precincts. And third, his deep anxiety concerning his future role in American society, which manifests itself on the emotional plane as a painful vacillation between hope and despair.

In her autobiography, *I Know Why the Caged Bird Sings*,[8] Maya Angelou describes a revival meeting in rural Arkansas. The preacher's text is Charity, but his not-too-secret theme is that "the mean whitefolks was going to get their come-uppance," if not in this world, surely in the next. "Charity," he intones, "is simple. . . . Charity is poor. . . . Charity is plain (107)." This is the rhetoric of Christian humility, but also of literary pastoral. "The Lord loved the poor and hated those cast high in the world. Hadn't He Himself said it would be easier for a camel to go through the eye of a needle than for a rich man to enter heaven (108)?" The last shall be first: such is the essence of the pastoral inversion.

Maya Angelou concludes her chapter with a passage which, in its illumination of the folk temperament, points implicitly to one major source of black literary pastoral: "They basked in the righteousness of the poor and the exclusiveness of the downtrodden. Let the whitefolks have their money and power and segregation and sarcasm and big houses and schools and lawns like carpets, and books, and mostly—mostly—let them have their whiteness. It was better to be meek and lowly, spat upon and abused for this little time than to spend eternity frying in the fires of hell (110-11)." This sentiment, in various secular metamorphoses, becomes the mainstay of much Afro-American short fiction.

To the extent of a black writer's disenchantment with his Protestant heritage, he is likely to incline toward antipastoral. Langston Hughes provides a case in point. Not without respect for the survival value of black religion, it is amply clear from the body of his work that he counts himself among the sinners rather than the saints of the black community. His poems and plays, novels and stories, are frequently irreverent in tone, and without exception lacking in the otherworldly (or Platonic) strain that underlies the pastoral ideal. Satire of the high and mighty, and a distinct readiness to challenge their supremacy in this world, is the hallmark of Hughes' fiction.

The alternating rhythm of pastoral and antipastoral likewise has its source in the black American's conflicting feelings toward the rural South. On the one hand, he is deeply moved by the natural beauty of the region, and on the other, repelled by its moral ugliness where his own existence is concerned. In a book like *Cane*, and especially its famous centerpiece, "Song of the Son," Jean Toomer apostrophizes the Southland in the accents of pastoral elegy. Yet Richard Wright's *Uncle Tom's Children*, whose mocking epigraph is taken from the popular song, "Is it true what they say about Dixie?" betrays an antipastoral bias so pronounced as to amount to a permanent revulsion from the black man's Southern homeland.

Beyond the matter of regional loyalty or its opposite lies the black man's deep ambivalence toward his position in American society. The oscillating pattern of pastoral and antipastoral originates in part in the black American's agonizing vacillation between hope and despair. Pastoral gives voice to his deepest yearnings for racial harmony and reconciliation, while antipastoral expresses his recurrent disillusionment, frustration, and despair. Neither mood is more authentic than the other; both have been experienced at one time or another by most black Americans. It follows that neither literary form is intrinsically superior; both are capable of rendering a profound psychological truth.

William Dawson's *Negro Symphony* has a movement entitled "Hope in the Night." This phrase seems to capture the spirit of much Afro-American writing. If a black author stresses the element of *hope* (the promise of America), he is likely to employ the pastoral mode. If he stresses *night* (the desecration of the Dream), he will move instinctively toward antipastoral. In our own era of disillusion and despair, it is tempting to endorse the latter mode. But before rejecting the pastoral tradition out of hand, we would do well to ponder what it means, even in the darkest night, to live devoid of hope.

We, here, are concerned with that early phase of Afro-American short fiction when hope was in the ascendancy and pastoral the predominant literary form. Either the vast majority of black Americans still lived in the rural South, or the Southern migrant, transplanted to the city pavements from the green fields of his youth, persisted in bestowing on the place of his nativity the affectionate epithet of "down home." It was a retrospective phase when Dunbar, writing at the turn of the century, looked back toward antebellum days, and when authors of the Harlem Renaissance, having congregated in the black metropolis, looked back with poignant yearning at the pastoral circumstances of their youth.

This penchant for idealizing the rural past is the very essence of the pastoral tradition. We are dealing here with two generations of black literary men who looked back on the rural South with much more fondness and affection than terror and revulsion. It was Richard Wright who pioneered the latter mode, and so we shall end this book short of *Uncle Tom's Children*, which marks the beginning of a new era in Afro-American cultural history. Henceforward urban styles of dress, manners, music, and literature would predominate. With the advent of Wright and his generation, black Arcadia may be said to have vanished. But while it persisted, it exercised a powerful hold on the black imagination.

Part I

The Masks of Slavery: 1885-1920

Disguise thyself as thou wilt, still, Slavery! said I, still thou art a bitter draught! and though thousands in all ages have been made to drink of thee, thou art no less bitter on that account.

—LAURENCE STERNE

Chapter 1

Literary Forebears

THE first short story to be published by an Afro-American has yet to be identified with any certainty. Until quite recently it was widely thought to be "Two Offers," by Frances Ellen Watkins Harper, which appeared in two installments in the *Anglo-African Magazine* of September and October 1859. Recent scholarship, however, has tended to press the claims of earlier and earlier prose narratives.

Several scholars, for example, have advanced the claim of "The Heroic Slave," by Frederick Douglass, which first appeared in *Douglass' Paper* of March 1853. But William Farrison, in his definitive study of William Wells Brown, demonstrates that Brown preceded Douglass with "A True Story of Slave Life," which was published in the *Anti-Slavery Advocate* of December 1852.[1] And William Robinson outbids all rivals by claiming short-story status for a very early narrative by Lemuel Haynes, entitled *Mystery Developed; or Russell Colvin (Supposed to be Murdered) in Full Life, and Stephen and Jesse Born, His Convicted Murderers, Rescued from Ignominious Death by Wonderful Discoveries* (Hartford, 1820).[2]

Not every short narrative, to be sure, is a short story. Given the difficulties of a strict generic definition, it may prove quite impossible to determine which of these early fictions or semifictions was the first authentic short story to be published by an American black. But it hardly matters, for the broad outlines of historical development are clear. The first generation of black writers, whose real achievement lay in other spheres, experimented briefly with the short-story form. But it remained for the second generation to employ that form with anything approaching professional skill.

The Black Abolitionists

The first group of black writers who can properly be called a literary generation flourished in the years 1845-1860.[3] These were the black abolitionists, whose poetry, fiction, and drama, no less than their essays, speeches, and autobiographies, were conceived as instruments of propaganda in the antislavery cause. After Emancipation, their output understandably declined, though some of them extended their careers to the early 1890's. Dominated by the leonine figure of Frederick Douglass, this early phase of Afro-American literary history may justly be regarded as the Age of Douglass.

Foremost among the Douglass generation were Martin Delany (1812-1885), William Wells Brown (1815?-1884), Frederick Douglass (1817?-1895), Frances Harper (1824-1911), and Frank Webb (dates unknown). These authors were born, it will be noted, between 1812 and 1824, and came to their majority in the 1830's and 1840's, when the antislavery movement was gathering momentum. Their role models were white abolitionists like William Lloyd Garrison, Wendell Phillips, and Harriet Beecher Stowe. They read and wrote for the abolitionist press, joined abolitionist societies, became effective platform speakers and pamphleteers, and in some instances emerged as major spokesmen of the antislavery cause.

Like all succeeding generations of Afro-American writers, the black abolitionists had their own publication outlets, on however modest a scale. Frederick Douglass' journal, the *North Star*, and its successor, *My Paper*, carried regular book reviews and literary essays, as well as occasional poetry and fiction. *The Anglo-African Magazine*, a monthly journal of politics and culture founded by Thomas Hamilton of New York, served briefly as a focal point for the Douglass generation. Its financially precarious career in 1859 and 1860 marked the high point of generational awareness and cultural collaboration among the black abolitionists.

The achievements of this generation in the literary sphere were limited, but by no means negligible. They will be remembered above all for the slave narratives, of which the *Narrative of the Life of Frederick Douglass, an American Slave, Written by Himself* (1845) is artistically the most successful. According to a recent critic, Douglass' *Narrative* represents a major contribution to the art of American autobiography.[4] Next in importance are their three novels: *Clotel* (1853), by William Wells Brown, *The Garies and Their Friends* (1857), by Frank Webb, and *Blake, or the Huts of America* (1859), by Martin Delany. Unfortunately, not much can be said for the quality of their shorter fiction.

Of the five leading figures of the Douglass generation, all but Martin Delany made some modest effort to write short fiction. Depending on one's definition of a story, William Wells Brown wrote one, Frederick Douglass one, Frances Harper two or three, and Frank Webb two.[5] From the early 1850's to the early 1870's, their total output in the genre amounted to perhaps six stories. By way of contrast, Charles Chesnutt, who began to write stories in the 1880's, published fifty-three, while Paul Dunbar, whose career began in the 1890's, published ninety-one.

Collectively, then, the first generation of black writers may be said to have pioneered in the short-story form. But a sense of proportion requires us to distinguish their production, which was sporadic and amateurish, from that of their successors, which was sustained and professional. Moreover, if we look for continuities between the two generations, they will not be found within the narrow compass of the short-story form. Since the short fiction of the Douglass generation was buried for the most part in obscure periodicals, it is doubtful whether Chesnutt and Dunbar were acquainted with their work. It was simply not a part of their usable past.

From a wider perspective, however, it seems clear that the lives and works of the black abolitionists were a source of inspiration to the next generation. In the same year, for example, that Charles Chesnutt published his first book of stories, *The Conjure Woman,* he also wrote a short biography of Frederick Douglass.[6] *The Conjure Woman* attacks the institution of slavery with a moral fervor stemming from the abolitionist tradition, and is saturated through and through with the sweet wine of freedom. Frederick Douglass, together with George Washington Cable and Joel Chandler Harris, was a major influence on the short fiction of Charles Chesnutt.

In 1885, Chesnutt placed his first apprentice tale with the McClure Newspaper Syndicate. By 1890 he had published twenty-five apprentice pieces in such newspapers and periodicals as the *Cleveland News and Herald, Family Fiction, Puck,* and *Tid-Bits.* In addition, three of his mature stories appeared in the *Atlantic Monthly* from 1887 to 1889. These conjure tales formed the nucleus of his first collection, *The Conjure Woman,* which was published in 1899. Later in the year, Houghton Mifflin brought out a second book of Chesnutt stories called *The Wife of His Youth.*

The years 1887-1889, when Charles Chesnutt published his first conjure tales in the *Atlantic Monthly,* mark the real beginnings of the Afro-American short story. Heretofore a few inconsequential pieces had been published in obscure newspapers and periodicals, but Chesnutt's appearance in the leading literary journal of his day was a major breakthrough for the black writer.

Chesnutt's apprenticeship in the short-story form did not materialize, to be sure, out of thin air. It was made possible by the publication in 1880 of the first book of Uncle Remus tales. Consider the chronology. *Uncle Remus: His Songs and His Sayings* appeared in 1880; *Nights with Uncle Remus* in 1883. Four years later, Chesnutt placed his first conjure tale in the

Atlantic Monthly. In the fullness of time, Houghton Mifflin, publishers of all the Uncle Remus books save one, brought out a collection of Chesnutt's conjure tales. It was Joel Chandler Harris, in short, who prepared the editors and publishers of a genteel era to accept the plantation lore of the folk Negro as a legitimate literary source.

Paul Dunbar's earliest efforts in the short-story form were made in 1890 and 1891, when he was still a student at Dayton's Central High. Primarily concerned in the early nineties with establishing his reputation as a poet, he postponed his serious apprenticeship in short fiction until after 1895. In 1898 *Folks from Dixie*, the first book of stories by a black American, was published by Dodd, Mead. By 1904, three more books of Dunbar stories had appeared.[7] From 1898 to 1904, Dunbar and Chesnutt published between them six volumes of short stories. Some fifty years after its earliest beginnings, the Afro-American short story had come of age.

Chesnutt and Dunbar were the advance guard of a literary generation whose ranks included such distinguished figures as Booker T. Washington, W. E. B. DuBois, and James Weldon Johnson. Emerging in the 1890's, this generation dominated Afro-American writing until the First World War. They were spokesmen of the rising Negro middle class, and their struggle to articulate the hopes and aspirations as well as the grievances of this class produced the first period of sustained writing in the history of Afro-American letters. This efflorescence—which occurred simultaneously in all genres—corresponded to Booker T. Washington's ascendancy as the political and cultural leader of the race, and thus may be denominated the Age of Washington.

The leading members of this generation were born between 1858 and 1872.[8] They thus reached their majority in the 1880's and 1890's, at the height of the post-Reconstruction repression. Yet despite the traumas of their early manhood, accommodation rather than protest was their characteristic tone.[9] The governing esthetic of the age was inspirational; its animating myth was embodied in the title of Washington's autobiography, *Up from Slavery* (1901). It was in literary outlook a retrospective age, in which the hardships of contemporary Negro life were overshadowed by the cataclysmic events of the not-too-distant past. Slavery and Reconstruction, rather than the harsh conditions of the present, were the focal points of their poetry and prose.

The Age of Washington was dominated in poetry by Paul Dunbar; in fiction by Charles Chesnutt and James Weldon Johnson; and in autobiography and the autobiographical essay by Booker T. Washington and W. E. B. DuBois. The enduring literary works produced by this generation are Washington's *Up from Slavery* (1901), DuBois' *The Souls of Black Folk* (1903), and Johnson's novel, *The Autobiography of an Ex-Colored Man* (1912), plus the best of Dunbar's poems and the best of Chesnutt's stories. By far the most distinguished single volume is Chesnutt's first book of stories, *The Conjure Woman* (1899).

The Local-Color School

When Chesnutt and Dunbar turned to story-writing in the 1880's and 1890's, they were not working in a cultural vacuum. The magazines in which they hoped to publish were most receptive to a type of fiction which stressed regional diversity. This emphasis on local color dominated the American short story from the end of the Civil War to the turn of the twentieth century. Associated with the rise of mass-circulation magazines like the *Atlantic Monthly* (founded in 1857), the *Overland Monthly* (founded in 1868), *Scribner's Monthly* (founded in 1870), and *Century Magazine* (founded in 1881), the local colorists set the tone of American magazine fiction for more than three decades.

The local-color vogue commenced in 1870 with the publication of Bret Harte's *The Luck of Roaring Camp and Other Sketches*. It was sustained through the seventies and eighties by such volumes as Sarah Orne Jewett's *Deephaven* (1877),

George Washington Cable's *Old Creole Days* (1879), Joel Chandler Harris' *Mingo and Other Sketches in Black and White* (1884), and Thomas Nelson Page's *In Ole Virginia* (1887). The vogue reached its peak in the nineties with such books as Hamlin Garland's *Main-Travelled Roads* (1891) and Stephen Crane's *Whilomville Stories* (1900), and entered its decline in the work of Jack London and O. Henry.[10]

Local-color fiction was a halfway house between romanticism and realism. Abandoning the Gothic tale of Poe, Hawthorne, and Melville, the local colorists moved in the direction of a greater specificity of physical setting and cultural milieu. To this end, all the distinguishing features of a region were brought into play: picturesque landscapes, native characters, provincial manners, quaint costumes, regional dialects, local legends or superstitions. It was all somewhat operatic, for the impulse toward realism was severely restricted by the provincialism of the Local-Color School, which tends to find its literary form in pastoral. This provincialism and its literary implications will be better understood if we review the historical circumstances that brought it into being.

The local-color movement had its source in a new regional awareness that sprang up in the aftermath of civil war. The chief political imperative of the postwar era was consolidation of the Union through reconciliation of the North and South. But paradoxically a stronger sense of nationhood could only be attained through a greater tolerance of sectional differences. In the legitimation of cultural diversity the local-color movement played a vital role. During a time of transition, when national loyalties were still tenuous, a regional literature offered a viable alternative. One's provincial roots might become a point of pride; one's unique traditions, the crux of his identity. Such was the psychological appeal of the Local-Color School.

These were the years, moreover, when the locus of American culture shifted from the eastern seaboard to the Mississippi valley and beyond. The challenge facing the

American imagination, no less than the American railroads, was the spanning of a continent. It was no accident that Bret Harte's story of a California mining camp launched the Local-Color School. The westward expansion reinforced the tendencies toward regionalism and cultural diversity in American letters. For as one commentator has observed, "It was clear that the continent was geographically, socially, and economically so varied that one could not entertain the idea of future unity or homogeneity."[11]

Back east, a rapid process of industrialization and urbanization had begun. These homogenizing forces tended to efface local manners and thereby render them more precious. As Louis Rubin notes, "The tranquil agricultural society of the republic in the days before the war thus became increasingly a lost paradise, and stories of outlying regions where life was still apparently easy and bucolic, without the complexities of postwar urban society, possessed a powerful appeal for the American imagination. Mark Twain, writing his tales of boyhood along the Mississippi while living in a brownstone mansion in Hartford, Conn., symbolized the yearning of an urban America for a lost rural innocence."[12]

This celebration of a pre-industrial America found its literary form in pastoral. The titles of such books as Sarah Orne Jewett's *Country Byways* (1881) and George Washington Cable's *Bonaventure: a Prose Pastoral of Acadian Louisiana* (1888) openly proclaim their pastoral intent. We must be wary, therefore, of attributing realistic motives to the Local-Color School. The pastoral convention imposes a certain ideality on materials drawn from rural or provincial life. For authors who adopt it, a tendency to prettify the countryside and its inhabitants is irresistible. The prettification of slavery is thus the point at which the Local-Color School and the Plantation School intersect.

The idyllic and realistic are incompatible perspectives. That was the fundamental contradiction of the Local-Color School. Their impulse toward a faithful recording of provincial life was constrained by a highly stylized literary mode. The result was a hybrid form of which Louis Rubin writes, "It provided close detail of setting and, within limits, a realistic descriptive texture, but these were grafted onto an essentially romantic plot structure, commonly a love story. The typical local-color story was a pastoral romance, with an emphasis on setting; if in their quaintness and simplicity the characters constituted something of a rebuke to the complexities of post-Civil War urban America, the rebuke was gently administered. . . ."[13]

The Local-Color School established a set of conventions and a cultural climate within which most short-story writers of the time felt constrained to work. Dunbar and Chesnutt, no less than their white contemporaries, published local-color stories in such journals as the *Atlantic Monthly, Overland Monthly,* and *Lippincott's.* They too utilized the form of the pastoral romance and employed "regional" (read "Negro") dialect in the manner of George Washington Cable and Joel Chandler Harris. Their image of the Negro, like that of other local colorists, stressed the picturesque, the quaint, and the exotic. A crucial theme in local-color fiction—the tolerance of differences and reconciliation of erstwhile enemies—was extended in their work to embrace racial as well as sectional animosities.

Like all local colorists, Dunbar and Chesnutt were torn between an urge toward realism and the constraints of a romantic form. Dunbar's dominant romantic strain may be seen—in addition, of course, to his plantation tales—in ten "Ohio Pastorals," published in *Lippincott's* from 1899 to 1905. These stories, whose characters are white, frequently employ the form of the pastoral romance. Dunbar's incipient realism may be found in seven tales of "Little Africa," scattered throughout his last three collections, which attempt to deal with Negro life in the embryonic northern ghettoes. Yet even here, a tendency to idealize or prettify his materials is irrepressible.[14]

In contrast to Dunbar, Chesnutt's dominant strain is realism. Despite a few romantic tales like "Her Virginia Mammy" or "Cicely's Dream," the bulk of his short fiction is realistic in treatment and satirical in tone. His first collection, *The Conjure Woman*, is much indebted to Joel Chandler Harris' *Free Joe and Other Georgian Sketches* (1887), whose title story is notable for its realistic and even satirical treatment of slavery times. His second collection, *The Wife of His Youth and Other Stories of the Color Line*, whose central theme is miscegenation and its consequences, owes a major debt to the fiction of George Washington Cable—not the pastoralist of *Bonaventure*, but the social commentator of *Old Creole Days*.[15]

Cable's influence on Chesnutt has been traced by Helen Chesnutt in her biography of her father.[16] Cable, who wrote Chesnutt a letter of congratulation after reading his conjure tales in the *Atlantic Monthly*, became his literary mentor and his friend. He played a major role in the younger man's apprenticeship, interceding with magazine editors, and providing criticism and advice. Through his Open Letter Club, an association of enlightened Southerners, he gave Chesnutt an opportunity to set forth his views on the race problem in a series of cogent essays. But most of all he imparted his own strongest virtues as a writer, including a meticulous sense of craft and a moral courage in dealing with socially controversial themes.

While Dunbar and Chesnutt were in part local colorists, too much can be made of this dimension of their art. Their commitment to the local-color vogue was at best half-hearted, for black writers of that generation were not inclined to flaunt their ethnicity or emphasize their deviations from the white cultural norm. They were not altogether comfortable, for example, with Negro dialect, which was corrupted on the minstrel stage and associated in their own minds with the Negro lower class. They were not completely happy, in short, with the necessity of being "picturesque." Yet they understood that these were the terms on which editorial acceptance could be won, and so conformed, at least in part, to the canons of the Local-Color School.

The Plantation School[17]

In the 1880's and 1890's a group of Southern writers appeared whose chief energies were devoted to the short-story form. Among the minor figures were James Lane Allen, Harry Stillwell Edwards, and Grace Elizabeth King. Foremost in their ranks were Joel Chandler Harris and Thomas Nelson Page, each of whom was the author of several books of stories. From one point of view, these authors comprised the Southern wing of the local-color movement, but in a longer perspective they represented a tradition in Southern writing which antedates the Local-Color School.

This is the so-called Plantation Tradition, whose principal exponents in the antebellum South were John Pendleton Kennedy, William Caruthers, John Esten Cooke, and William Gilmore Simms. These men, who were primarily novelists (though Simms published over sixty stories), were pioneers in a type of romantic fiction, closely modeled on the work of Walter Scott, which has aptly been called "the Confederate romance." Their costume dramas, set for the most part in the eighteenth century, featured a more or less flattering portrait of plantation life and a more or less vigorous defense of slavery.

The eighties and nineties witnessed a revival of the plantation legend among the writers of the New South. If anything, the legend had a stronger hold than ever on the Southern imagination after the destruction of the old regime. Postwar Southern writing was suffused with nostalgia for a bygone era, and with romantic melancholy, stemming from devotion to the Lost Cause. Pastoral was the ideal vehicle for these emotions. In the poetry of Irwin Russell and the fiction of Harris and Page, plantation life was celebrated as the incarnation of a Golden Age. Yet whatever the sentimental motives of these authors, political considerations were decisive in the timing and tenor of their art.

In 1876, withdrawal of the occupying armies from the South was followed by the virtual collapse of Reconstruction. In the decades that ensued, a brutal repression, whose purpose was the restoration of white supremacy, was unleashed against the former slaves. The complicity of the Plantation School in this political repression is not to be denied. Their major theme, other than a celebration of plantation life, was reconciliation of the Blue and Gray. This seems innocent enough, until it is remembered that in actuality reconciliation was effected through the abandonment of Reconstruction, the disfranchisement of blacks, and the ruthless reestablishment of white supremacy.

The strategy of the Plantation School, in short, was a strategy of masking. "America," as Ralph Ellison has instructed us, "is a land of masking jokers. We wear the mask for purposes of aggression as well as for defense."[18] No less than their contemporaries of the Ku Klux Klan, Southern writers of the post-Reconstruction era donned a mask to keep the Negro in his place. That mask consisted of a false image of the benevolent slaveholder and his contented slave. For to justify the current political repression it was necessary to maintain the fiction that the black man was a helpless child unworthy to be free.

The truth is that Harris, Page, & Co. were the chief ideologists of the New South. As Charles Nichols has observed, "There is little doubt that these Southern writers succeeded in persuading most of America that the radical Republican program of Reconstruction was a ghastly mistake. Indeed, the American people began to feel that the Union armies, led on by fanatical abolitionists, had swept away a noble civilization. Ideologically speaking, the South had won the war."[19]

Their role as propagandists notwithstanding, it would be an error to dismiss the Plantation School on narrow political grounds. These writers saw their own work not so much as a defense of white supremacy as of a rural and patriarchal way of life which white Southerners had inherited from their English forebears. Harris and Page, like their predecessors of the antebellum South, were committed to a cultural ideal whose birthplace was the English countryside and whose natural medium was pastoral. To trace the Plantation Tradition to its source, we must take a closer look at the antebellum generation of John Pendleton Kennedy and William Gilmore Simms.

Men of letters in the antebellum South were for the most part members of the planter class. They were the descendants of court favorites who emigrated to Virginia or the Carolinas under the protection and patronage of English kings.[20] Who among the English upper classes emigrated to the Colonies? Younger sons deprived of land by the laws of primogeniture. Their object in the New World was to reestablish a way of life as close to English norms as possible. Central to these norms was the manorial estate or country seat which formed the basis of a family dynasty. Such was the concept of the Great House, as celebrated in Elizabethan pastoral.[21]

The Southern plantation, with its Big House at the vital center, was the New World incarnation of this ideal. Black slaves, to be sure, replaced the English peasantry, but that was a minor variation. What persisted was a vision of the good society, based on an agrarian economy, a stable moral order, and a rigid social hierarchy. The cultural orientation of the planter class was English, but at the same time provincial. Their role model was the English country gentleman, with his love of horses, hounds, and books, in that order. This cultural ideal was transmitted from father to son, and reinforced among the antebellum generation by their reading of eighteenth-century English authors.

Jay Hubbell, in his comprehensive work *The South in American Literature* (1954), places great stress on this influence.[22] English authors who exerted the strongest hold on the imaginations of Southern literary men were Oliver Goldsmith and Thomas Gray, and the works that seemed most relevant to them were *The Vicar of Wakefield,* "The Deserted Village," and the "Elegy Written in a Country Churchyard." These works came closest to expressing the Southern writer's agrarian values and his sense of provincial isolation. He was attracted, in short, to a pastoral strain which appeared in the late eighteenth century in response to the then incipient Industrial Revolution.

This pastoral strain was the literary source of the Plantation Tradition. Southern writers of the early national period found in Goldsmith and Gray a stance from which to oppose industrial development, which they perceived as a Yankee heresy, menacing to their rural and patriarchal way of life. They discovered in the English pre-romantics a set of values to counterpose to those of the Machine Age. In imitation of these models, they produced a literature that was agrarian in outlook, sectional in politics, neo-Platonist in philosophy, romantic in idiom, and pastoral in form.

It remains to establish a direct link between the late eighteenth-century pastoral tradition and the Plantation School of Joel Chandler Harris and Thomas Nelson Page. Among the journalistic, editorial, and belletristic talents of the Old South was Joseph Addison Turner, the owner of a large cotton plantation in central Georgia called Turnwold, where he edited and published a literary weekly called *The Countryman.* Of this venture Turner wrote, "Our aim is to model our journal after Addison's Little Paper, *The Spectator,* Steele's Little Paper, *The Tatler,* Johnson's Little Papers, *The Rambler* and *The Adventurer,* and Goldsmith's Little Paper, *The Bee.*"[23]

"In the fall of 1862," according to Jay Hubbell, "Turner printed in the *Countryman* his long poem, 'The Old Plantation,' in old-fashioned heroic couplets and confessedly modeled upon Goldsmith and Gray."[24] In the previous year, 1861, Turner had employed as an apprentice typesetter a fatherless boy of thirteen named Joel Chandler Harris. It was from

Turner's well-stocked library that Harris gleaned his literary education. At Turnwold he encountered Uncle George Terrell, the model for Uncle Remus, who told quaint stories to the Turner children. And there he heard for the first time those folktales of the Negro slaves which he would one day introduce to all the world.

A line of descent can be traced from Turner's poem, "The Old Plantation" (1862), to the poetry of Irwin Russell, whose work was a major force in refurbishing the plantation legend. In 1876 Russell published a dialect poem called "Uncle Cap Interviewed" in *Scribner's Monthly*, an event widely regarded as marking the birth of the Plantation School. Russell's verse, with its plantation setting and pastoral assumptions, was a major influence on the fiction of Harris and Page, not to mention the poetry and prose of Paul Laurence Dunbar.[25] Thus the long arm of the eighteenth century stretched from Goldsmith and Gray through the generation of Kennedy, Simms, and Turner, to that of Russell, Harris, and Page, and beyond them to black writers of the Age of Washington.

By 1885 or 1890, when Chesnutt and Dunbar arrived on the literary scene, the plantation myth had acquired the force of orthodoxy. If one wished to write of Negro life in the mass-circulation magazines, the approved formula included (1) a setting in the antebellum South; (2) a plot shaped by the requirements of the pastoral romance; and (3) an image of the Negro that deprived him of dignity, maturity, or capacity for independent judgment. These were the expectations of editors and audience alike. Yet a fundamental freedom was available within these narrow limits: the freedom to choose the genre or countergenre, the modes of pastoral or antipastoral.

Dunbar chose to work substantially within the former mode. Of his 73 collected stories, 31 are plantation tales with settings in the antebellum South. These tales, which for the most part are pastoral romances, conform in all respects to the plantation myth, and owe a major debt to the short fiction of

Thomas Nelson Page. Chesnutt, on the other hand, chose to work primarily through antipastoral. His major work, *The Conjure Woman*, has a plantation setting, but the owners are transplanted Northerners during Reconstruction times. What they learn of antebellum days from the stories of their black coachman is calculated to destroy rather than sustain the plantation myth.

When Chesnutt and Dunbar began their work in the short-story form, there were two available traditions, represented by the Local-Color and Plantation Schools. Writers exposed to these influences alone would be predisposed to pastoral. The Afro-American oral tradition, however, functioned as a counterforce. This immemorial tradition of oral storytelling, which stemmed from remote slavery times, was antipastoral in tendency. For the black slave's existence in America, while sylvan and agrarian, was something less than idyllic, and his earliest, preliterate attempts to fictionalize his experience were hardly governed by the white man's notion of Arcadia.

Chapter 2

The Oral Tradition

JOEL CHANDLER HARRIS is in bad odor among the younger generation of literary men. The blacks, who tend to equate Uncle Remus with Uncle Tom—sometimes, one suspects, without having read either Harris or Stowe—reject the Uncle Remus books out of hand. And sympathetic whites, who hope thereby to ingratiate themselves with the black militants, are fond of giving Harris a gratuitous kick in the shins. Both responses are regrettable, for they blind their victims to the archetypal figure of Brer Rabbit, who is not only a major triumph of the Afro-American imagination, but also the most subversive folk hero this side of Stagolee.

Harris did not invent the animal fables that constitute the imaginative center of the Uncle Remus books. But he did transpose them to the written page, thus saving them from possible oblivion. It was through Harris that a major figure in the pantheon of American folk heroes saw the light of day. Brer Rabbit, who has kindled the imagination of black writers for almost a century, came loping into view in 1880. But Clio, the muse of history, is no respecter of race. It was a white man of the deep South who forged the missing link between the Afro-American folktale and the Afro-American short story.

The rehabilitation of Joel Chandler Harris was no part of my original intent. As a journalist, after all, he was an active propagandist in the cause of white supremacy, and as a literary man, a leading proponent of the plantation myth. Still less did I intend—nor do I now propose—to serve as an apologist for Uncle Remus, who is principally a figment of the white imagination. But the Brer Rabbit tales themselves are something else again. A product of the Afro-American oral tradition, these magnificent folktales must not be allowed to languish simply on the grounds that a white Georgian was the first to write them down.

So perhaps some modest effort at rehabilitation will be tolerated by the young. Out of simple justice, then, let it be entered on the record that, whatever else he was, Joel Chandler Harris was a complicated man, full of neurotic conflicts and self-deceiving ways; a Southern maverick, capable of stubborn orthodoxies and equally tenacious heresies where black people were concerned; an admirer of black folklore, and an ethnologist of strict integrity, to whom black Americans owe a considerable debt for the preservation of their folk heritage; and a catalytic agent of prime importance in the history of the Afro-American short story.

Our final judgment of this man and his work cannot be a simple one. If the Uncle Remus books perpetuate the pro-slavery myths of the plantation tradition, they also contain one of the sharpest indictments of the institution in American literature. Perhaps we cannot improve on the formulation of William Stanley Braithwaite, who wrote in 1925, ". . . in the Uncle Remus stories the race was its own artist, lacking only in its illiteracy the power to record its speech. In the perspective of time and fair judgment the credit will be divided, and Joel Chandler Harris regarded as a sort of providentially provided amanuensis for preserving the folk tales and legends of a race."[1]

The Afro-American Folktale

Modern folklorists, both black and white, have attested to the storytelling powers of the folk Negro. A large body of material has been collected in the field, and a good deal is known about its scope and variety.[2] The repertory includes animal fables, trickster tales (*e.g.*, the John-and-ole-Marster cycle), conjure stories, preacher tales, jokes, proverbs, anecdotes, and plantation lore of every description. Wonder tales, horror stories, voodoo legends, and what Zora Hurston calls "just plain lies" have passed from mouth to mouth in the black community for generations.

The origins of the Afro-American folktale may be traced to West Africa, where a rich tradition of storytelling flourished for centuries. Especially prominent in this repertory was a large body of animal fables. But what precisely is the relationship of the Brer Rabbit tales to the animal legends of West Africa? Do the folktales of the American Negro represent a survival of African culture in the New World? Joel Chandler Harris was inclined to think so. Basing his opinion on the latest findings of contemporary scholarship, he wrote of the animal tales, "One thing is certain—the Negroes did not get them from the whites: probably they are of remote African origin."[3]

At the same time, Harris recognized that some Afro-American folktales were more African than others. He knew, for example, that the stories told on the cotton plantations of central Georgia were strikingly different from those recounted in the rice-growing districts of the Georgia coast. To accommodate these differences in his fiction he invented Daddy Jack, a narrator who came straight from Africa and told his tales in Gullah dialect. By creating a coastal counterpart of Uncle Remus, Harris anticipated, if only at the level of artistic intuition, some of the conundrums that have yet to be resolved by modern scholars.

Scientific folklorists are divided on the issue. Melville Herskovits leans to the theory of African origins while Stith Thompson points to the existence of European cognates. Richard Dorson argues that the tales are drawn from multiple sources which include Africa, Europe, the West Indies, and white American folk traditions. After weighing the available evidence he concludes that "the New World Negro repertoire falls into two groups of stories, one pointing toward Africa and one pointing toward Europe and Anglo-America."[4] Northeastern South America, the Caribbean and Atlantic islands, and the Gullah districts of the Georgia and Carolina coast produced the first group; the plantation states of the American South the second.

What seems beyond dispute is that a very ancient African tradition survived the middle passage, and served as a basis for renewed creative efforts in the Western Hemisphere. At the same time, we must insist that the Brer Rabbit tales were conceived not by Africans, but Afro-Americans. For these tales reflect the social conditions and historical experience of black slaves on the continent of North America. They represent the first attempt of black Americans to define themselves through the art of storytelling; a heroic effort on the part of chattel slaves to transmute the raw materials of their experience into the forms of fiction.

Chesnutt and Dunbar were of course exposed, personally and directly, to this folk tradition. Teaching as a young man in the Freedman's Bureau schools of North Carolina, Chesnutt was fascinated by the conjure stories of emancipated slaves. Dunbar heard stories of plantation life from his own mother, who had been a house servant in a prominent Kentucky family. But for the most part their knowledge of the Afro-American folktale was vicarious and literary. Like other middle-class Americans of their time and place, they came to know the power of the folk imagination through the Uncle Remus books. It was Joel Chandler Harris who aroused their emulation by demonstrating the potential of the folktale as a literary form.

There was nothing unusual in this cultural dialectic. The postwar era was one of widespread interest in Afro-American folklore, popularized for the most part by white authors. As early as 1867, Thomas Wentworth Higginson contributed an essay on the spirituals to the *Atlantic Monthly*, and that same year W. F. Allen published his still valuable *Slave Songs of the United States.* In 1877 William Owens wrote an article for *Lippincott's* entitled "Folklore of the Southern Negroes," which inspired Harris to undertake the Uncle Remus books. It therefore seems historically appropriate that we, like Chesnutt and Dunbar themselves, should approach the archetypal figure of Brer Rabbit through the mediating vision of Joel Chandler Harris.

The problem of authenticity will instantly arise. How faithful was Harris to his folk sources? In the process of writing down the animal fables, and providing them with a narrative frame, to what extent did he impose his own values and point of view as a white Southerner? At this point, a crucial distinction must be drawn between the kernel and its husk. It is undeniable that the external wrappings of the Brer Rabbit tales function to perpetuate the plantation myth. But the tales themselves were never tampered with. As a conscientious if amateur ethnologist, Harris respected their integrity.

Harris himself vouches for their authenticity. In his introduction to *Nights with Uncle Remus* (1883) he asserts that "The thirty-four legends in the first volume were merely selections from the large body of plantation folk-lore familiar to the author since his childhood. . . ." No tale, he continues, was included without being verified, either by his own extensive practice of yarn-swapping with the blacks, or by correspondence with other folklorists. He insists, moreover, on his fidelity to the originals: "Not one of them is cooked, and not one nor any part of one is an invention of mine. They are all genuine folk-tales."[5]

These claims to authenticity have been fully substantiated by modern scholarship. J. Mason Brewer, a Negro folklorist, confirms in his *American Negro Folklore* (1968) that "The first, and still the most significant and authentic volume of Negro animal tales is Joel Chandler Harris' *Uncle Remus: His Songs and His Sayings.* . . ." Richard Dorson, a white scholar, and former president of the American Folklore Society, offers evidence of a more objective kind. In *American Negro Folktales* (1967), Dorson has collected 1,000 stories, tape-recorded on field trips to Michigan, Arkansas, and Mississippi in the early 1950's. Of his thirty-four animal tales, nine are variants closely related to the Harris versions.

There is lastly the internal evidence of the Brer Rabbit tales themselves. They depict, as we shall see, the master-slave relation from the slave's point of view. Their central emotion is hostility toward the powerful and strong. Their moral code is that of an oppressed people; their hidden motives are such as no white man could entertain. The world of Brer Rabbit, in short, is an unmistakable projection of the black imagination. The adjacent and enfolding world of Uncle Remus is something else again. The moment that we move from the folktale to its narrative frame, we enter a fictive world entirely of the white man's making.

Afro-American animal tales belong to the genre of the beast fable, which is a species of satiric allegory.[6] They are allegorical by virtue of their veiled presentation of the slave's situation through images drawn from the animal world. They are satirical by virtue of their veiled attack on ole Massa. To attribute human traits to animals is one of those devices of indirection which are the trademark of the satirist. This indirection springs, in all literatures, from the fear of censorship, suppression, or retaliation· from the high and mighty. Never was this fear more justified than in the case of the chattel slave, who found himself in the absolute power of his owner.

The Brer Rabbit tales have been widely misconstrued, for the good and sufficient reason that they constitute a secret code. The slaves who created these remarkable fictions were under the life-and-death necessity of masking in the presence of white power. To express openly the subversive sentiments concealed in these animal tales would have invited instant retaliation from the Big House. The bitter truths of the slave's existence were too dangerous to acknowledge in the master's presence, and too painful to acknowledge even to the conscious self. The result was a set of fables notable for their subliminal method of communication.

It was a white critic who first noted the subversive character of the Brer Rabbit tales. In a brilliant essay called "Uncle Remus and the Malevolent Rabbit,"[7] Bernard Wolfe has shown that these animal fables, far from being harmless children's tales, and still farther from being a defense of Southern orthodoxy, constitute a covert assault on white power. Brer Rabbit, according to Wolfe, is a projection of the slave's festering hatred of his master, a means of giving vent to his aggressive impulses. The animal tales are a type of masquerade: what they reveal to posterity is "the venomous American slave crouching behind the Rabbit."

Brer Rabbit is a symbol of covert resistance to white power. As the crimes of slavery were manifold, so the modes of resistance were many. The heroism of the slave revolt is not that of the underground railroad, and neither encompasses the brand of heroism that stands its ground and fights the system from within. The trickster-hero represents a mode of resistance, not submission or accommodation. To neglect the Brer Rabbit tales because a white man was the first to write them down is to betray the black man's folk tradition. For the American Negro's heritage from slavery times is neither negative nor negligible, and one of its most precious features is precisely the figure of Brer Rabbit.

From a literary point of view, the importance of the animal fables lies in the outlaw code that they espouse. This code of conduct, embodied in the figure of Brer Rabbit, was forged in the crucible of slavery, and cannot be understood apart from the brutalities that gave it shape. Living in the shadow of lash and gun, black storytellers had no choice but to formulate an outlaw code. For a master's sense of right and wrong is hardly suited to a slave. A man on short rations is bound to steal chickens. The only moral code he can afford to entertain is one that helps him to survive.

The Brer Rabbit tales are a celebration of this survival code. Stressing such qualities as slickness, deceit, evasiveness, and ruthless self-interest, the code is profoundly anti-Christian. It is this feature that makes the animal tales a more authentic product of the slave imagination than the more familiar spirituals. For the spirituals embody the official morality to which the bondsmen formally subscribed, while the folktales have immortalized the survival ethic that they actually practiced. If this code ran counter to Christian values, that was because the slave system which gave it birth was itself demonic.

The black man's folktales are his Handbook of Survival. Everything that he has been compelled to hide—his anger and resentment, his hatred and malevolence, his scheming and duplicity, his male aggressiveness and sexuality, his yearning for revenge—has been projected into the mythic world of the Brer Rabbit tales. Through the ritual of storytelling these illicit feelings have been safely drained away. At the same time the tales define a stance, a posture, a model of behavior, a means of preserving one's integrity even in the face of overwhelming odds. This role model is embodied in the figure of Brer Rabbit, the trickster-hero of an enslaved people.

The trickster-hero, based on the archetypal figure of Brer Rabbit, reappears in the short fiction of Charles Chesnutt and Paul Dunbar. Chesnutt's Uncle Julius, the narrator of his conjure tales, is such a hero. Uncle Julius might be described as Uncle Remus revamped according to the specifications of the Afro-American oral tradition. Dunbar too has produced a handful of trickster tales of which one, "The Scapegoat," is his best story. Both writers have thus been responsive, although in varying degrees, to their folk tradition, and both have been inspired by an oral literature whose crowning glory was the creation of the Brer Rabbit tales.

Of crucial importance to the present study is the point in time when this oral tradition surfaced, transcended its folk origins, and became incorporated into the literary culture of nineteenth-century America. That moment occurred in 1880, with the publication of the first book of Uncle Remus tales. Because of the cultural significance of this event, as well as its neglect by literary men, the remainder of this chapter will be devoted to a close inspection of *Uncle Remus: His Songs and His Sayings.* While this effort will involve us briefly with the life and career of Joel Chandler Harris, our primary aim is to illuminate the storytelling genius of the black slave.

Mask and Countermask

Joel Chandler Harris (1848-1908) was born in Putnam County, central Georgia. According to Jay Hubbell, "His mother, Mary Harris, had fallen in love with an Irish day laborer and in spite of strong family opposition had gone off to live with him. When he deserted her and their child, she settled in Eatonton with her mother and earned her living by sewing."[8] Harris attended school irregularly until the age of thirteen when, as we have seen, he undertook an apprenticeship in the printing trades at the Turner plantation. The boy who grew to manhood at Turnwold was lonely, shy, and insecure. Something of an outcast by virtue of his bastardy, he turned for solace to the Negro slaves.

This emotional attachment to a pariah class was to manifest itself in his writings as a strange ambivalence. On the one hand he is the conscientious ethnologist who presents "uncooked" folktales to the world. On the other, he is perfectly capable of using Uncle Remus, in the columns of the *Atlanta Constitution*, as a counter in the white man's game of Reconstruction politics. So deep is this fissure in his personality that it is not extravagant to speak of schizoid tendencies. Harris acknowledges as much in a letter to his daughter: "You know all of us have two entities or personalities."[9] Only a split personality can account for an author who juxtaposes such antithetical images of Negro life as Uncle Remus and Brer Rabbit!

In 1867 the *Countryman* went under, and Harris was forced

to leave Turnwold. For the next ten years he knocked about the South, working as a typesetter and journalist in Macon, New Orleans, and Forsyth, Georgia. In 1876, having married a woman of French Canadian antecedents, he settled in Atlanta, where he joined the staff of the *Atlanta Constitution.* As early as January 1877, Harris printed songs in Negro dialect in his regular column. During the next two years he published character sketches of Uncle Remus and an occasional animal tale. In 1880 he selected from the *Constitution* files the proverbs, songs, and stories which comprise the first of his Uncle Remus books.

Uncle Remus: His Songs and His Sayings (1880) was an instantaneous popular success. Within a matter of months the book passed through four editions. It was soon followed by a second volume, *Nights with Uncle Remus* (1883). Six such books eventually appeared, whose impact on American culture has yet to be properly assessed. Harris had established a new literary mode whose first fruits included Charles Chesnutt's *The Conjure Woman* (1899) and Don Marquis' *The Lives and Times of Archie and Mehitabel* (1916). Later works in the same line of descent would include William Faulkner's *The Sound and the Fury* (1929), Ralph Ellison's *Invisible Man* (1952), and John Updike's *Rabbit Redux* (1971).

Uncle Remus: His Songs and His Sayings was the book that launched the plantation revival of the 1880's. It was, in point of fact, the first major literary statement of the New South. As such, it bore the historic burden of revealing to the nation the current state of the Southern soul. Was the defeated South in a repentant frame of mind, or unregenerate in its defense of slavery? The answer, when it came, seemed unequivocal. The new generation of Southern writers, by their revival of the plantation myth, seemed determined to idealize the old regime, mitigate its harshness, cloak it in a haze of nostalgia, and thereby justify the restoration of white supremacy.

Joel Chandler Harris, who was, after all, a political commentator for a major Southern newspaper, was entirely orthodox in this respect. There is nothing in his characterization of Uncle Remus that violates the spirit of the plantation myth. On the contrary, it is the author's avowed purpose to create a sympathetic, nostalgic, and untroubled portrait of plantation life before the war. The point of view, he tells us frankly, will be that of an old Negro "who has nothing but pleasant memories of the discipline of slavery—and who has all the prejudices of caste and pride of family that were the natural results of the system. . . ."[10]

Harris' unconscious motivations were something else again. Guilt is an elusive state of mind, whether in a man or nation. Seldom appearing to the conscious mind in its own guise, it assumes a thousand Protean shapes and forms. Dramas of the soul involving guilt are more likely to be enacted in the dark than before the bright glare of television cameras. Hence Harris' fascination with the subliminal world of the black folktale. Folktales are allied to dream states, and possess something of the magical fluidity of dreams. Precisely because they deal with buried feelings, they confront us with blurred outlines, veiled analogies, hints and correspondences. They thus permit us to know and not to know at the same time.

At some deeper level of artistic intuition, Harris must have known that Uncle Remus was not the whole story, and perhaps not even the true story, of slavery times. Through the character of Uncle Remus he gave form to the white man's fantasy of being loved by his slaves. But there was another perspective from which to view chattel slavery, as Harris was well aware from his lonely adolescent years at Turnwold. That was the black slave's point of view, as embodied in his folklore. Try as he would, Harris could not bring himself to suppress it. This ghost is present in the Uncle Remus books, just as inescapably as it is buried in the nation's consciousness.

Whatever the intentions—conscious or unconscious—of Joel Chandler Harris, the Uncle Remus tales confront us with two distinct, and ultimately irreconcilable, versions of reality. One is white, the other black, and they are embedded in a two-tier or split-level structure consisting of (1) a narrative frame, and (2) an animal tale. Dramatically, the tales shift from the human to the animal plane; from Uncle Remus and the little boy to Brer Rabbit and the other woodland creatures. Linguistically, they shift from standard English to Negro dialect, so that the very texture of the prose announces unmistakably the transition from a white to a Negro world.

The two fictive worlds of the Uncle Remus tales are in fact the divided worlds of the American South. They are the segregated and yet curiously interlocking worlds of the two races, of the Big House and the slave quarters, of Euro-American and Afro-American culture. Their uneasy coexistence in the Uncle Remus books is a tribute to the capacity of the human mind for self-deception. For if the one world is nostalgic and sentimental, the other is utterly subversive; if the one is steeped in fantasy and wish-fulfillment, the other is immersed in the harsh realities of American slavery. On the literary plane, these tensions are reflected in the conventions of pastoral and antipastoral.

Consider the tableau that sets the tone of the Uncle Remus books. The figures of Uncle Remus and Miss Sally's little boy cling to one another in pastoral innocence and peace. The boy rests with his head against the old man's arm or sits on his knee, as Uncle Remus strokes and caresses the child's hair. It is a picture of utter confidence and trust, mutual tenderness and love. In a word, the scene is idyllic. What it proclaims to the reader is this: "There is nothing to be afraid of, or even upset by, in these animal fables; they are merely quaint legends or harmless children's stories."

Now consider the central images of the folktales themselves. Far from creating an atmosphere of tranquility and love, they convey a world of unrelieved hostility and danger, violence and cruelty, terror and revenge. In one tale, Brer Rabbit lures Brer Wolf into a large wooden chest, bores holes in the top, and scalds him to death with boiling water. In another, he persuades the animals whom he has robbed to submit to an ordeal by fire, and as a consequence, the innocent Brer Possum is killed. In a third, having caused Brer Fox to be beaten to death, Brer Rabbit attempts to serve up his enemy's head in a stew to his wife and children.

The tales are full of beatings, tortures, savage assaults, and deadly ambushes. They reproduce, in their jagged images of violence, the emotional universe of the Negro slave. How else should the black imagination respond to the brutalities of the American slave system? What other images would be commensurate with its inhumanity? If the flagrant sadism of the Brer Rabbit tales offends, it is well to remind ourselves that violence and cruelty were the mainstays of the institution. If the white imagination is content to linger over the smiling aspects of the slave estate, it would be strange indeed if the black storyteller should follow suit.

The Brer Rabbit tales preserve not so much the dramatic features as the moral atmosphere of slavery. What they are about, in the last analysis, is the black slave's resistance to white power. Hence the effort to "contain" this subversive theme in a pastoral frame. But in the tales themselves, an unrelenting state of war obtains between Brer Rabbit and his powerful antagonists. It is a war to the knife, without truce or quarter or forgiveness. The moral vision projected in these tales is that of men who have been brutalized, degraded, rendered powerless—and yet who manage to survive by dint of their superior endurance and mother wit, their cunning artifice and sheer effrontery.

The world of Brer Rabbit is a pathological world, both emotionally and morally. There is nothing normal about being a slave, and nothing normal about the black man's response to an intolerable situation. Absolute power produces absolute desperation; all moral scruples are discarded in a fierce effort to survive. This is the explanation for the code of conduct that is celebrated in these tales. Deceit and trickery, theft and betrayal, murder and mayhem are endorsed as appropriate responses to the slave condition. Such are the ruthless expedients of Brer Rabbit, who can survive in Hell by outsmarting the Devil. Having been raised in a brier patch, he is one tough bunny.

Uncle Remus and Brer Rabbit stand in the relationship of mask to countermask. Uncle Remus, the creation of Joel Chandler Harris, is one of many masks employed by the Plantation School to justify the restoration of white supremacy. But Brer Rabbit, the creation of anonymous black slaves, may be thought of as a countermask which contravenes the pastoral charade and exposes the harsh reality. A closer look at the first book of Uncle Remus tales will serve to substantiate this claim. An exhaustive survey of the Uncle Remus books would be beyond the scope of this study. A suggestive treatment of selected tales is our intent, and for this purpose a generous sampling of the first volume should suffice.

The Brer Rabbit Tales

Slavery was first of all a system of compulsory labor. A number of the animal fables are thus devoted to methods of survival which include shirking and malingering, "going fishing," and similar evasions of brutal toil in the hot sun. In one tale the animals are clearing new ground that they intend to plant in corn. Feigning an injury, Brer Rabbit slips off to take a nap in the shade. In another, they are patching up the leaky roof of their communal storehouse. On the pretext that his wife is ill, Brer Rabbit deserts the scene, steals down to the spring house, and consumes the community's entire supply of butter.

The most impressive of the work tales is "A Story About the Little Rabbits." Brer Fox drops in on Brer Rabbit and finds no one at home except the rabbit children. His mouth waters in anticipation, but some sort of pretext is required before he can devour them. He imposes three unreasonable tasks, which he expects to be beyond their strength or capacity. They are ordered to break a piece of sugar cane, carry water in a sieve, and put an enormous log on the fire. Each time a little bird instructs them in the art of the impossible:

> Sifter hold water same ez a tray
> Ef you fill it wid moss en dab it wid clay.
> De Fox git madder de longer you stay—
> Fill it wid moss en dab it wid clay.[11]

This tale is a parable of survival under a forced labor system. Brer Fox is assigned the role of tyrannous overseer, working his charges to the point of exhaustion: "Hurry up dar, Rabs! I'm a waitin' on you." To survive in such a situation, the slave had to be capable of accomplishing the impossible. If the externally imposed conditions of work were cruel and unalterable, then the only recourse was to alter one's own attitude. That is the burden of the little bird's song about the huge log:

> Spit in yo' hans en tug it en toll it
> En git behine it, en push it, en pole it;
> Spit in yo' hans en r'ar back en roll it (110).

Chronic undernourishment of the labor force was a common feature of the slave economy. For the closer a planter could drive his slaves to the margin of subsistence, the faster he could grow rich. If the Brer Rabbit tales are any indication, a constant hunger stalked the slave's imagination, producing what amounts to an obsession with images of food. In many of the tales, the action is devoted to the acquisition of a supplemental food supply, sometimes through hunting or fishing but more often through stealing. The theft of food was the archetypal plantation crime; its penalty was customarily exacted by the lash. Savage beatings thus provide the dominant images of several tales.

Typical of this crime-and-punishment motif is the tale "Mr.

Fox Gets Into Serious Business." The story opens with an unmistakable delineation of the master-slave relationship:

> "Hit turn out one time dat Brer Rabbit make so free wid de man's collard patch dat de man he tuck'n sot a trap fer ole Brer Rabbit."
>
> "Which man was that, Uncle Remus?" asked the little boy.
>
> "Des a man, honey. Dat's all (140-41)."

When the little boy persists, Uncle Remus parries with the comment, "Now den, less des call 'im Mr. Man en let 'im go at dat."

Having trapped the culprit in a snare, Mr. Man goes off into the brush to cut himself some switches. In his absence, Brer Fox passes by. Through an involved maneuver that plays on his victim's sexual appetites, Brer Rabbit tricks Brer Fox into taking his place in the noose. When Mr. Man returns he is astonished at the change that has overtaken his captive, but he proceeds with the whipping on general principles: "en wid dat he lit inter Brer Fox wid de hick'ries, en de way he play rap-jacket wuz a caution ter de naberhood." No doubt it was often thus in slavery times, when the guilty party escaped his punishment by tricking an innocent bystander into assuming the scapegoat role.[12]

Before proceeding it may be well to enlarge our cast of characters. While resisting the temptation to allegorize, we may yet observe that the animals can be divided into two distinct groups. In addition to the wily Rabbit, Brer Possum and Brer Terrapin may be regarded as folk heroes. Brer Fox and Brer Wolf, on the other hand, are a constant source of fear to the sympathetic characters. It is clear that the former group would offer many possibilities of identification to a slave audience, while the latter would tend to be regarded as dangerous foes or menacing authority figures.

Brer Possum, that artful dodger, is a symbol of survival-by-illusion. In the story "Why Mr. Possum Loves Peace," Mr. Dog attacks Brer Coon and Brer Possum. Brer Coon, who "wuz cut out fer dat kinder bizness," puts up a pretty stiff fight, but Brer Possum plays dead. He embodies the slave's knowledge that he cannot hope to offer a frontal challenge to white power. But by "playing possum," or in other words *by creating a fiction*, he can escape the worst excesses of that power. Fiction, in short, is perceived as a mode of survival. With this perception, we are very close to the sources of the black man's storytelling art.

Brer Terrapin is a symbol of survival-by-endurance. With his notoriously long life and his impenetrable armor, he represents the slave's ability to outlast trouble:

> "Tuck a walk de udder day, en man come 'long en sot de fiel a-fier. Lor', Brer Fox, you dunner w'at trubble is," sez Brer Tarrypin, sezee.
>
> "How you git out de fier, Brer Tarrypin?" sez Brer Fox, sezee.
>
> "Sot en tuck it, Brer Fox," sez Brer Tarrypin, sezee.
>
> "Sot en tuck it, en de smoke sif' in my eye, en de fier scorch my back," sez Brer Tarrypin, sezee (60).

Short in stature and slow of foot, Brer Terrapin compensates for his lack of size or speed by clever stratagems. In a race with Brer Rabbit, he places wife and children at every marker and successfully carries off the impersonation. (All us Terrapins look alike!) In a contest of strength with Brer B'ar, he challenges his opponent to pull him out of the branch with a long cord. Diving to the bottom, he ties the cord to a husky tree root and humiliates the bear. The object lesson of these tales is clear: the slave is not a passive victim. He can survive and even prevail by learning to overcome his handicaps and limitations.

What of the figures of the Fox and Wolf? Beasts of prey, carnivores endowed with an appropriate strength and ferocity, they are exteriorizations of the slave's sense of danger. It is tempting to conclude that they are symbols of white power: certainly they become the principal targets of aggression and revenge. It may be closer to the truth, however, to suggest that slavery creates a situation where every black man is a wolf to his neighbor. For slavery abrogates community, destroys solidarity, and pits each slave against his fellows in a fierce struggle to survive. Hence the atmosphere of distrust and suspicion of which these tales are a projection.

Brer Fox and Brer Wolf, it is worth noting, are tricksters in their own right. They are forever trying to "put up a game on Brer Rabbit." In the tale "Mr. Wolf Makes a Failure," they attempt to lure him into the house of Brer Fox:

> "How you gwine git 'im dar?" sez Brer Fox, sezee.
> "Fool 'im dar," sez Brer Wolf, sezee.
> "Who gwine do de foolin'?" sez Brer Fox, sezee.
> "I'll do de foolin'," sez Brer Wolf, sezee, "ef you'll do de gamin'," sezee (54-55).

The game consists of a scheme to trap Brer Rabbit by persuading him that Brer Fox is dead. The intended victim spoils the game, however, by inventing a countergame that penetrates his enemy's disguise.

Games and countergames, jokes and counterjokes, masks and countermasks: these are the stock-in-trade of the Brer Rabbit tales. To what cultural reality do these literary devices correspond? Once again we must turn to Ralph Ellison's comment that "America is a land of masking jokers." As if it were not enough for the slave to contend with raw white power, he finds himself controlled and manipulated, disarmed and disoriented, by white hypocrisy. Ellison has of course devoted an entire novel to the subject. Suffice it to observe of the Brer Rabbit tales that the white man's disingenuous treatment of the black supplies the delicious motive of the masker unmasked, the deceiver deceived.

In the deadly game of masking and countermasking, the slave's most powerful defense is a knowledge of his master's weaknesses. Like all tricksters, Brer Rabbit exploits the vices of his victims: their pride and vanity, greed and lust. Through studying the foibles of his masters, the slave becomes a natural satirist, as the dance form of the cakewalk demonstrates. Armed with this secret weapon he employs a kind of spiritual judo, whereby the white man's own momentum can be used against him. Prevented from asserting his own will, the slave learns to manipulate his master's to his own advantage.

This spiritual judo is the subject of the story "Mr. Rabbit Grossly Deceives Mr. Fox." Brer Fox invites Brer Rabbit to a party, where he intends to humiliate him in front of "Miss Meadows en de gals." But Brer Rabbit, scenting trouble, insists that he is too sick to attend. After much negotiation he agrees to go, but only if Brer Fox will tote him on his back, fully equipped with saddle and bridle. Brer Fox, intent on establishing his reputation with the ladies, readily submits. In an ironic reversal typical of the Brer Rabbit tales, it is Brer Fox, spurred mercilessly by the triumphant Rabbit, who is humiliated in the end.

The linguistic mode of the Brer Rabbit tales is derived from the principle of masquerade. That mode is irony, a form of verbal masking. In the world of Brer Rabbit, words seldom mean what they appear to mean. For the slave who takes his master's words at face value is a fatally disoriented man. He must learn instead to probe beneath the surface, assess the white man's motives, and adapt himself accordingly. In such a situation, mutual deceit becomes the norm Masks proliferate and ambiguity prevails. The ever-changing guises of reality are reflected in the shifting façades of language. Irony thrives in such an atmosphere, as the ties that bind word and deed are dissolved.

It is in his fantasies of revenge that the black man's irony attains its maximum intensity. In a tale called "The Awful Fate of Mr. Wolf," Brer Rabbit kills off his hereditary enemy by scalding him to death. A sinister exchange takes place in the midst of Brer Wolf's agony. It is a scene that could have been imagined only by a race that has suffered from centuries of white hypocrisy. Revenge is sweet, and sweetest at its most ironic. Here the dislocation of word and deed reaches pathological proportions. And yet the dialogue that follows is no more cruelly cynical than the practice of enslaving blacks and calling it salvation.

> Den Brer Rabbit git de kittle en fill it full er water, en put it on de fier. "W'at you doin' now, Brer Rabbit?" "I'm fixin' fer ter make you a nice cup er tea, Brer Wolf." Den Brer Rabbit went ter de cubberd en git de gimlet, en commence fer ter bo' little holes in de chist-lid. "W'at you doin' now, Brer Rabbit," "I'm a bo'in' little holes so you kin get bref, Brer Wolf. . . ." Den Brer Rabbit he got de kittle en commenced fer to po' de hot water on de chist-lid. . . . "W'at dat I feel, Brer Rabbit?" "You feels de fleas a bitin', Brer Wolf. . . ." "Dey er eatin' me up, Brer Rabbit," en dem wuz de las' words er Brer Wolf, kase de scaldin' water done de bizness (66-68).

The most profound of the Brer Rabbit tales is the famous story of the Wonderful Tar-Baby. Brer Fox, hoping to trap Brer Rabbit, makes a figurine of sticky tar and places it in his victim's path. Brer Rabbit, attempting to exchange polite salutations with the stranger, is infuriated by his silence: "Ef you don't take off dat hat en tell me howdy, I'm gwineter bus' you wide open." But the Tar-Baby maintains his silence, so Brer Rabbit lams him with one fist. "Ef you don't lemme loose, I'll knock you agin," says Brer Rabbit, and the other fist is stuck fast. Whereupon he kicks and butts, only to find himself completely mired in the tar.

Hubris is the subject of this story. For once Brer Rabbit

oversteps himself, taking on the white man's ways of arrogance and willfulness, and bullying the tarry representative of blackness. To bully is to be cruel and overbearing to others weaker than oneself, and for this psychological indulgence Brer Rabbit pays with one of his few abject defeats. On a deeper plane, the tale is concerned with the relationship of will and circumstance. To *force* circumstance, to browbeat or intimidate it, to want one's way no matter what, is a fatal attitude. For circumstance is sticky stuff that seems pliable enough, but leaves us, if we fight it, with a nasty problem of extrication.

The sequel to this tale, "How Mr. Rabbit Was Too Smart for Mr. Fox," delineates the proper relationship of will to circumstance. Brer Rabbit has been trapped, but he retrieves his error by *collaborating* with the force of circumstance, now embodied in the figure of Brer Fox. He manipulates his adversary by appealing to what Poe has called the imp of the perverse. As Brer Fox casts about for a means of killing his captive, Brer Rabbit counters each proposal by saying in effect: burn me, hang me, drown me, skin me, but whatever you do, don't fling me in that brier-patch. Which of course is the inevitable outcome, and Brer Rabbit skips off shouting triumphantly, "Bred en bawn in a brier-patch, Brer Fox— bred en bawn in a brier-patch!"

The brier-patch is an eloquent image of the uses of adversity. Lacking the defensive equipment of the porcupine, the rabbit borrows his defense from his environment; a hostile universe is thus converted to a sanctuary and a home. Such is the nature of antagonistic cooperation, as defined by Albert Murray in *The Hero and the Blues.* The nimble footwork, quick wit, and boundless invention of Brer Rabbit are called forth precisely by adversity. He is thus the forerunner of the blues hero who is equal to all emergencies and can extricate himself from any difficulty. This quality of improvisation in the face of danger, or as Hemingway would put it, grace under pressure, is in Murray's view the basis of the blues tradition.[13]

The Tar-Baby stories bring our discussion of the Brer Rabbit tales to a fitting close. For these are the supreme fictions of the folk imagination, as memorable for their esthetic form as for the wisdom they impart. When we consider that the artists who created these and similar animal fables were illiterate slaves, we can only stand in awe of their achievement. By this act of creativity they vindicated their humanity and established their claim upon the highest faculty of man: the moral imagination. In so doing they transformed their lives and overcame the limits of their low estate. They accomplished, in short, the crucial metamorphosis of a fate endured into a fate transcended.

In a poem called "O Black and Unknown Bards of Long Ago," James Weldon Johnson pays a moving tribute to the nameless authors of the Negro spirituals. Yet surely his sense of awe is no less appropriate to the anonymous creators of the animal tales:

> There is a wide, wide wonder in it all,
> That from degraded rest and servile toil
> The fiery spirit of the seer should call
> These simple children of the sun and soil.[14]

Johnson does in fact pay homage, if not to these black storytellers, at least to the folk hero that they made famous. In an early dialect poem, written in the manner of Paul Dunbar, he tells of a meeting in the forest where all the animals have gathered to decide "Who is de bigges' man." Judge Owl nominates Brer Rabbit, but this decision provokes so much jealousy that the animals fall to fighting among themselves. The outcome, as Johnson describes it, offers us a memorable image of the trickster-hero:

> Brer Rabbit he jes' stood aside an' urged 'em on to fight.
> Brer Lion he mos' tore Brer B'ar in two;

W'en dey was all so tiahd dat dey couldn't catch der bref
Brer Rabbit he jes' grabbed de prize an' flew.

> Brer Wolf am mighty cunnin',
> Brer Fox am mighty sly,
> Brer Terrapin an' Possum—kinder small;
> Brer Lion's mighty vicious,
> Brer B'ar he's sorter 'spicious,
> Brer Rabbit, you's de cutes' of 'em all.[15]

Chapter 3

Paul Dunbar

IN *Doctor Faustus,* Thomas Mann describes a butterfly whose wings resemble a leaf, "not only in shape and veining, but in the minute reproduction of small imperfections, imitation drops of water, little warts and fungus growths, and more of the like. When this clever creature alights among the leaves and folds its wings, it disappears by adaptation so entirely that its hungriest enemy cannot make it out."

Protective mimicry is the key to Dunbar and his age. In the post-Reconstruction era, hungry enemies were everywhere, and they were determined to reduce the blacks to something like their former state of servitude. In the face of this onslaught, it often seemed the better part of valor to blend with one's surroundings, and to seek sanctuary through invisibility. Even the blemishes of the environment—including the fungus growths of racism—were incorporated into this ingenious adaptation. Thus the Negro minstrel troupes, who blackened their own dark skins with burnt cork, and distorted their own features to conform to the white stereotype.

In Paul Dunbar's shorter fiction, protective mimicry consisted (1) of imitating the Plantation School, and (2) utilizing the conventions of the minstrel stage. Some thirty of his stories are historical romances with settings in the antebellum South, while twenty more are minstrel travesties. These forms offered safety and protection to a black author because they were firmly established in the popular culture of the day. In so merging with his cultural surroundings, Dunbar was assured of popular success, but he paid an awesome price for this protective coloration. Like the black minstrels, he collaborated in the defamation of his own people.

Dunbar's protective adaptation to a hostile environment was not at all unique. His was an age of accommodation, presided over by the imposing figure of Booker T. Washington. The Founder of Tuskegee, whose racial policies were formulated in his Atlanta speech of 1895, dominated Negro thought and action for a generation. He exerted a profound influence on the cultural expression of American Negroes, including their imaginative literature. There is no point in trying to ignore or minimize this influence. Dunbar was Washington's disciple, and no amount of sophistry will transform an advocate of compromise and reconciliation into a racial militant.

Yet such an effort has been made by Darwin Turner, who argues that Dunbar's work is "much more a part of the protest tradition than his reputation suggests."[1] As his principal supporting evidence, he cites five or six of Dunbar's stories, published in *The Strength of Gideon*. It cannot be denied that Dunbar wrote a handful of protest stories, representing approximately 7 percent of his output in the genre. But most of his tales are so accommodationist in tone as to be embarrassing to modern readers. Only by ignoring the overwhelming mass of evidence is it possible to classify him as a protest writer.

To rank Dunbar on some sort of militancy scale is to do him a disservice, for in any scrupulous and conscientious reckoning, he is bound to be the loser. This approach, moreover, is open to the charge of provincialism, insofar as it imposes the values of the present on the past. Every age has a right to be judged on its own terms; and every writer, by the canons of his chosen genre. That, in Dunbar's case, is the pastoral, rather than the protest mode. Ultimately we must weigh his substance as a pastoralist, assessing him by what is central, and not tangential to his art.

The challenge of Dunbar criticism is to disengage his art as far as possible from the imperatives of ideology, and judge it as an act of the imagination. This procedure will require us to be sympathetic, and yet critical; to make historical allowances, and yet to take his measure by the realistic standard of what was possible for a man of his time. If, for example, Dunbar's reputation suffers from comparison with that of his contemporary, Chesnutt, that is because the latter strove to rise above his era and transform its consciousness, while the former was content for the most part to reflect the social prejudices of his age.

Life and Work

Paul Laurence Dunbar (1872-1906) was born and raised in Dayton, Ohio.[2] The son of former slaves, he was often entertained as a boy with stories of plantation life. Joshua and Matilda Dunbar, however, were exposed to very different aspects of the slave experience; their attitudes toward the past were sharply divergent; and their son was the baffled recipient of a divided heritage. Dunbar has portrayed his parents' respective situations in "A Family Feud" and "The Ingrate."[3] The contrasting tone of the two stories is a good point of departure for understanding what Saunders Redding calls the schizoid tendency of Dunbar's art.

Matilda Dunbar was a house servant in one of Kentucky's leading families. She was proud of her exalted status, completely loyal to her white folks, and if not entirely reconciled to her situation as a slave, at least able to view it in retrospect without bitterness. She transmitted these attitudes and values to her son, whose conciliatory version of plantation life is unique among Afro-American authors. In poetry or prose, Dunbar drew heavily for plot material on his mother's memories. These consisted of sentimental and nostalgic anecdotes which stressed the humorous and lighthearted aspects of the slave estate.

Joshua Dunbar, on the other hand, was a runaway who escaped to Canada by way of the underground railroad. A skilled plasterer, he was hired out by his master and taught to read and cipher, to prevent his being cheated by the neighbors. He expressed his gratitude by forging a railway pass and lighting out for freedom shore. He returned to the United States to enlist in the Union Army, and following his discharge settled in Dayton, where he married Dunbar's mother. Unfortunately, the couple separated when their son was only four or five, and his father died when Dunbar was still a boy of twelve. He was thus deprived of an influence that might have served to counter the racial conservatism of his mother.

Dunbar's formal education was accomplished in the Dayton public schools. He began to write in high school, where he became editor of the student newspaper, president of the literary club, and class poet. His mother cherished hopes of a ministerial career, but these ambitions were defeated by the boy's determined opposition. In any case, the money for a higher education was simply not available. His mother had supported him in high school on her earnings as a laundress, but now it was imperative that Dunbar seek employment. Barred from office work by the prejudices of the day, he was forced to take a job as an elevator boy.

He persisted, however, in his efforts to become a poet. His literary models were the successful newspaper poets of the nineties: Eugene Field, Ella Wheeler Wilcox, and James Whitcomb Riley. Dunbar's first book of poems, *Oak and Ivy*, was printed at his own expense in 1893. A second volume, *Majors and Minors*, was published in 1896 with the help of a white patron. This book was favorably reviewed by William Dean Howells in *Harper's Weekly*, and Dunbar's career was launched. He soon established a connection with Dodd,

Mead, and Co., who brought out several volumes of his verse, four novels, and four collections of short stories.

By his middle twenties Dunbar had become a national celebrity. In 1897 Robert Ingersoll procured a post for him in the Library of Congress. A year later he married Alice Ruth Moore, a schoolteacher, poet, and short-story writer. They established a home in Washington, D.C., where they cultivated the genteel and imitative life-style of the black bourgeoisie. The marriage was undermined, however, by ill health and incompatibility, and they separated in 1902. By this time Dunbar's drinking was a problem, and his health was seriously impaired by the lung disease that would take his life in 1906 at the age of thirty-four.

Dunbar was primarily a poet, but he soon discovered that poetry was easier to write than sell. He assumed the burden of marketing his first two books of verse, but his best efforts met with small success. Even when these meager earnings were supplemented by recitals at Negro churches, lodges, and civic groups, they were far from providing the means of self-support. Yet Dunbar was responsible for the needs of an aging mother, as well as the desires of an ambitious wife. In proportion as these financial pressures mounted, he turned increasingly to prose. The short story, in particular, was a source of ready cash, and in the form of a collection, offered the prospect of steady royalties as well.

Dunbar's career as a short-story writer began while he was still a student at Central High. The not-yet-famous Wright brothers (Orville was his friend and classmate) were publishing a weekly journal, and Dunbar proposed to do the same for Dayton's black community. In 1890 he organized *The Dayton Tattler*, where his own apprentice fiction first appeared. In 1891 he sold two "Westerns" to the Kellogg newspaper syndicate. These stories were the first writing of any kind for which he was paid, and they not only inspired him with the notion that a writer might earn a living at his trade, but imbued him with a permanent respect for the commercial possibilities of short fiction.

A more serious apprenticeship ensued, once his reputation as a poet was assured. From 1895 to 1897 Dunbar published several stories in *Cosmopolitan*, the *Independent*, and the *New York Journal*. Dodd, Mead, and Co. then suggested that if he would add a few stories to this nucleus, they would undertake a volume. The result was *Folks from Dixie* (1898), the first collection of short stories to be published by a black American. The book, which combined sentimental images of slavery times with a conciliatory treatment of the Reconstruction era, was a popular success. It was followed by a second volume, *The Strength of Gideon* (1900), in which plantation tales and protest stories, mingling in equal proportions, neutralize each other as a base an acid.

Meanwhile George Lorimer, editor of *The Saturday Evening Post*, offered to publish a sequence of plantation tales. These stories, after appearing in the *Post*, provided the main bulk of a third volume, *In Old Plantation Days* (1903). In his fourth collection, *The Heart of Happy Hollow* (1904), Dunbar abandoned the plantation scene for a portrait of contemporary Negro life. In the last six years of his career (1899-1905), he published fourteen stories which have never been collected. They appeared in such periodicals as *Lippincott's Magazine*, the *Smart Set*, and *Metropolitan Magazine*. *Lippincott's* predominates, by virtue of a series of "Ohio Pastorals," whose themes are nonracial and whose characters are white.

Dunbar is by far the most prolific of Afro-American short-story writers. His four collections alone contain a total of seventy-three stories. If we add to these his apprentice work, uncollected stories, and unpublished manuscripts, the grand total comes to ninety-seven tales. Of these, about a third are pastorals. A still larger proportion of Dunbar's verse, and three of his four novels, belong to the same genre. What emerges from an overview of his career is a basic dedication to the pastoral ideal. He is a writer of provincial consciousness who celebrates the rural life in forms deriving from the pastoral tradition.

Dunbar's affinity for pastoral had many roots, perhaps the taproot being his smalltown, Midwest origins. As a dialect poet, he was influenced by a long tradition, stretching from Theocritus to Robert Burns, in which the use of country dialect supports the poet's pastoral intent. As novelist and storyteller, he was exposed to the pastoral conventions of the Plantation and Local-Color Schools. Reinforcing these influences from the wider culture, moreover, were certain forces indigenous to Negro life in the United States. To understand these forces, we will need to take a closer look at Booker T. Washington and the racial strategies that he devised to cope with the post-Reconstruction repression.

The Age of Washington

The most important public utterance of Booker T. Washington's career was made in Atlanta at the Cotton States Exposition of 1895. Like any major historical address, it cannot be understood apart from the context of the times. In the years from 1876 to 1900, the foundations of the American caste system were being laid. Following the withdrawal of federal troops from the South, the forces of white supremacy launched a massive repression against the emancipated blacks. Peonage, disfranchisement, segregation laws, lynching, and other forms of physical intimidation by the Ku Klux Klan, were among the means employed. The Negro leadership was under an excruciating pressure, and Washington was forced to formulate his policies at a time when there was little room for political maneuver.

At the heart of Washington's survival strategy was a gesture of propitiation. As a primitive tribe might make a ritual sacrifice to an offended god, hoping thereby to avert his greater wrath, so Washington's Atlanta speech was designed to propitiate the white power structure. His famous metaphor specified the nature of the sacrifice: "In all things that are purely social we can be as separate as the fingers, yet one as the hand in all things essential to mutual progress." Given the desperate circumstances of the moment, Washington was prepared to renounce, at least momentarily, the black man's claim to social equality and first-class citizenship.

The essence of Washington's Atlanta Compromise was a trade-off with the white South. In exchange for limited but crucial economic gains, he relinquished for the moment any higher goals: "The chance to earn a dollar in a factory just now is worth more than a chance to spend a dollar in an opera house." As with economics, so with education. In exchange for limited training in the industrial arts, Washington was willing to suspend for the time being any claim to higher education. At the center of this strategy, in short, was an act of renunciation. By abandoning the high ground to the whites, he hoped to win their consent to certain minimal demands.

If there is a higher and a lower road to freedom, Washington chose the lesser way. In this he was opposed by W. E. B. DuBois, who was committed from the outset to the high road of manhood suffrage. In *The Souls of Black Folk* (1903), DuBois took Washington to task for imposing on his people a permanent condition of inferiority.[4] The battle lines were drawn, and a bitter schism appeared in the ranks of the black intelligentsia. On one side was Washington and the so-called Tuskegee machine; on the other, DuBois and men like Monroe Trotter, editor of the Boston *Guardian*, who collaborated in the founding of the militant Niagara Movement, later to be absorbed by the NAACP.

Much has been written of the ideological aspects of the Washington-DuBois controversy. The literary implications of the schism, on the other hand, have been ignored. Yet no less is at issue than a choice between two basic literary modes. To choose the high road or the low is not without linguistic consequences, and the differing approaches of the two men are nowhere more apparent than in their contrasting rhetorical styles. The epic intentions of DuBois are unmistakable: his style is characterized by lofty thoughts, lofty aspirations, and a lofty rhetoric. Washington, however, eschews the high ground of epic for the humbler strains of pastoral.

Consider the language of Washington's Atlanta speech:

> Our greatest danger is, that in the great leap from slavery to freedom we may overlook the fact that the masses of us are to live by the production of our hands, and fail to keep in mind that we shall prosper in proportion as we learn to dignify and glorify common labor, and put brains and skill into the common occupations of life; shall prosper in proportion as we learn to draw the line between the superficial and the substantial, the ornamental gewgaws of life and the useful. No race can prosper till it learns that there is as much dignity in tilling a field as in writing a poem. It is at the bottom of life we must begin, and not at the top.[5]

This is the rhetoric of pastoral. Washington casts the black man in the role of humble swain, content to find his place at the bottom of American society. Like all pastoralists, he eschews the "ornamental gewgaws" of courtly life and exalts the "common occupations" of the countryman. It was natural enough that Washington should clothe his thoughts in shepherd's garb: his constituency, after all, consisted of rural Negroes, and his program was designed to conform to the agrarian traditions of the white South. Beyond the matter of audience rapport, however, lay a serious attempt to grapple with the problem of Negro aspiration.

Washington's principal challenge as a leader was to reconcile the success-drive of the rising Negro middle class with the restrictive practices of the American caste system.

There is a tension in the rhetoric of his Atlanta speech which reflects this dilemma. On the one hand, he stresses the freedom to rise and prosper; on the other, he is careful to reassure his audience that blacks do not propose to rise too fast, nor prosper too convincingly. *Limited aspiration* is the note that he intends to strike. That, of course, is the essence of his educational philosophy, whose stress on agricultural and industrial training represents an effort to contain Negro aspiration within the boundaries of caste.

To be sure, Washington's grand design contained more than an element of duplicity. A close student of Brer Rabbit and his ways, the Founder of Tuskegee understood that there is safety in the guise of harmlessness. Behind a humble stance, the Negro middle class could pursue its true objectives. Washington assumed the mask of humility as a means of disarming the opposition. He employed the pastoral convention, with its implicit condemnation of ambition, as a form of reassurance—a pledge that white supremacy would not be placed in jeopardy if minimum concessions were granted to the blacks. The danger in this strategy, as in all forms of masking, was that in the end the black man might become his mask.

However one evaluates Washington's racial policies, the fact remains that he was a major influence on the black writers of his time. For Washington was the voice of Negro aspiration. As Principal of Tuskegee, he was the black man's symbol of hope for a better life. As the author of *Up from Slavery* (1901), he gave the epoch its sustaining myth. Chesnutt, Johnson, and DuBois played their own distinctive variations on this theme, but Dunbar was a true disciple, who stood at the center of the Washington tradition.

Washington and Dunbar

Dunbar's career was just commencing when Washington delivered his Atlanta speech of 1895. The young man was deeply moved by this address, whose contents appealed to his conservative instincts.[6] The speech became in fact the ideological foundation of his art. The overwhelming mass of Dunbar's poetry and fiction displays the same humble stance, the same conciliatory tone, the same protestations of loyalty, the same renunciations and compromises, and the same pastoral assumptions as the famous declamation of his mentor. So striking are the similarities in the careers of these two men that they are worth examining in some detail.

Washington and Dunbar, to begin with, were both accommodationists. Both were acting under duress; seeking to accommodate to the superior strength of their antagonists. Just as the black leader confronted a political repression, so the black author faced its cultural equivalent. Throughout the post-Reconstruction era, American popular culture was inundated by a flood of anti-Negro stereotypes. The purpose of these racial caricatures, whether disseminated through the minstrel shows, the songs of Stephen Collins Foster, the poetry and fiction of the Plantation School, or the new medium of cinema, was quite simply to traduce the Negro, and thereby fix him firmly in his place.

The coercive power of these false images was enormous. However counterfeit, they won acceptance as coinage of the realm, and woe to the black writer who tried to undermine or circumvent them! Chesnutt, as we shall see, managed to adapt the outward forms of the Plantation School to his own subversive ends. But Dunbar more or less capitulated, leaving the stereotypes largely undisturbed. His response to the situation was, in short, accommodationist. As Washington accepted caste and worked within its limitations, so Dunbar accommodated to the false images of Negro life that permeated his environment. He offered up these self-derogatory images as a gesture of propitiation to the gods.

Dunbar's accommodation to the minstrel tradition is well known. Over a period of years he collaborated with the black composer Will Marion Cook, on a number of music-hall entertainments familiarly known as "coon shows." Dunbar contributed most of the lyrics to "Clorindy, the Origin of the Cake-Walk" (1898), and some of the lyrics to "Jes' Lak White Folks" (1900) and "In Dahomey" (1902). In 1899 he wrote a vaudeville sketch called "Uncle Eph's Christmas" for Ernest Hogan, a veteran minstrel singer and former star of "Clorindy." Here is a sample of the dialogue: "Pappy, where was de first possum perskivered?" "Don't you know dere's no sich word in the dictionumgary as perskivered?"[7]

Dunbar persisted in these collaborations despite the active opposition of his wife. They became in fact a major source of conflict in his marriage. Alice Dunbar and her rather aristocratic family objected that such activities were beneath the dignity of a serious poet. They felt entirely justified in this opinion when a Boston reviewer of "Uncle Eph's Christmas" called Dunbar "Prince of the coon song writers." In January 1900, Alice accompanied her husband on a business trip to New York where she tried to break off his relationship with Hogan. A bitter quarrel ensued, and the breach in their marriage was never altogether healed.[8]

Dunbar's insensitivity to the implications of the minstrel stereotype is nowhere more apparent than in the illustrations that adorn the four collections of his stories. The drawings of his white illustrator, Edward Windsor Kemble, are travesties of Negro life, blatantly racist in their impact.[9] They are at best comic stereotypes and at worst vicious caricatures. It would be damaging enough if, against his better judgment, Dunbar had been forced to accept such a collaboration by his publishers. But what are we to say of a black writer who so admired these racist drawings that he asked the artist to let him frame the originals for his den?[10]

Equally accommodationist was Dunbar's response to the Plantation School. These writers were the chief propagandists of the New South, and as such, their object was to win the acquiescence of the North in the disfranchisement of Southern blacks. To this end they portrayed the former slaves as feckless and irresponsible, and altogether incapable of self-government. For such childlike and dependent wards, freedom was illusory, and Negroes who migrated to the North were seized (especially at Christmas time) with paroxysms of nostalgia and regret. So ran the fantasies of Southern writers whose poetry and fiction amounted to a literary version of keeping the Negro in his place.

Dunbar's culpability in parroting the propaganda of his racial enemies is not to be denied. There are few clichés of the Plantation School, however anti-Negro in their implications, that he hesitates to use. In "Viney's Free Papers" he portrays a slave who revokes her manumission rather than confront the ambiguities of freedom. In "Silas Jackson" he warns against the folly of abandoning the South for the lure of "false ambitions" in the North. In "An Old Time Christmas" he depicts the yearning of Northern migrants for the old plantation, not scorning to support his point with a few lines from "Suwanee River." Dunbar's images of Negro life in these and many other tales cannot be distinguished from those of Thomas Nelson Page.[11]

In accordance with his tactic of accommodation, Dunbar was prepared, like Washington, to sacrifice the greater for the lesser good. Just as Washington renounced the ballot box and opera house in order to achieve a modest economic gain, so Dunbar renounced his highest ambitions as a writer and settled for a modest reputation as a dialect poet and local colorist. The point in each case was to win a limited acceptance by a gesture of propitiation. Like Washington, Dunbar was prepared to recognize his "place." As the black leader accepted a subordinate position for his people, so the black writer for his art.

True to the spirit of the Atlanta Compromise, Dunbar consistently abandoned the high road for the low. The high road, linguistically speaking, was standard English; the low road, Negro dialect. Such, at any rate, was Dunbar's understanding of the matter. He regarded Negro dialect as an inferior speech, limited in emotional range and detrimental to his serious ambitions as a poet. He preferred to write in standard English, but grudgingly acceded to the expectations of the white world. He has expressed the bitterness of this accommodation in his famous lines:

> He sang of love when earth was young,
>   And Love itself was in his lays.
> But, ah, the world, it turned to praise
> A jingle in a broken tongue.[12]

The high road, culturally speaking, was the literary world of Boston and New York, presided over by William Dean Howells. But Dunbar's affinities were rather with the dime novels and newspaper romances, the minstrel shows and sentimental magazine verse—in short, the popular culture of his day. Just as DuBois and Washington embodied the divergent ideological tendencies of the age, so Chesnutt and Dunbar its artistic polarities. Chesnutt, like DuBois, was determined to travel the high road come what may. He aspired to meet the critical standards of the *Atlantic Monthly*, the leading literary journal of his time. Dunbar, by way of contrast, found his natural audience among the readers of *Lippincott's* and *The Saturday Evening Post*.

The high road, in literary terms, was the epic mode; the low road, the less pretentious mode of pastoral. Just as Washington avoided lofty sentiments in his Atlanta speech, turning instinctively to the rhetoric of pastoral, so Dunbar shunned the heroic possibilities of Negro life, limiting himself to subjects that would not alarm the whites. The essence of the Washington approach was to settle for limited aspiration, limited education, and limited participation in social and political affairs. Such an ideology found its natural expression in pastoral where, as William Empson has observed, ". . . you take a limited life and pretend that it is a full and normal one."[13]

Washington's Atlanta speech called for peaceful coexistence of the races in a rural setting. This is the very stuff of pastoral. Traditionally the genre has served as a cohesive force, binding together the potentially divisive segments of society. Reconciliation is thus the keynote of Dunbar's poetry and fiction. Erstwhile enemies forgive and forget, as they overcome their personal, sectional, or racial animosities.[14] As in all pastoral, present conflicts are resolved in terms of an idyllic past. Hence Dunbar's evocation of the antebellum South. Through the depiction of a Golden Age, he sought to plead the cause of racial harmony among his own contemporaries.

"The central meaning of pastoral," according to Hallett Smith, "is a rejection of the aspiring mind."[15] The pastoralist admonishes the lower orders to shun ambition, and to recognize that true contentment lies in humble circumstances. This, as we have seen, is the burden of Washington's Atlanta speech. "Cast down your bucket where you are," he exhorts the younger blacks, as he warns them to forgo illusory adventures in the urban North. Renounce "the ornamental gewgaws" of the city, and settle for the elemental satisfactions of country life.

Dunbar's art, like Washington's politics, rested on pastoral assumptions. A pronounced anti-urban bias is evident throughout his work. Aspiration beyond a certain point is condemned as a form of hubris. Much of Dunbar's fiction constitutes a warning to younger blacks against "the false ideals and unreal ambitions" to which they might succumb in the Northern cities.[16] The pastoral convention, in Dunbar's hands, served as a restraint on Negro aspiration. Some such restraint was essential to the black bourgeoisie, whose aspirations were restricted by the stubborn realities of caste.

Washington and Dunbar, though active in separate spheres, faced a common task. The reconciliation of Negro aspiration with the principle of white supremacy was the focal point of both careers. In this they embodied the historical dilemma of the social class from which they sprang. The rising

Negro middle class found its journey up from slavery blocked at every turn by the artificial barriers of caste. They were torn, in consequence, between a desire to succeed, and a fear of retaliation in the event that they should succeed too well. It was to this agonizing conflict that Dunbar addressed himself in his short fiction.

Dunbar and the Minstrel Mask

At bottom Dunbar's stories represent a quest for a solution to the problem of Negro aspiration. Four alternatives were possible in Dunbar's time: (1) the Negro might accommodate to caste by curbing his ambition; (2) he might conceal his true motives behind a minstrel mask; (3) he might sound the protest note and challenge the restrictive practices of caste; (4) he might turn to illicit forms of aspiration when he found the normal channels closed. Dunbar explores all of these alternatives, not without considerable confusion and inconsistency. The contradictory impulses that assailed him will be better understood if we trace the conflict with his mother that gave rise to Dunbar's art.

From his childhood Dunbar was a victim of his mother's fierce ambition. As a schoolboy he was under constant pressure to succeed, to be a credit to his race, to prove to whites that he was worthy of acceptance. He was educated for the ministry, which Matilda Dunbar regarded as "the one cultured profession in which a Negro could reach the top."[17] Dunbar's mother was a devout woman who raised her son according to a strict puritanic regimen. A stern disciplinarian, she outlawed many boyish pleasures, and implanted the success virtues in her son with an unremitting zeal. So drastic a repression was bound to produce a passionate rebellion in the end.

At first the boy accommodated to his mother's expectations. He assumed a mask of goodness and propriety, becoming a model pupil and devoted son. The truth is that Dunbar was something of a mama's boy—a fact that explains much of the inauthentic nature of his life and art. Yet even as a boy he developed modes of resistance to his mother's iron will. He found that being ill or "delicate" might exempt him from the household chores. "Getting his lessons" might achieve the same effect. The child, it seems, was father to the man. Combine malingering with intellectual attainment and what results? A tubercular poet!

During adolescence, open rebellion flared. Dunbar's apostasy has been recorded in his novel, *The Uncalled* (1898). The plot concerns a youth and his female guardian, who raises him relentlessly to be a minister. Although the characters are white, the autobiographical basis of the book is obvious. The same pattern may be discerned in Dunbar's "Ohio Pastorals." In story after story, there is a mother-figure who embodies the Protestant ethic, and a male protagonist (usually a henpecked husband) who seeks some relaxation of the rigid code that oppresses him. No one who peruses these materials will doubt that Dunbar's conflict with his mother was the psychological foundation of his art.

Dunbar was a man divided against himself. His mother required him to aspire in order to be loved, but a sound instinct for psychological survival prompted him to balk. The result was a profound ambivalence. There was one Dunbar who aspired and another who resisted aspiration. But which was the authentic self? It was a question that many Americans were asking of themselves toward the turn of the century. The minstrel shows, which played so prominent a role in the popular culture of the day, addressed themselves to this conundrum. For on the minstrel stage a complicated drama of the soul was being acted out, through which Americans—black and white alike—might discover who and what they "really" were.

In a brilliant chapter of his book *Harlem Renaissance*, Nathan Huggins has analyzed the origins of minstrelsy.[18] The power and tenacity of this theatrical tradition, he argues, derived from the fact that it served a deep psychological need.

In a culture obsessed with success, the possibility of failure posed a devastating threat to the psyche. To cope with this anxiety, white Americans projected an antiself: "White men put on black masks and became another self, one which was loose of limb, innocent of obligation to anything outside itself, indifferent to success (for whom success was impossible by racial definition) and thus a creature totally devoid of tension and deep anxiety."[19]

An aspect of the minstrel shows that Huggins overlooks is their relationship to pastoral. In the pastoral tradition, courtiers masquerade as shepherds, assuming an antiself in order to define, by contrast and antithesis, their own essential selves. Blackface is the American equivalent of this European form. The use of a theatrical mask to achieve a deeper sense of self is among the oldest of literary conventions. In *As You Like It*, for example, Rosalind assumes the guise of a youth in order to confirm her femininity, just as the Duke pretends to be a commoner in order to discover the true meaning of nobility. Assumption of the antiself, in short, expedites the process of self-definition.

The minstrel shows amounted to a rite of exorcism. The actors, wearing blackface, embodied those traits of indolence, self-indulgence, and comical ineptitude which would guarantee failure in a social system oriented toward success. These negative qualities, invested with a symbolic blackness (that is, associated with the devil), thus were exorcised. For this projective mechanism to succeed, it was necessary to maintain a proper distance between the self and antiself. The mask must never be mistaken for the man. This was the function of minstrel humor which, by making the stage Negro an object of derision, forestalled the possibility of psychological confusion.

The form employed, in order to maintain the necessary distance between the self and antiself, was travesty. "Travesty," according to Huggins, "turns on the disparity between the actor and his costume which thinly disguised pretense.

The small girl with her face powdered and rouged, in the high heels, furs, and baubles of her mother; the jester wearing the king's crown; the peasant in the robes of nobility; transvestites (men in chorus lines, women acting as 'toughs') are classical sources of comedy. To make travesty work, however, the disproportion must be obvious. No matter how she stretches and struts and preens herself, it is impossible for the little girl to be her mother."[20]

On the minstrel stage, the disproportion was made obvious by various devices essentially mock-heroic in character. Thus a minstrel "darky" might be dressed a notch above the height of fashion (Jim Dandy), or be made to utter ponderous and Latinate malapropisms, or be named, in the mocking fashion of the antebellum South, for a Roman aristocrat. The stage Negro was made to seem ridiculous when thrust into roles that in real life were reserved for whites. Laughter arose when the audience perceived a gap between the affectation and the actuality. Pretentiousness is thus the chief ingredient of travesty, whose aim is to keep the pretender in his place.

Such were the conventions of the minstrel stage, as exploited for the psychological aggrandizement of whites. But how can we account for the phenomenon of black minstrelsy, with its self-demeaning images of Negro life? How account for the theatrical careers of George Walker and Bert Williams, Bob Cole and Rosamond Johnson, Will Cook and Paul Dunbar—all of whom employed the caricatures and stereotypes of minstrelsy? Commercial motives surely played a part, but they alone will not explain this self-betrayal. Rather we must look to the social class from which these artists sprang. For the situation of the Negro middle class was not so different, after all, from that of its white counterpart.

On the minstrel stage, white men assumed the mask of blackness in order to confirm their dedication to the Protestant ethic. But the need was no less urgent for the Negro middle class. They too suffered the anxieties of an achievement ethic, and required the reassurance of an antiself. Their problem was compounded, however, by a need to differentiate themselves from the "lazy nigger" of the minstrel shows. Black artists who utilized the minstrel form were hard put to keep a proper distance between the self and antiself. Their solution was precisely to exaggerate the caricature, and then adopt a tone and posture of superiority so unmistakable that no one could possibly confuse *them* with the objects of their travesty.

This necessity accounts for the worst excesses of Dunbar's art. Some twenty of his tales are travesties deriving from the minstrel tradition. These stories are rituals of exorcism in which certain traits of the Negro personality, developed during slavery times, are being cast out and replaced by the success virtues. On the face of it, these travesties seem to uphold the principle of caste. The stage Negro is a comic figure, after all, precisely because he is out of the running. But if the minstrel "darky" is perceived as an antiself, then Dunbar's travesties may be read as an expression of Negro aspiration, concealed behind a minstrel mask.

Always we return to the ruthless success-drive of the rising Negro middle class. As a boy, Dunbar was a victim of his mother's inordinate ambition. As an artist, his own ambivalent feelings toward success enabled him to cope with the historical dilemma of the black elite, caught between the opposing vectors of success and caste. History gave Dunbar his subject: Negro aspiration. His tragedy consisted of the fact that the major forms available for dealing with this subject had been preempted by the whites. Locked into the stereotypes of the Plantation School and the minstrel tradition, Dunbar was able only on rare occasions to achieve authenticity.

Representative Stories

We are now ready to survey Dunbar's short fiction, and discuss briefly a number of representative tales. His four collections contain a total of seventy-three stories, which may be divided, according to historical setting, into thirty-one antebellum and forty-two post-emancipation tales. The former are historical romances which conform in all respects to the plantation myth. The image of plantation life that they convey would cause no disturbance at a convention of the Knights of the White Camelia. These plantation tales may be found in all four volumes, but are concentrated in the third, *In Old Plantation Days* (1903). In terms of genre, they consist primarily of pastorals and travesties.

The stories with a post-emancipation setting deal somewhat more authentically with Negro life. Yet even here, stereotypes of the Plantation School and the minstrel tradition intrude between Dunbar and his material, obscuring his vision and distorting his sense of truth. Only in a handful of stories does he succeed in circumventing these false images. The settings of his post-emancipation tales include the rural South (principally smalltown Kentucky), metropolitan New York and Washington, and the generic "Little Africa." This euphemism for the urban ghetto reflects Dunbar's rather gingerly approach to material with which he felt considerably less at ease than the plantation scene.

To Dunbar's seventy-three collected stories must be added ten uncollected tales, which he himself has designated as "Ohio Pastorals."[21] These stories, most of which appeared in *Lippincott's* from 1901 to 1905, have a common setting in the Ohio village of Dorbury, and an overlapping cast of characters, all of whom are white. Linguistically they belong to the "b'gosh" and "I vum" school of country dialect. The Ohio pastorals are highly autobiographical, being transparent projections of the author's emotional conflict with his mother. As in his first novel, *The Uncalled* (1898), Dunbar assumes the mask of whiteness when writing of intensely personal emotions.

So much for an overview of Dunbar's short fiction. Six basic story-types encompass most of his output in the genre. First there are the pastorals (32), deriving essentially from the Plantation School. Next the travesties (20), deriving from the minstrel shows. Third, protestations of loyalty (8), which offer reassurance to the whites in the Washington tradition. Fourth, stories of uplift (6), which celebrate the success virtues. Fifth, protest stories (6), which challenge the artificial barriers of caste. Sixth, stories of illicit aspiration (5), which are close in spirit to the Brer Rabbit tales. We will now discuss these story-types *ad seriatum*, illustrating each with one or more representative tales.

In his short stories and his novels, Dunbar employs three distinct varieties of pastoral. According to their basic thrust, I have called them pastorals of release, pastorals of reconciliation, and pastorals of place. The first type predominates among the Ohio pastorals; the second, among the antebellum tales; the third, among the post-emancipation stories. Each type, moreover, is associated with a particular Dunbar novel. Thus the pastorals of release may be thought of as spin-off from *The Uncalled* (1898); the pastorals of reconciliation, from *The Fanatics* (1901); and the pastorals of place, from *The Sport of the Gods* (1902).

The pastorals of release have their source in the strict authoritarian controls of Dunbar's youth. They celebrate his liberation from the Protestant ethic of hard work and self-denial, from the competitive pressures of the Negro middle class, or in other words, from his mother's tyranny. Truancy is the central metaphor of these stories, and in this respect they anticipate the fiction of Claude McKay. Their tone is one of genial humor, deriving from a leniency and mellowness of spirit. They advocate a tolerance of human weakness, and a generous forgiveness of venial sins. These stories are designed, in short, to mitigate the rigors of the puritan tradition.

"The Independence of Silas Bollender" will serve to illustrate the type.[22] An Ohio farmer with a nagging wife defies her wishes and attends a country fair, where he indulges in the harmless pleasures that such occasions offer: "Anyway, he enjoyed himself. He ate gingerbread, rode the merry-go-round, and someone even saw him coming out of one of the

many minstrel shows with a seraphic smile on his face (380)."
At the racetrack, however, a pickpocket relieves him of his
watch and wallet, and he returns in disgrace to his morally
complacent but forgiving spouse. This emotional syndrome
of rebellion, guilt, and reconciliation is typical of Dunbar's
Ohio pastorals.

The pastorals of reconciliation have their origin in this
syndrome. Revolt against maternal domination produces
guilt, which in turn necessitates a reconciliation with the
mother. "The White Counterpane,"[23] for instance, depicts the
reconciliation of a mother and her son, after a breach occasioned by the son's marriage. It is the mother's recollection
of her own courtship that effects the reconciliation: ". . . she
sat for a space, her mind roaming the green pastures of the
past (508)." Sentimental memories of the past, in short,
perform a harmonizing function. This motif, projected on
the historical plane, accounts for most of Dunbar's antebellum
tales.

Breach-and-reconciliation constitutes the plot of these
plantation tales. Typically they open with a feud or bitter
quarrel between two lovers or their families; between Blue-
and-Grey, master-and-slave, or east-and-west plantations. In
the end a reconciliation is effected, often through the in-
tervention of a faithful servant. The moral injunction implicit
in these tales is to forgive and forget. The spirit of dissension,
or faction, or die-hard conservatism is condemned, while the
virtues of conciliation and openness to change are celebrated.

The pastorals of place are concerned with exposing false
ambition or restraining the aspiring mind. Working within
the conventions of the Plantation School, Dunbar subscribes
—or pretends to subscribe—to Southern agrarian values. He
thus portrays the Great Migration as a moral disaster. At the
same time, the Northern movement that he condemns
functions in his fiction as a metaphor of social mobility. The
moral of these stories is: know your place, be content with
what you have, and resist the temptation to aspire above your

station. The pastorals of place, in short, subserve the Washingtonian doctrine of limited aspiration.

Throughout Dunbar's fiction, the Northern city is depicted as a repository of false ideals. Anti-heroes, or negative exemplars, are created to embody these false values and illusory goals. Typically they are youthful migrants who succumb to the temptations of gambling, drinking, street crime, disease, or promiscuity. "Silas Jackson" is the purest story of its kind.[24] It deals with a Virginia farmboy who becomes a waiter at a resort hotel. Eventually he is corrupted and destroyed by an opportunity to join a troupe of Negro singers in New York. Like Silas Bollender, he returns from his excursion in disgrace: ". . . spent, broken, hopeless, all contentment and simplicity gone, he turned his face toward his native fields (362)."

A variation on the theme of false ambition is what might be called the carpetbagger theme. Here the protagonist is tempted by a get-rich-quick scheme which promises to bring success without the trouble of hard work. Such a scheme might involve political patronage ("Mr. Cornelius Johnson, Office Seeker"), real estate manipulation ("The Promoter"), or the policy game ("The Trustfulness of Polly"), but always the protagonist falls victim to his own avarice. In the end his Eldorado vanishes, and he is brought low. The moral of these tales is Washingtonian: only through hard work and sacrifice can the black man hope to improve his lot.

Some of Dunbar's overly ambitious blacks are undone by their own pretentiousness and pride. These are the boastful ones, who insist on flaunting their prosperity. Success turns their heads; they put on airs, become pompous, and adopt a condescending attitude toward their less fortunate brothers. In imitation of the white aristocracy they buy expensive clothes, assume fancy names, cultivate impressive manners, and in short become dandified. Such stories as "The Wisdom of Silence," "Johnsonham, Jr." and "The Home-Coming of 'Rastus Smith" warn the blacks to keep a low profile and do nothing to arouse the envy of their enemies.

Pastoral and travesty are closely related literary forms. Both employ the device of masquerade, but so to speak, in opposite directions. When a courtier pretends to be a shepherd, the result is pastoral, but when a shepherd pretends to be a courtier, the result is travesty. In travesty the masker "dresses up," while in pastoral he "dresses down." But in either case, the form depends on audience recognition that the masquerader is not what he pretends to be.

Travesty moves from the sublime to the ridiculous. A form of parody, it implies a moral norm beyond itself, of which it is a humorous burlesque. It posits an exalted sphere of human conduct from which its own sphere represents a falling-off. The victims of travesty are brash pretenders to that higher sphere. They are built up for a fall, which occurs when their pretensions are unmasked. The form depends, in short, on that deflationary movement known as *bathos* (from the Greek, *depth*), which may be defined as anticlimax, or comedown. It is through this reductive mechanism that the pretender is brought low.

In minstrel travesty, the moral norms of course are white. It is to white standards of dress, language, and deportment that the "darkies" of the minstrel stage aspire. Imitation of the white ideal is the crux of minstrel humor, for it is thought to be an imitation doomed in advance. The little girl, no matter how persuasively she dresses up, cannot be her mother. The Negro's imitation is *necessarily inferior*: that is the essential point. His pretensions are ludicrous in light of his inevitable failure. He is a comic figure insofar as he falls short of the white ideal.

Dunbar's travesties run true to form. They stress the imitative, or derivative, or secondhand features of Negro life. The key characters are those members of the black community—headwaiters, butlers, and body servants—who have the freest access to white culture. This dimension of Dunbar's art is closely related to the popular diversion of the cakewalk. He was familiar with the form through his efforts in the field of musical comedy. The cakewalk, in which Negro slaves parodied the elegance and formal manners of the Big House, was a standard ingredient of every minstrel show. If we recognize its equivalent in Dunbar's fiction, we cannot fail to be impressed with the affinity of his art to minstrelsy.

"A Supper by Proxy" is the purest of Dunbar's travesties.[25] It presents us literally with a dress-up affair, in which slaves momentarily assume the outward semblance of their masters. A Virginia planter and his wife announce their intentions of making an extended trip to Philadelphia. During their absence, the house servants prepare a lavish banquet to which they invite the entire "black aristocracy" of the neighborhood. In the midst of the festivities, their childish world of make-believe is rudely shattered. Old master returns in disguise, and much to their chagrin the pretenders are unmasked.

"A Supper by Proxy" is a classic example of social travesty, whose comedy derives from the attempt to rise above one's station. He who imitates his betters, like Malvolio, runs the risk of ridicule. This is the source of humor in such post-emancipation tales as "A Judgment of Paris," "The Deliberation of Mr. Dunkin," and "The Way of a Woman." What is really at issue in these tales is the former slave's desperate quest for a code of manners, a model of deportment, a standard of taste appropriate to his new status as a freedman. That this painful effort on the part of black folks to become "respectable" should be perceived as comical by Dunbar is a measure of his psychological assimilation to the white man's point of view.

Dunbar's religious travesties constitute a variation on the theme. Here a comic disproportion arises between saintly pretensions and human frailties. These stories contrast the high road of salvation with the low road of appetite. They move from a lofty spiritual plane to a mundane level of petty intrigue, ulterior motive, courtship rivalry, or venial sin. Thus a convert is not so much "under conviction" as in search of a husband ("Anner 'Lizer's Stumblin' Block"); or what seems to be a miracle turns out to be a prank ("The Walls of Jericho"). Often these stories have a bathetic ending which provides a naturalistic explanation for a seemingly supernatural event.

Most of Dunbar's religious travesties are antebellum tales whose common setting is the Virginia plantation of Stuart Mordaunt.[26] The central figure in the Mordaunt series is old Parker, the plantation exhorter. Mordaunt's Jim, who represents the unregenerate element among the slaves, is Parker's foil. A devoted servant of the Lord, Parker is sometimes guilty of the sin of overzealousness. From time to time he is taken down a peg by being discovered in some embarrassing or apparently compromising position. These travesties derive from the folk form of the preacher tale, in which the black preacher's alleged pomposity, greed, unchastity, or hypocrisy provides a source of deflationary humor.

A few religious travesties have post-emancipation settings. Their plots generally turn on some form of rivalry in church governance. But the tone is comic; the issues trivial or insignificant. These stories proclaim above all that the lives of black folk are lacking in high seriousness. We are presented not with Negro church life, but a parody thereof. Dramatic conflict may be present, but it is unworthy of mature minds. Of these undignified portrayals, "The Trial Sermon on Bull-Skin" is perhaps the most representative, while "Mt. Pisgah's Christmas 'Possum" is closest to the minstrel stereotype.

Dunbar's loyalty tales are best approached by way of a passage from Washington's Atlanta speech:

> . . . you can be sure in the future, as in the past, that you and your families will be surrounded by the most patient, faithful, law-abiding, and unresentful people that the world has seen. As we have proved our loyalty to you in the past, in nursing your children, watching by the sick bed of your mothers and fathers, and often following them with tear-dimmed eyes to their graves, so in the future, in our

humble way, we shall stand by you with a devotion
that no foreigner can approach, ready to lay down
our lives, if need be, in defense of yours . . .[27]

Eight of Dunbar's tales are protestations of loyalty along
these lines. Some are set in the antebellum South; others
follow the fortunes of a Southern family beyond the Civil
War, in order to demonstrate the loyalty of former slaves
through thick and thin. All reflect the house-servant orientation inherited by Dunbar from his mother.[28] "At Shaft 11"
constitutes a special case. This story, which deals ostensibly
with labor strife in the West Virginia coalfields, has been
praised as an extension of Dunbar's range and a clear break
with the Plantation School. In actuality, the old plantation has
simply been transposed from Virginia to West Virginia. Despite this metamorphosis, loyalty to white power remains the
story's theme.

In its offensiveness to modern readers, "The Strength of
Gideon" is typical of Dunbar's loyalty tales. Modeled closely
after Thomas Nelson Page's "Meh Lady,"[29] the story is concerned with a loyal slave who is the mainstay of his master's
womenfolk throughout the Civil War. Even as the Yankee
troops advance, and his beloved Martha urges him to join her
in deserting to the Yankee camp, Gideon remains loyal to his
white folks. At the moment of decision, the voice of Duty, in
the person of ole Missy, calls. Gideon's response must surely
be the saddest line in Negro literature: "Yes, Mis' Ellen, I'se
a-coming."[30]

Six of Dunbar's stories are concerned with the theme of
moral uplift. Inspirational in tone, they seek to redeem the
darker brother from his backward ways. Their origin can thus
be traced to the missionary impulse of the planter class, which
would not rest content until its slaves were Christianized. This
impulse toward salvation has been secularize 'n Dunbar, and
amounts to little more than the inculcation of h~ 'rgeois
values. These stories are little sermonettes on the dangers of

gambling, alcohol, and sex, or the vices of shiftlessness, irresponsibility, and wife-desertion. They are dedicated to the dissemination of what might be called the Booker-T virtues.

"The Ordeal at Mt. Hope" will serve to illustrate these principles.[31] The story depicts a young minister, educated in the North, who goes South during Reconstruction to work among his benighted people. He finds them shiftless and improvident, and somewhat given over to dissipation. The son of his hosts, in particular, has fallen into evil ways. By befriending the boy, Reverend Dokesbury inspires him to raise a few chickens. He then persuades him to attend an industrial training school to learn the trade of carpentry. Galvanized by this example, the whole town prospers: "Let the leaven work . . . and all Mt. Hope must rise."[32]

Despite his natural inclination to accommodate, Dunbar is not entirely lacking in rebelliousness. While ordinarily his true feelings are well masked, on occasion the mask slips, and we catch a glimpse of the authentic self. Six of his stories, for example, are concerned with voicing historic grievances, protesting current injustices, and defending his race from the ravages of the post-Reconstruction, repression. Two of these ("The Ingrate" and "The Easter Wedding") attack the institution of slavery; two ("The Tragedy at Three Forks" and "The Lynching of Jube Benson") are antilynching tracts; and two ("One Man's Fortunes" and "A Council of State") are direct assaults on the barriers of caste and the bastions of white supremacy.

"One Man's Fortunes" is typical of Dunbar's protest tales. Autobiographical in origin, it reflects the young poet's bitterness, following his high-school graduation, when he was unable to find a decent job. Bert Halliday, the hero of the story, is a graduate of the state university who leaves his alma mater full of hope, but is brought to the verge of despair by a series of disillusioning encounters with white discrimination and hypocrisy. Thwarted ambition is the story's theme. The hero insists upon his due, and a lower level of aspiration, symbolized by teaching in the South, is accepted only under duress. Perhaps in this astringent tale Dunbar discloses what he truly feels about the Washington doctrine of limited aspiration.

If legitimate ambition is thwarted by the color line, then illicit forms of aspiration are certain to appear. A new type of hero is required to dramatize this theme. In Dunbar's early stories the heroes are paragons of virtue, as virtue would be understood by whites. In certain of his later tales, however, a hero of a different stamp appears. This is a man whose character and actions are shrouded in moral ambiguity. With his appearance, the moral certainties of melodrama are dissolved, and the outlines of a more sophisticated moral vision are revealed. Dunbar is striving to transcend the official (or white) morality of which he has been heretofore a captive, and an outlaw (or Negro) code is beginning to emerge.[33]

Thus we have the confidence man, the racetrack tout, or the convicted felon cast in the heroic role. These are metaphors, or ritual masks, behind which lurks the elusive figure of Brer Rabbit. For it was the signifying Rabbit who first embodied this outlaw code. In a social order where the white man possesses all the power, writes all the laws, and formulates the moral code, the black man is pushed beyond the pale of conventional morality. He becomes a moral outlaw. So it is with Dunbar's disreputable heroes: the trickster with his signifying ways is a threat to the white man's moral order; the racetrack tout is a challenge to white respectability; the convict is a victim of the white man's law.

The figure of the trickster emerges slowly in Dunbar's fiction. His first treatment of the theme, "Aunt Mandy's Investment," is little more than a sentimental portrait of the con man with a heart of gold. In "The Mission of Mr. Scatters," however, we are confronted with a genuine rogue-hero. A similar progression may be seen in Dunbar's treatment of the racetrack milieu. In "The Finish of Patsy Barnes" an adolescent boy earns money for his mother's medical expenses by the "questionable" expedient of becoming a jockey. But in "Schwallinger's Philanthropy" a racetrack tout is developed as a full-fledged trickster-hero.

Dunbar's best story, "The Scapegoat," represents the culmination of this tendency.[34] The plot concerns a political boss in Little Africa who is betrayed by his white associates when the city is seized by a momentary passion for reform. Convicted of election-rigging, Robinson Asbury serves a year in the penitentiary. On emerging he announces his retirement from politics, but secretly he works for the defeat of the machine. On election day it rains black voters, and Asbury enjoys the full measure of revenge. In his slickness, duplicity, and ruthless survival code, Asbury is a lineal descendant of Brer Rabbit. The blunder committed by his enemies is to toss him back in the brier patch!

How shall we assess Dunbar's work in the short-story form? Much of it is inauthentic, in the sense that it reflects the white man's definitions of reality. Much of what remains is parochial or topical, and does not survive its own historical epoch. Very few of Dunbar's stories escape the limitations of a facile commercialism: they were mass-produced, written to standard specifications, and packaged for a quick sale. The truth is that Dunbar was a black businessman working in the literary line.

Despite these strictures, it cannot be denied that Dunbar played an important role in the evolution of the Afro-American short story. He established a pastoral tradition that would come to fruition in the era of the Harlem Renaissance. He was the founder, moreover, of a populist and anti-intellectual tradition that descends through Langston Hughes to the revolutionary writers of the Black Power movement. Finally, in his focus on the theme of Negro aspiration he identified a subject to which generations of black storytellers would return.

On balance, however, the verdict must be negative. In the short-story field, Dunbar will be remembered chiefly as a purveyor of dead forms. Plantation tales, minstrel travesties, loyalty sagas: these were the sterile fantasies of a nation engaged in a hollow ritual of self-justification. That they survived at all in the fiction of a black American is testimony to the coercive power of the white man's literary forms.

There is a moribund quality in Dunbar's art, attributable at least in part to the limitations of his age. To overcome those limitations, to make the most of his restricted possibilities, to stretch the imaginations of his contemporaries and thereby enlarge their moral horizons, it would have been necessary for Dunbar to adopt a sharply different literary stance. Romanticism would have had to yield to realism; loyalty to satire; pastoral to antipastoral. Such were the expedients of Charles Chesnutt, as he undertook to breathe new life into the dead forms of the Plantation School.

Chapter 4

Charles Chesnutt

PAUL DUNBAR'S undoing was his willingness to fulfill the expectations of the white world. Charles Chesnutt, a man of tougher moral fiber, was uncompromising in his opposition to anything that threatened his essential dignity. From the outset he refused to lie in the Procrustean bed prepared for him by partisans of the Plantation School. In a letter to George Washington Cable, he denounced the current literary portraiture of Negroes: ". . . their chief virtues have been their dog-like fidelity to their old masters, for whom they have been willing to sacrifice almost life itself. Such characters exist. . . . But I can't write about those people, or rather I won't write about them."[1]

In rejecting the myth of the faithful black retainer, Chesnutt was striking at the heart of Southern pastoral. For the pastoral ideal, according to Empson, assumes "a proper or beautiful relation between rich and poor."[2] If the master-servant relation is portrayed as other than idyllic, the effect is antipastoral. Chesnutt's antipastoral intentions are most explicit in a story called "The Passing of Grandison," which is best described as a loyalty tale turned inside out.[3] Here Chesnutt pushes the stereotype of the loyal slave to the point of absurdity, whereupon the tale, yielding to ironic pressure, is transformed into mock-pastoral.

Chesnutt's masterpiece of antipastoral is *The Conjure Wom-*

an. Set in rural North Carolina, and dealing ostensibly with grape cultivation, this book of stories is designed to expose the serpent in the Southern garden. It constitutes, in fact, a devastating parody of Southern pastoral. Arcadia lies in ruins in the aftermath of civil war. Hence the images of dilapidation and decay that permeate these tales. The author's aim is to force us to confront the destruction of the Garden, ponder its fundamental cause, and trace it in the end to chattel slavery, the fatal flaw in the *ancien régime*.

Enough has perhaps been said to indicate that Chesnutt's art is rooted in antithesis and opposition. If the Plantation School inclines toward pastoral, he employs the counter-genre. If white audiences object to mulatto characters, he devotes a whole volume to stories of the color line. Nor is Chesnutt's contrariety exclusively a racial stance. In "The Wife of His Youth" and "A Matter of Principle," he satirizes the color prejudices of the Negro middle class. In "The Web of Circumstance" he challenges the Washington formula of education and property as a panacea for racial ills. Chesnutt chose, in short, to work against the grain.[4]

This cantankerous streak is the mark of a born satirist. A gift for satire was in fact Chesnutt's major contribution to Afro-American letters. Drawing on the satirical resources of the black folktale, he founded a tradition that descends through Langston Hughes and George Schuyler to William Melvin Kelley and Ishmael Reed. As a writer of satirical tales, Chesnutt was by far the most accomplished literary artist of the Age of Washington. His chef d'oeuvre, *The Conjure Woman*, is a tart confection of sly derision and purgatorial laughter. Unmatched for subtlety, sophistication, and depth of moral vision, this book is the most important product of the black imagination prior to the First World War.

Life and Work

Charles Waddell Chesnutt (1858-1932) was born in the city of Cleveland where he was to spend the greater portion of his life. His family roots, however, were in Fayetteville, North Carolina, where his father and mother had been born. In 1856 his parents—not yet married—joined a wagon train of free colored persons who were headed north and west in an effort to escape the intolerable restrictions that threatened to reduce them to the status of the slaves. The young traveling companions fell in love, married, and settled down in Cleveland where the first of their seven children was born.

In 1866, when Chesnutt was eight years old, his parents returned to Fayetteville to look after the boy's paternal grandfather. Chesnutt remained in North Carolina for seventeen years. He attended school until the age of fourteen, when he was obliged to help with the family expenses. For the next eight years he was employed as teacher and principal in schools established by the Freedman's Bureau. At the age of twenty-two he was appointed principal of the State Normal School at Fayetteville.

This was a remarkable appointment for so young a man, but it did not satisfy Chesnutt's ambition. He grew increasingly restive in the South, especially after his marriage and the birth of a first child. He decided to teach himself stenography as a guarantee of future employment and a means of escaping to the North. In 1883, after a brief interlude as a journalist in New York, he settled with his wife and children in the city of his birth. There he studied for the bar in the office of a corporation lawyer. For the remainder of his life, with the exception of a few years when he tried to support himself by writing, he earned his living as a lawyer and court stenographer.

Cleveland and Fayetteville are the twin poles of Chesnutt's imagination. They are the "Groveland" and "Patesville" of his major stories. The dual rhythm of his life—partly Southern and partly Northern, partly rural and partly urban, accounts for the broad historical perspective that enriches Chesnutt's fiction. It accounts as well for his famous detachment and objectivity. Virtually all critics have commented on his aloofness of tone, his esthetic distance from his characters and their experience. It flows from his social marginality, for he never belonged completely to a Southern or a Northern world.

The seventeen years that Chesnutt spent in North Carolina supplied him with two of his essential subjects: slavery and the Reconstruction South. As a teacher in remote country districts he came into daily contact with emancipated slaves. He absorbed their tales of slavery times, their wonder stories, their talk of magic and conjuration. From these folk materials he was to fashion a remarkable series of conjure tales. Meanwhile, during his most impressionable years he was exposed to the hardships and vicissitudes of Reconstruction. This too would provide material for several of his finest stories.

Cleveland offered Chesnutt his third major subject: the foibles of the Negro middle class. He himself was a classic example of the type. He was of free-colored parentage—a group that had been manumitted for the most part because of kinship ties with their former masters. Like many members of the embryonic Negro middle class, Chesnutt's physical appearance was Caucasian. The ambiguities and ironies of race thus became a chief preoccupation of his fiction. Two of his best stories, for example, satirize the Blue Vein Society, an exclusive social club whose members draw a color line within the race.

His satirical bent notwithstanding, Chesnutt subscribed in the main to the value system of the rising Negro middle class. He was, after all, a self-made man in the nineteenth-century American tradition. His father had been an unskilled laborer, but he was able to educate his own children at Smith, Harvard and Western Reserve. Chesnutt himself was every inch the Victorian gentleman. He aspired to a style of life that encompassed an exclusive social set, a proper church affiliation, a summer cottage on Lake Erie, and European travel. He differed from his own milieu principally by virtue of a serious commitment to his art.

Like other writers of the Age of Washington, Chesnutt

peopled his stories and novels with doctors, lawyers, and businessmen. His heroes were men of wealth and station who had risen from lowly origins to establish a secure position in the upper-middle class. Chesnutt's style was designed in part to proclaim his gentility; to differentiate him from the uneducated mass. In his journal, he criticizes a book by the black abolitionist, William Wells Brown, for its lack of style: "The book reminds me of a gentleman in a dirty shirt. You are rather apt to doubt his gentility under such circumstances."[5] Chesnutt, who was a careful stylist, saw to it that his own gentility could not be called into question.

What distinguished Chesnutt from the other Negro writers of his day was a superior devotion to his craft. He kept a journal from the age of seventeen in which he recorded his literary progress. He brought to his apprenticeship that formidable discipline of which his social class was capable: "I have formed a general plan—one hour daily to Latin, one to German, and one to French, and one to literary composition."[6] In the last sphere, he formed the habit of writing several drafts, making frequent revisions, and subjecting his prose to a ruthless scouring. He became, in short, a serious professional who pressed his talent to its outer limits.

Chesnutt's literary apprenticeship began in 1885, when he submitted a story to a newspaper syndicate recently organized by S. S. McClure. In the next four years he placed a total of twenty-eight stories, principally in the McClure Syndicate and *Family Fiction*, a weekly published in Washington, D.C. Several humorous sketches found an outlet in *Puck* or *Tid-Bits*, but his real breakthrough came in the years 1887-1889, with the publication of three conjure tales in the *Atlantic Monthly*.[7] Some ten years later, after much negotiation, and what amounted to a further probationary phase, Houghton Mifflin agreed to publish a volume of Chesnutt's conjure tales.

Thomas Bailey Aldrich had published Chesnutt's conjure tales in the *Atlantic* without disclosing his racial identity. Walter Hines Page, fearing that such a revelation might harm the reception of *The Conjure Woman*, likewise refrained from mentioning the author's race. Chesnutt, for his part, acquiesced in the charade because he wanted his first book to be judged entirely on its merits. The subtitle of his second volume, *The Wife of His Youth and Other Stories of the Color Line*, came close to giving the game away, but it was not until both books were reviewed by William Dean Howells in the *Atlantic* of May 1900 that Chesnutt's racial background was generally known.

1899 was Chesnutt's banner year. In addition to his two books of stories, he brought out a short biography of Frederick Douglass. 1900 witnessed the appearance of his first novel, *The House Behind the Cedars*. Its theme was miscegenation, and its form evolved, after several unsatisfactory versions, from a short story called "Rena Walden," begun in 1889. These four books were the fruits of Chesnutt's early manhood. Retrospective in nature, they looked back on slavery or Reconstruction times. They were written in the eighties or nineties, but their publication was delayed until the timidity of editors and publishers was overcome.

In 1901, Chesnutt's writing took a new direction with the publication of his second novel, *The Marrow of Tradition*. This book, prompted by the massacre of black voters in Wilmington, North Carolina, during the Presidential elections of 1898, was an angry protest at the disfranchisement of Southern blacks. A third novel, *The Colonel's Dream*, whose aim was the exposure of peonage and convict lease, appeared in 1905. Thereafter Chesnutt published very little, though he lived for another twenty-seven years. In 1928 he received the Spingarn Medal from the NAACP for his pioneering role as a literary artist. In 1932 he died, never having surpassed the achievement of his first book of conjure tales.

The Conjure Woman

Chesnutt's first book of stories could not have been conceived without the prototype of the Uncle Remus tales. He himself acknowledges as much in an essay on Negro folklore which appeared in 1901: "Mr. Harris, in his Uncle Remus stories, has, with fine literary discrimination, collected and put into pleasing and enduring form, the plantation stories which dealt with animal lore, but so little attention has been paid to those dealing with so-called conjuration, that they seem in a fair way to disappear, without leaving a trace behind."[8]

In retrospect, however, Chesnutt draws a sharp distinction between the Uncle Remus stories and his own conjure tales. In an essay published a year or two before his death, he discusses the genesis of his conjure stories: "They are sometimes referred to as folk tales, but while they employ much of the universal machinery of wonder stories, especially the metamorphosis, with one exception, that of the first story, 'The Goophered Grapevine,' of which the norm was a folk tale, the stories are the fruit of my own imagination, in which respect they differ from the Uncle Remus stories which are avowedly folk tales."[9]

This crucial distinction, which ostensibly concerns the use of folk material, in fact reflects a difference of esthetic creeds. Harris, operating from a set of assumptions that might be described as representational or naturalistic, strives to preserve the authenticity of black folktales by leaving them "uncooked." Chesnutt, whose working assumptions are Coleridgean, stresses the primacy of the imagination and improvises freely on his folk materials. It is true, in short, that *The Conjure Woman* is based on an authentic body of plantation lore that deals with witchcraft and conjuration. But Chesnutt is correct to insist that his primary interest in this material is literary, not ethnological.

Chesnutt is in debt to Harris, but only for the outer trappings of his art. The Uncle Remus books consist of a narrative frame and a set of "inside" stories; *The Conjure Woman* has a similar design. Harris employs the venerable Uncle Remus as his narrator; Chesnutt, a similar figure named Uncle Julius. Both narrators recount a series of plantation legends in Negro dialect to a white audience. These resemblances, however, are superficial. Certain forms are employed by Harris in the service of a pastoral ideal. But Chesnutt takes these neutral forms and fills them with the demythologizing spirit of antipastoral.

The truth is that Chesnutt used Harris as a protective mask. His strategy, in the face of a racist culture unwilling to accept him on his own terms, was to present himself in the guise of the harmless and familiar. He was able to appropriate a literary form made popular by Harris and infuse it with a content that was not only strikingly original, but profoundly subversive of the smiling face of slavery put forward in the Harris books. Against great cultural odds he managed to pursue his own artistic ends, which were not the concealment, but precisely the exposure of the cruelties and injustices of chattel slavery.

The Conjure Woman consists of seven stories, bound together by a common principle of plot construction, a common cast of characters, and a common theme. In each story there is an outside plot, narrated in standard English by a white Northerner, and an inside plot, narrated in Negro dialect by Uncle Julius. Typically an action is undertaken in the outside plot (frequently a carriage drive), in the course of which an occasion arises for the telling of a conjure tale. This inside story, told by Uncle Julius, contains at its core some act of metamorphosis, such as the transformation of a slave into a tree, a man into a mule, or a child into a bird.

The plan of the book, then, is anything but simple, as several critics have mistakenly averred. On the contrary, it is a rather intricate affair, based on the sophisticated device of the parallel plot. It cannot be too heavily stressed that Chesnutt, at a time when most Negro writers were still learning to tell a simple story, was constructing plots within plots, and compelling his readers to respond to complex analogies. Nor was this a matter of mere virtuosity. The function of the outside plot is to provide a clue to the meaning of the metamorphosis, and thereby to control our reading of the fable.

Chesnutt confronts us in *The Conjure Woman* with two radically divergent fictive worlds. That of the outside story is the world of actuality, the domain of the ordinary and the commonplace. It is preeminently a world of *economics*: of crop rotation, improvements to the land, and projects for increasing revenue. Its spiritual qualities, as embodied in the white narrator (a gentleman farmer, transplanted to Patesville from his native Ohio), include a naïve faith in rationality, and a dogged skepticism toward anything that smacks of magic or conjuration. It is the world, in short, of capitalist enterprise as it invades the Reconstruction South.

The inside story represents the realm of the imagination, the domain of the wonderful and marvelous. It is a fairy-tale universe of grotesque transformations and Gothic horrors. Its gruesome violence reminds us of its kinship with the black folktale. The world of the conjure tale confronts us not with the present but the past; not with realism but romanticism; not with reason but emotion; not with calculation but accident. The central values of this world are not progressive but traditional. *The Conjure Woman* thus projects the crucial tensions of the nation in the decades following the Civil War.

The book is designed, with its movement from the husk to the kernel, to lead us toward the fabulous and fanciful. The white narrator, and to a lesser extent his wife, represent what Wallace Stevens calls "the world without imagination." Their civilization, lacking in imagination except where it came to making money, did not hesitate to trade in human flesh. Their lack of moral vision, even after Emancipation, continues to insulate them from comprehending the enormity of this historic crime. It is the function of the black storyteller, drawing on the imaginative resources of his folk tradition, to arouse the white man from his moral lethargy. Such were the politics of the imagination, as Chesnutt conceived of them in 1899.

The relation of Uncle Julius to his white employers is emblematic of the artist-audience relation. The black story-teller functions as a kind of proxy for Chesnutt, while John and Annie serve as stand-ins for Chesnutt's white audience. The impact of the conjure tale on its auditors is thus as much a part of Chesnutt's meaning as the tale itself. What John and Annie understand or fail to understand is often the dramatic center of the story. In Chesnutt's parable, the art of fiction serves as a corrective to the moral vision. John and Annie are the see-ers; chattel slavery the thing seen. Julius is the intermediary, or artist, who supplies the means of superior sight, or insight.

The role of the black writer, as Chesnutt conceives of it, is conveyed through the metaphor of conjuration. For Julius is a kind of conjurer, who works his roots and plies his magic through the art of storytelling. The point is that he succeeds in manipulating his white audience, in ways both small and large. He thus provides a model of how to conjure or bewitch the white folks. Through the medium of fiction, Chesnutt proposes to create a moral revolution, by enlarging the white man's sympathies and sharpening his moral vision.[10]

The instrument of improved vision is the metamorphosis found at the center of each conjure tale. But why should a mere conjurer's trick—an alteration in the shape of things—enable us to see them better? Because fiction is concerned with the truth that lies beyond the form. It alters forms, in order to reveal essences. The artist will not suffer us to live in a world of surfaces; he insists on probing for a deeper reality. It is the reality of chattel slavery that interests Chesnutt, and he employs a series of brilliant transformations in exposing it to view.

The concept of metamorphosis is crucial to the thematic unity of *The Conjure Woman*. Beginning with a theory of the imagination, Chesnutt extends its working principle to the spheres of morality and politics. At the core of each conjure tale is a transformation that reveals some essential truth concerning slavery times. But the magical power of fiction as wielded by Uncle Julius is immediately felt in the hearts of his white listeners. There a moral transformation begins to occur. Projected on the historical plane, this transformation constitutes the Reconstruction. For Chesnutt understands that white Americans as well as black were in need of moral reconstruction after the Emancipation.

So much for the book's general design; we must now examine certain of the stories in detail. The basis of selection is somewhat arbitrary, for all but one of the seven stories that comprise *The Conjure Woman* are achievements of the first rank.[11] Limitations of space, however, preclude a full discussion of six conjure tales. Perhaps four will serve to illustrate the possibilities inherent in the form, as well as indicate, without belaboring the point, the stature of the book as a work of art.

"The Goophered Grapevine" is the most widely anthologized of Chesnutt's conjure tales. Since it is the opening story, it bears the burden of setting forth the basic situation and launching most of the principal themes. John, the white narrator, and Annie, his wife, have come to Patesville from Ohio in search of a tract of land suitable for cultivating grapes. As they survey a ruined plantation with an eye to its purchase they come upon an elderly Negro enjoying a hatful of scuppernong grapes. In response to their queries concerning the history of the vineyard, he tells them a tale of slavery times.

This very vineyard, Julius explains, was "goophered" by a conjure woman in the days before the war. To prevent his slaves from stealing grapes, Mars Dugal' hired Aunt Peggy to cast a powerful spell on his vineyard. According to the terms of the goopher, any slave who ate the grapes would be certain to die within a year. The goopher worked entirely to the satisfaction of old master, who was heard to remark to his overseer that "fifteen hund'ed gallon er wine wuz monst'us good intrus' on de ten dollars he laid out on de vimya'd (18)."[12]

When a newly purchased slave eats the grapes in ignorance

of their magical properties, Aunt Peggy is persuaded to suspend the power of the conjure. If Henry will anoint his bald head every spring with the sap of the pruned vines, he will escape the consequences of his misdeed. Through the workings of this new conjure, Henry comes to share the properties of a grape plant, his life rhythms tied to the seasonal changes of the vines. When the plant sends forth its leaves and tendrils in the spring, Henry's hair grows thick and he is young and spry again. When the leaves fall and the grapes shrivel in the autumn, he becomes bowed and rheumatic; his hair falls out; and his physical strength declines.

Mars Dugal', who was never known to let a dollar slip by him in the dark, takes advantage of the situation to do some shrewd slave-trading. For five seasons he sells Henry in the spring and buys him back at a lower price in the fall, realizing a profit of a thousand dollars on each complete transaction. All goes well until a strange Yankee appears on the plantation. This high-pressure salesman bedazzles Mars Dugal' with promises of greater productivity if he will invest in a new wine press and adopt the latest methods of scientific farming. He persuades old master to push the vines beyond their limits, and in the end they are destroyed, along with Henry, who is linked symbolically to their fate.

What is the meaning of Chesnutt's fable, with its magical transformation of a black slave into a grape plant? Beneath the comic surface of the tale is a lesson in the economics of slavery. The slaves were in fact worth more in the spring, with the growing season still to come; in the fall prices declined, for an owner was responsible for supporting his slaves through the unproductive winter season. These fluctuations in price underscore the slave's status as *commodity*; his helpless dependence on the impersonal forces of the market. The target of Chesnutt's satire is the dehumanizing system that reduced the black man to the level of the crops that he was forced to cultivate.

"The Goophered Grapevine" is concerned with the moral

dangers of a market economy abandoned to the trade in human flesh. Through the figure of Mars Dugal', Chesnutt satirizes a capitalist culture obsessed with a good return on its investment. But the institution of chattel slavery, operating within the capitalist ethos, produced an historical disaster. The story of Mars Dugal' and the Yankee swindler is a parable of greed. Slavery was a case of pruning the branches too close to the vine. Through a desire for excess profits and a total ruthlessness toward its black labor force, the white South brought about its own destruction.

The moral atmosphere of slavery, as Chesnutt re-creates it, is one of mutual deception, slyness, and intrigue. It is a world of masking jokers in which everyone—white and black alike— is trying to outsmart or swindle everybody else. It is in short the world of Brer Rabbit, where the devil takes the hindmost and the height of folly is to trust your neighbor. A secondary theme, which will reverberate throughout *The Conjure Woman,* is the deceitfulness of appearances and the necessity of a certain skepticism where human motives are concerned. Thus the white narrator discovers that Julius has been exercising squatter's rights on the ruined plantation and deriving a substantial profit from the goophered grapevine.

"Sis' Becky's Pickaninny" is a moving tribute to the sorrow songs. It is a celebration of the slave imagination which produced the spirituals and, by converting suffering to sorrow, enabled an oppressed people to survive. Sis' Becky is a field hand who is callously traded by her master, Colonel Pendleton, for a prize racehorse. Her infant son, Little Mose, is not a part of the bargain, and so the slave mother and her child suffer the agonies of separation when she is removed to the next county. In the end they are reunited, but not until the devious maneuvers of a conjure woman trick the white folks into canceling the trade.

The center of the fable consists of two metamorphoses performed by Aunt Peggy, the plantation conjure woman. She transforms little Mose into a hummingbird, then a mockingbird, and sends him on each occasion to pay a visit to his mother. Sis' Becky hears the birds humming or singing and imagines them to be her son. Her heart is thereby comforted and fortified against despair. The birds are emblematic of the black man's musical imagination. Music did not alter the slave's external circumstances, but it did offer consolation to his wounded spirit. Which is why, after all, his songs are called *spirituals.*

Human slavery, Chesnutt seems to imply, is a crime against human love. But behind the crime is a failure of imagination. Colonel Pendleton and his associates are portrayed as men of no imagination who cannot distinguish between trading in horses and trading in human beings. They represent a culture exclusively concerned with cash values. Men of prosaic and utilitarian temper, they hold in contempt the superstitions of their Negro slaves. The blacks, however, with their belief in magic, conjuration, and the like, are seen to possess in ample measure the saving quality of imagination.

The outside story corroborates this reading of the fable. At the outset the narrator's wife, Annie, is suffering a deep depression. Eventually she is aroused from "her settled melancholy" by hearing Julius' conjure tale. The art of storytelling is thus presented as a balm to the sick soul. Annie's mysterious malaise is cured only when she listens to a tale about a conjure woman, who is a symbol of the artist, or maker of metamorphoses. As the story unfolds, it becomes clear that Annie's ailment is likewise emblematic: it represents the inability of her society to take what Coleridge has called the esemplastic power seriously. Bourgeois civilization, in short, suffers from a contempt for the imagination.

Exemplary of this malaise is her husband's attitude toward Julius and his rabbit foot: "Your people will never rise in the world until they throw off these childish superstitions and learn to live by the light of reason and common sense. How absurd to imagine that the forefoot of a poor dead rabbit, with which he timorously felt his way along through a life surrounded by snares and pitfalls, beset by enemies on every hand, can promote happiness or success, or ward off failure or misfortune (135)!"

We need only be reminded of Chesnutt's admiration for the Uncle Remus books to scrutinize a passage concerning rabbits with extraordinary care. It was the Negro slave, after all, who "timorously felt his way along through a life surrounded by snares and pitfalls, beset by enemies on every hand. . . ." If Brer Fox, like Colonel Pendleton and the white narrator, is a symbol of power without imagination, Brer Rabbit, like Sis' Becky and Uncle Julius, is a symbol of the imagination without power, which sometimes manages to turn the tables, but always enables its possessor to endure.

Julius remarks toward the end of the story that "Ef Sis' Becky had had a rabbit foot, she nebber would a' went th'oo all dis trouble." We are to understand, however, that she had a good luck charm or fetish all along. Her rabbit foot was the power of imagination that enabled her to transform a hummingbird or mockingbird into her lost child. It is no accident, then, that John should discover a rabbit foot among his wife's effects, shortly after her condition takes a permanent turn for the better. As for Julius, his rabbit foot is his power as a storyteller: it is that which has kept him out of trouble with the white folks for more than forty years.

"The Conjurer's Revenge" is the subtlest and most difficult of Chesnutt's conjure tales. Designedly so, for the author means to place the burden of interpretation squarely on the reader, and thereby to compel the active involvement of his imagination. The inside story is based on two metamorphoses. Having offended a conjure man, a slave named Primus is turned into a mule. On his deathbed the conjure man relents, and determines to restore him to his human form. Unfortunately he dies before the second transformation is complete, and Primus is left permanently crippled by a club foot. Unfinished metamorphosis is thus the dominant conception of the story.

Muledom is developed as the metaphorical equivalent of slavery. From the first the mule is linked to the black man as a beast of burden. Julius remarks, for example, "eve'y time I cuts a mule wid a hick'ry, 'pears ter me mos' lackly I's cuttin' some er my own relations (106)." Now let the metaphor expand: slavery is itself an act of conjuration, for it attempts, in effect, to turn a man into a mule. That is the point of the comical sequence in which Primus, turned mule, raids a tobacco patch, gets drunk on fermenting wine, and attacks a man who is courting his former sweetheart. A social system may change a man into a beast of burden, but his human traits will nonetheless persist.

In Chesnutt's fable, the man who conjured Primus into muledom undergoes a conversion to Christianity. Overcome by remorse, he hopes to atone for the harm that he has done by turning the mule back into a man. It is not so easy, however, to wipe the slate clean. Once a man has been a mule, he bears the scars of that condition in the form of a club foot. His Reconstruction, so to speak, is incomplete. Slavery has left the black man psychologically handicapped in his situation as a freedman. Chesnutt's unfinished metamorphosis, on its primary level of meaning, is an emblem of the unfinished business of American democracy.

Meanwhile the outside story is concerned with another kind of unfinished metamorphosis. As the story opens, it is a dull Sunday, and Julius' white employer seeks amusement in "the impossible career of the blonde heroine of a rudimentary novel." Exasperated, he throws the book aside and welcomes the diversion of a conjure tale. His wife too has been bored, but for once she is not amused by Julius' narrative: "That story does not appeal to me, Uncle Julius, and is not up to your usual mark. It isn't pathetic, it has no moral that I can discover, and I can't see why you should tell it. In fact, it seems to me like nonsense (127)."

What follows is a brilliant defense of the art of fiction. Through a strategy and style deliberately evocative of Cervantes, Chesnutt establishes his theme: the deceitfulness of appearances. Whether it is a question of horse trading, or the apparent rising and setting of the sun, sense impressions are not to be trusted. It is the special virtue of fiction, precisely by manipulating appearances, to lead us to a deeper truth. But for this mode of knowledge to be viable, it is necessary that the reader see beyond the surfaces of things. Annie has failed to penetrate the surface of Julius' fable. The force of the tale is therefore lost on her and she must suffer, like all literal-minded men, the doom of nonsense.

Fiction is a joint enterprise: that is Chesnutt's essential point. It can succeed only by engaging the reader in an act of imaginative collaboration. If the reader fails to do his part, the metamorphosis will be incomplete. That is the secondary meaning of Primus' club foot. The conjure-man, or artist, initiates the transformation, but if the reader refuses to participate, the tale will limp along to a sorry conclusion. Something akin to Chesnutt's theme is expressed in Robert Frost's "The Grindstone," when the poet remarks of his own honings and sharpenings, "I was for leaving something to the whetter."

"The Gray Wolf's Ha'nt" explores the relationship of the imagination to the moral life. In this cautionary tale of a man who is turned into a wolf, Chesnutt warns us of the bestiality that must ensue if we neglect the proper uses of imagination. His ultimate reference is the crime of human bondage, for it was a mammoth failure of imagination on the white man's part that made possible the cruelties of chattel slavery. The story may thus be seen as a deeper probing of themes set forth in "The Conjurer's Revenge." There a white woman's failure to penetrate the meaning of a conjure tale brings upon her head the doom of nonsense. Here a similar failure of imagination calls down upon a black slave the doom of wolfishness.

Dan, who is annoyed by a free Negro's unwelcome attentions to his wife, accidentally kills the man with his fist. Unhappily, the victim is the son of a conjurer, and despite

Dan's efforts to protect himself with a life-charm, the father takes a terrible revenge. He turns his son's slayer into a gray wolf and his wife into a black cat. By persuading Dan that the cat is a witch, he lures him into slaying his own spouse. The wolf, having discovered the conjure man's treachery, attacks and kills him, but not before he pronounces an incantation that will fix the charm forever: "Wolf you is en wolf you stays / All de rest er yo' bawn days (189)."

Of what does Dan's "wolfishness" consist? He commits three murders, and on each occasion acts precipitately, on the basis of appearances alone. His tragic flaw is an inability to penetrate the various disguises in which evil may present itself. Like Othello, he falls prey to a satanic figure who manipulates appearances and tempts him into murdering his own wife. At bottom his crimes represent a failure of imagination, for that is the faculty by which we move beyond appearance to a deeper truth. Lacking in imagination, man declines to the level of a beast. Properly employed, the imagination is a "life-charm" which protects its possessor from every kind of evil, injury, or harm.

In customary fashion, Chesnutt controls the meaning of his fable through a set of clues embedded in the narrative frame. The outside story begins and ends in a Gothic atmosphere evocative of Poe and Hawthorne. A certain tract of land, according to Uncle Julius, is haunted by a howling wolf. Like the Southland which it represents, this haunted ground has been the witness of unutterable crimes. Maule's curse, or something like it, lies upon the land. These Gothic devices point the way to Chesnutt's wider philosophical concerns. For the Gothic mode is essentially a means of penetrating mere appearances and striking to the heart of things.

These concerns are made explicit in a passage of philosophy read by the white narrator to his wife. The passage is concerned with the problem of essence and existence, and the difficulty of deducing essence from the shifting appearances of things. The abstract language of philosophy at once gives way to the concrete imagery of fiction: "Some one was coming up the lane; at least, a huge faded cotton umbrella was making progress toward the house, and beneath it a pair of nether extremities in trousers was discernible (163-64)." From these outward manifestations we are to deduce the essence of Julius. It is Chesnutt's playful way of suggesting that in the fable which ensues we must penetrate to the essence of slavery, whatever the disguises that it may assume.

One such disguise confronts us in the inside story. When the conjurer determines to revenge himself on Dan, he begins with an act of demonic possession: "So dis conjuh man 'mence' by gwine up ter Dan's cabin eve'y night, en takin' Dan out in his sleep en ridin' 'im roun' de roads en fiels ober de rough groun' (177)." What is slavery, Chesnutt invites us to perceive, but a form of witchcraft in which one man takes possession of the body of another and uses it for his own purposes? Through such brilliant transformations Chesnutt forces us to look at a familiar evil with fresh eyes.

That slavery is Chesnutt's ultimate concern is apparent from a passage toward the end of Julius' tale: "Mars Dugal' tuk on a heap 'bout losin' two er his bes' han's in one day, en ole missis 'lowed it wuz a jedgment on 'im fer sump'n he'd done. But dat fall de craps wuz monst'us big, so Mars Dugal' say de Lawd had temper' de win' ter de sho'n ram, en make up ter 'im fer w'at he had los' (191)." The nameless crime that Mars Dugal' has committed is of course the crime of holding slaves. What was involved, as in the case of Dan's murders, was a failure of empathy. To temper the wind to the shorn ram is to be capable of empathy, or the imaginative projection of one's consciousness into that of another being.

The great testimonial to empathy in English literature is Laurence Sterne's *A Sentimental Journey* (1768). It is Sterne's ruined maiden, Maria, who observes that "God tempers the wind . . . to the shorn lamb."[13] Through this allusion, Chesnutt alerts us to a major source of inspiration for *The Conjure Woman*. We can imagine the shock of recognition as he read of

Sterne's journey to Paris and his trip to the Bastille, discovered his parable of the captive starling, and finally perused the words: "Disguise thyself as thou wilt, still, Slavery! said I, still thou art a bitter draught! And though thousands in all ages have been made to drink of thee, thou art no less bitter on that account."[14]

"The Gray Wolf's Ha'nt" is Chesnutt's finest conjure tale; in it he comes closest to defining his essential theme. His intent throughout *The Conjure Woman* is to penetrate the disguises of the demon, Slavery. His assumption is that evil presents itself to men in the guise of innocence. The Plantation School, for example, was concerned entirely with the innocent surfaces of slavery. But the Brer Rabbit tales, which formed so crucial a part of Chesnutt's heritage, penetrated to the essence of the crime. Like the anonymous creators of the slave tales, Chesnutt was determined to strike through the mask. In pursuing this objective he developed a technique that made him an impressive master of the short-story form.

The Wife of His Youth

Chesnutt's second book of stories, while containing some of his best work, is disappointing as a whole. *The Wife of His Youth* includes fewer major stories than *The Conjure Woman*, and is lacking in the unity of design that was a central source of strength in its predecessor. The second work, moreover, is seriously marred by a sentimentality that only slightly damages the first. It is tempting to attribute these weaknesses to a shift in the direction of Chesnutt's career, but the truth is that the two books appeared almost simultaneously, and the stories that comprise them were a part of the same creative surge.

The Wife of His Youth and Other Stories of the Color Line was published in December 1899, less than a year after the appearance of *The Conjure Woman*. Like the conjure tales, these stories of the color line had been accumulating for a dozen years, awaiting the imprint of a reputable publisher. In the fall of 1897 Chesnutt submitted virtually his entire output of short stories to Houghton Mifflin. The firm, moving cautiously, delayed decision for about a year. Meanwhile Chesnutt's hand was greatly strengthened by the magazine publication of what was destined to become the title story of his new collection.

"The Wife of His Youth" appeared in the *Atlantic* of July 1898. The public response to this impressive story was immediate and enthusiastic. James Lane Allen wrote to Walter Hines Page at Houghton Mifflin: "It is the freshest, most admirably held in and wrought out little story that has gladdened—and moistened—my eyes in many months."[15] Throughout the summer, favorable notices and reviews poured in. Editors and publishers began to approach Chesnutt with a variety of literary projects. "Taking it all in all," he wrote to Page, "I have had a slight glimpse of what it means, I imagine, to be a successful author."[16]

This was the breakthrough that Houghton Mifflin had been hoping for. In September 1898 they decided to proceed with the publication of *The Conjure Woman*, and within a year Chesnutt was negotiating the terms for a second volume. The new book would be built around the story that had won such praise when it appeared in the *Atlantic*. The new stories would deal not with antebellum days, but with postwar life among the colored people, whether of the North or South. They would be written in a realistic vein, and their purpose would be to "throw a light upon the great problem on which the stories are strung; for the backbone of the volume is not a character, like Uncle Julius in *The Conjure Woman*, but a subject, as indicated in the title—*The Color Line.*"[17]

Chesnutt's second collection contains nine stories, of which four add substantially to his reputation. "The Sheriff's Children" is a poignantly ironical treatment of the origins of the mulatto middle class. "The Wife of His Youth" and "A Matter of Principle" are companion pieces which satirize the follies of that class a few decades after the Emancipation. A fourth story, "The Passing of Grandison," is an amusing inversion of the plantation myth, but once the plot has been retold, there is little scope for critical commentary. Pressed for space, we will rely on the first three stories to impart a flavor of the volume.

"The Sheriff's Children" is one of Chesnutt's earliest as well as strongest efforts.[18] Published in the *Independent* of November 1889, it belongs to that period in the late eighties when Chesnutt emerged as the progenitor of the Afro-American short story. Set in North Carolina during Reconstruction, the story is concerned with the symbolic rejection by a white man of his mulatto son. The father, however, is the focus of dramatic interest. Chesnutt's theme is the corrosiveness of racism in the white man's soul; the decay of moral sensibility that is an inevitable consequence of caste; the tragic spectacle of a man of decency and conscience who is warped by his environment.

That environment is delineated at the outset through a studied parallel with the opening passages of Irving's "Legend of Sleepy Hollow." As the Dutch hamlets of the Hudson Valley were untouched by the ferment of the Revolution, so Branson County has remained immune to the changes wrought by the Civil War. This somnolent community—isolated, backward, and morally lethargic—pursues its traditional ways oblivious to the great moral crisis that has shaken the nation. Chesnutt's hero, like Irving's, is an idealist defeated by the forces of convention. But above all Chesnutt's tone derives from Irving: that gentle and yet piercing irony which serves to distance so many of our nineteenth-century authors from the follies of their countrymen.

As the story opens, a white man has been murdered, and a strange mulatto taken prisoner on the basis of circumstantial evidence. A mob surrounds the jail and attempts to lynch the Negro, but the sheriff stands his ground and drives them off. Thereupon the prisoner seizes a revolver and, disarming his captor, reveals himself to be the sheriff's son. In the confrontation that ensues, the embittered black is shot and wounded by his white half-sister. The sheriff bandages the wound and retires for the night, to struggle with a *crise de conscience*. He resolves to atone for his cowardly betrayal of his black son, but it is too late: the youth has killed himself by opening his wound.

Irony permeates every level of "The Sheriff's Children." Structurally speaking, the story consists of two crises: one when the sheriff faces the mob; the other when he faces his son. The discrepancy in his conduct on these two occasions is the source of the story's central irony. The sheriff is afraid of no man save himself: he possesses a great deal of physical, but not much moral courage. The son, who is a mirror-image of the father, is a physical coward but a moral hero. The crowning irony is that the sheriff's decision to atone for the past comes too late to save his son.

A tissue of ironies is woven around the symbol of the jail. The point is that the sheriff is a prisoner of his own racial fictions. Father and son share the same prison, and the name of that prison is caste. In the course of the dramatic action they reverse positions, as each one gains the upper hand. Handy-dandy, as King Lear would say: which is the jailer and which the prisoner? There is, however, one crucial difference in their situations: it is the father who holds the keys. "We want the jail keys," says a leader of the mob. "They are not here," the sheriff's daughter responds. "The sheriff has them himself (73)."[19]

The rich verbal ironies with which the story is infused can be illustrated from a passage in which the sheriff addresses the mob: " 'All right, boys, talk away. You are all strangers to me, and I don't know what business you can have.' The sheriff did not think it necessary to recognize anybody in particular on such an occasion; the question of identity sometimes comes up in the investigation of these extra-judicial executions (74)."

It is the sheriff's son, of course, who in another context is a *stranger* to him, and whom he has not thought it necessary to *recognize.* The question of the boy's *identity* will rise to haunt the father, for it is quite true that such problems may result from certain *extra-judicial* activities. Chesnutt the lawyer is at some pains to stress the inconsistencies in the sheriff's attitude toward law. Illegal lynchings, it would seem, are one thing; illicit intercourse another. And yet in both situations the sheriff plays the role of masking joker that is so frequent an artifice in the white South. It is precisely these pretenses, charades, and hypocrisies that are the target of Chesnutt's satire.

Chesnutt's larger meanings are supported by image patterns calculated to intensify his ironical effects. The story opens, for example, with images of somnolence and stagnation, and closes with images of arousal and awakening, but as we have seen, the sheriff's moral awakening occurs too late. An elaborate pattern of blood imagery points toward the final episode in which the mulatto dies of a symbolic wound inflicted by his own flesh and blood. Images of war and combat, centering upon the Civil War, delineate a culture that possesses the military, but not the moral or domestic virtues.

"The Sheriff's Children" springs, we may be sure, from Chesnutt's sense of personal injury. The story does not wholly escape from the stereotype of the tragic mulatto, but the pervasive irony which is its central feature enables Chesnutt to transcend the personal and achieve a universal meaning. The moral paralysis that overtakes the sheriff when confronted by his son is emblematic of a nation that will not face its historical responsibilities. The sheriff's repudiation of his paternal role is symbolic of America's rejection of her black minority. Chesnutt is thus the first black story-writer to employ the archetypal figure of the Negro as rejected child.

"The Wife of His Youth" consists of three sections which serve the classical ends of exposition, complication, and resolution. Part I introduces us to the milieu of the Groveland Blue Veins, or near-whites. Mr. Ryder, the leader of this exclusive set, is about to give a ball in honor of a young widow whom he hopes to marry. As he makes his preparations for a gala evening, we are given a satirical but not unkindly portrait of the rising Negro middle class. We observe in Mr. Ryder both the strengths and virtues and the narrowness and folly of his social group. What stands out in this realistic portrait is the hero's assimilationist perspective, his hope of being absorbed "upward" into the white race.

Part II contains an episode that reminds him of his true identity in the most compelling terms. A black woman of a certain age presents herself on Mr. Ryder's porch to inquire about a missing husband. According to her tale, she was married to a mulatto man while still a slave, but she and her husband have been separated for twenty-five years by the cruelties of slavery and the fortunes of war. As we slowly realize that Mr. Ryder is the missing man, we begin to comprehend the full dimensions of his moral dilemma. He must choose between two women—one old and black, the other young and almost white—who represent two different sets of values and styles of life.

His choice is rendered still more poignant if we recognize in the title an allusion to the Book of Proverbs. The passage contains an ancient wisdom that Chesnutt has transposed into racial terms: "Let thy fountain be blessed; and rejoice with the wife of thy youth. Let her be as the loving hind and pleasant roe; let her breasts satisfy thee at all times; and be thou ravished always with her love. And why wilt thou, my son, be ravished with a strange woman, and embrace the bosom of a stranger?"[20]

Mr. Ryder's conflict is dramatized by a stunning tableau that sums up the meaning of the tale. As he prepares a toast for the ladies, he takes down a volume of Tennyson, turning first to "A Dream of Fair Women," and then to the famous description of Queen Guinevere. The lines embody all of the loveliness of white womanhood. Even as Mr. Ryder pays obeisance to this sexual and cultural ideal, he is interrupted by the black woman who turns out to be his wife. Point by point

Chesnutt relentlessly contrasts the dress and bearing of the white Queen with that of the impoverished black woman. It is one of the most affecting scenes in Afro-American fiction.

The danger of internalizing the white ideal is Chesnutt's major theme. Up to a point, he warns, the black man can play at being white, but in the end reality will overtake him. The story thus amounts to an attack on the assimilationist perspective and an exposure of its source in fantasy and wish-fulfillment. The story's secondary theme has to do with the black man's sense of history. The wife of Mr. Ryder's youth is a symbol of his obligation to the past. The heritage of slavery is a painful one, and yet the old and ugly wife must be embraced. For the impulse to deny the past is a form of spiritual suicide.

Part III concludes on a note of Jamesian renunciation. At the height of the festivities Mr. Ryder renounces his love for the young widow and acknowledges the wife of his youth. What are the symbolic implications of the hero's choice? Mr. Ryder's dilemma is essentially that of the "voluntary Negro" who is light enough to pass and therefore free to choose his race. But Chesnutt is concerned more broadly with relations between the black elite and the black masses. In "The Wife of His Youth" he celebrates the values of group solidarity, *noblesse oblige*, and a loyalty that is unwilling to betray its own.

"A Matter of Principle," Chesnutt's second treatment of the Blue Vein milieu, is a comedy of manners in the fashion of Molière. The social custom under satirical attack is a tendency among the near-whites to discriminate against their darker brothers. They do so in the vain hope that this will make them more acceptable to white society. Chesnutt brings a devastating ridicule to bear upon this point of view. He hopes to exorcise the demons of genteel racism through a cleansing laughter. He is concerned, as a satirist, with correcting the moral vision of his fellow Blue Veins, disabusing them of the notion that white is right, and helping them to perceive the realities of their social situation.

Ambiguity is Chesnutt's chief device. As a man of light

complexion, frequently identified as white, he was an expert in the field. The story turns on ambiguity, uncertainty, and mistaken identity; a comedy of errors unfolds because the complexion of a certain stranger is cloaked in mystery. But we are in danger of outrunning the plot. Mr. Clayton is a successful *restaurateur* who labors under the illusion that he is not a Negro. He lives in splendid isolation with his family and friends, refusing all social intercourse with those of a darker complexion than himself. His daughter Alice, facing a restricted marriage market, makes a trip to Washington in order to expand her circle of eligible suitors.

Upon her return Alice receives a flattering letter from a Negro Congressman. Having met her at a ball, he desires to call upon her in her home. Alice, however, remembers Mr. Brown only indistinctly and cannot recall whether he is dark or fair. When a preliminary investigation suggests that he is of an eligible hue, the family prepares to receive him as a house guest and Mr. Clayton arranges to meet his train. Arriving at the depot he perceives a very black Negro standing guard over two valises, one of which is plainly marked with the Congressman's name. Assuming that a frightful error has been made he withdraws without making his presence known.

To extricate himself from the situation Mr. Clayton invents a fiction. He sends a note to Mr. Brown explaining that his daughter has come down with a case of diphtheria. Naturally they will have to abandon their plans for his entertainment. In order to validate his fiction—to create verisimilitude and preserve the unities—Mr. Clayton is compelled to remain at home for a few days, bribe a doctor into placing them in quarantine, and pack Alice off to bed with a putative sore throat. As the sorry farce is played to its conclusion, we learn that the dark man at the station was in fact Mr. Brown's traveling companion. Through her father's fateful error Alice loses her suitor to her nearest rival.

The theme of the story is the nature of fiction and of social fiction. As a writer of fiction and a serious student of the craft,

Chesnutt understands the putative nature of reality. He thus perceives that race is nothing but a social fiction. He also understands that art coerces life: if the scenario calls for a sore throat, Alice will contract a sore throat. And if the scenario calls for a black man, one becomes for all practical purposes black, even if in fact one's complexion, features, and hair are utterly Caucasian. With this insight we begin to comprehend the curious world of ambiguity and absurdity that is the natural habitat of the black American.

Race, Chesnutt shows us, is America's supreme fiction. He understands, moreover, the consummate artistry of the national charade. When white men in the decades following Emancipation rebuffed the advances of near-whites and rejected their pleas for special treatment, they were simply preserving the unities, and defending the integrity of their racial fictions. To these men the mulattoes represented not merely an embarrassing reminder of their own sexual hypocrisy, but a threat to the very concept of race. They would never rest until their social fiction was made consistent and complete by classifying the near-whites as Negroes.

"Baxter's Procrustes"

No account of Chesnutt's short fiction would be complete without some mention of his uncollected stories. Thirty-eight in number, twenty-five are more or less inept apprentice tales. Of the remainder, ten are undistinguished, but three must be counted among the author's most impressive work. "Dave's Neckliss" and "The March of Progress" are similar in theme and execution to the best stories of *The Conjure Woman* and *The Wife of His Youth*. The third story, however, breaks new ground. "Baxter's Procrustes" is Chesnutt's richest story, and as such it merits full consideration.[21]

"Baxter's Procrustes" is the story of a literary hoax. A club of bibliophiles called the Bodleian goes in for fine bindings, handmade linen paper, uncut edges, numbered editions, and similar appurtenances of the literary art. One of the members, named Baxter, known to have composed a poem in blank verse, is asked to supervise its publication under the club's imprint. He agrees, and in due time distributes a handsome edition of fifty numbered copies. The books are sealed, for if uncut pages bring a higher price, how much higher a sealed volume! A night is appointed for review of the Procrustes, but at the height of the festivities a stranger inadvertently reveals that the pages are entirely blank.

On its surface the story is a satire of Anglophiles and book collectors, critics and reviewers, and the whole tribe of bourgeois pretenders who reduce art to the status of a commodity. The target of satirical attack is a kind of fetishism, which operates according to the principle of contiguity: "[The club] possesses quite a collection of personal mementos of distinguished authors, among them a paperweight which once belonged to Goethe, a lead pencil used by Emerson, an autographed letter of Matthew Arnold, and a chip from a tree felled by Mr. Gladstone (52)."[22] These fetish-objects distract us from the author's *meaning*. The writer in bourgeois society suffers, in short, from what Marx has called the fetishism of commodities.

Fetishism may be defined as the worship of external forms. Baxter's "Procrustes," with its handsome cover and blank pages, is a fitting symbol of these hollow forms. Members of the Bodleian are objects of the author's ridicule because, mistaking form for essence, they settle for the surfaces of things. In this they resemble racists, who think to know a book by its cover, or a man by the color of his skin. These gentlemen of culture are actually fools: they are victims of a hoax in whose perpetration they have willingly collaborated. Their proper emblem is the cap-and-bells border with which the binding of Baxter's slender volume is embossed.

In their metaphorical dimension, however, Chesnutt's literary fetishists are not so much fools as victims of a cosmic joke. What if the universe is in effect a sealed book? What if ultimate reality, despite the efforts of philosophers to apprehend it, is unattainable, offering to man only a tantalizing glimpse of transcendental meanings? Then we have a universe of which Baxter's "Procrustes" is a brilliant image: "Each number was wrapped in a thin and transparent but very strong paper, through which the cover design and tooling were clearly visible (57)." Yet this is just a teaser, since the wrapper is transparent while the cover is opaque.

What are we to make of this false transparency, which amounts to a kind of mask? The list of prior publications undertaken by the Bodleian provides a clue. These include Coleridge's "Ancient Mariner," an essay by Emerson, another by Thoreau, and the "Rubaíyat" of Omar Khayyám.[23] All of these authors view Nature as a mere integument, capable of being pierced by the mind's eye. But some suspect that the great Bookmaker has employed his skill in such a way as to allow mankind at best a limited or partial access to the heart of things. To the deeply pessimistic, who suspect that the pages may be blank, God will appear as a masking joker, whose chief legacy to humankind is the principle of ambiguity.

Baxter is the avatar of such a God. That is the point of a brief episode concerning the club porter's crippled child, in which Baxter masks his true feelings and confronts the world with an enigmatic smile.[24] As author of a hoax, Baxter plays a godlike role, for he creates a fictive world in which the mask alone is real. The success of his scheme, however, depends on the willingness of the little society of Bodleians to endorse it. So long as every member of the club subscribes to Baxter's fiction, the mask remains intact. The story thus is centrally concerned with the process of public endorsement by which a fiction may acquire the force of truth.

The tyranny of social preconception is Chesnutt's central theme. "Society was the Procrustes which, like the Greek bandit of old, caught every man born into the world and endeavored to fit him to some preconceived standard . . . (55)." These rigid molds, or ritual masks, or fetish-objects, or stereotypes are mere fictions, as Chesnutt demonstrates convincingly in the case of racial categories. Buttressed by the herd instinct, however, and the will of fools to believe, they harden into tribal truth. Once granted collective sanction they become a Procrustean bed, brutally effective in suppressing individuality.

The power of the social lie is one of the great themes of *Huckleberry Finn*.[25] Since Chesnutt mentions Mark Twain in the opening paragraph, we are not surprised to find, toward the end of the story, that Baxter's hoax is exposed by a young Englishman, "a very jolly boy with a youthful exuberance of spirits and a naïve ignorance of things American, that made his views refreshing and, at times, amusing (60)." It is this naïf who, with his simple and direct approach to life, punctures the social fiction so carefully contrived by the sophisticated Baxter. The young man's name is *Hunkin*, an anagram of Huck Finn.[26]

Along with Twain, Emerson and Thoreau are mentioned several times. Chesnutt thus establishes the two poles of his American tradition. The Transcendentalists represent an unjustified optimism that the Book of Nature, if properly scanned, will reveal its deepest secrets to mankind. Twain, in his late and disillusioned phase, voices the pessimistic view that the Book may contain only blank pages. In "Baxter's Procrustes," at the very end of his career, Chesnutt associates himself with the pessimistic outlook of Mark Twain, and more precisely, with that masterpiece of antipastoral, *Huckleberry Finn*.

The source of Chesnutt's bitterness and disillusionment is obvious enough. In the fall of 1899 he gave up his legal work and tried to earn a living entirely by his pen. In 1902, after the failure of his books to sell in sufficient quantity, he reluctantly resumed his law career. "Baxter's Procrustes" was Chesnutt's revenge. He had brought a talent of the first rank to American letters, and his best efforts were greeted with indifference and neglect. His response was to write a magnificent swan-song portending his retirement from the literary life.

In 1900, after two volumes of Chesnutt's stories had appeared, William Dean Howells undertook an appraisal of his work in the pages of the *Atlantic Monthly*. In a generous and laudatory essay, he welcomed Chesnutt into a very exclusive company: "Mr. Chesnutt seems to know quite as well what he wants to do in a given case as Maupassant, or Tourguénief, or Mr. James. . . ."[27] Had "Baxter's Procrustes" been available at the time of this review, Howells might have felt confirmed in his high estimate of Chesnutt's art.

Howells, it may be argued, was guilty of a double standard in respect to black writers. But I have tried to show that his sense of Chesnutt's stature was substantially correct. Let me be precise. Before the Civil War, the American short story had three major practitioners: Poe, Hawthorne, and Melville. In the period between the Civil War and World War I, there were four: Henry James, Mark Twain, Stephen Crane, and Charles Chesnutt.

There is nothing "compensatory" or condescending in this claim. Afro-American writing of the nineteenth century, from a literary point of view, was a rather bleak affair. By the turn of the century, however, black America produced a literary artist of the first rank; a major American writer; and an early *Meistersinger* in the short-story form.

Part II
The Masks of Arcady:
1920-1935

By Mystic's banks I held my dream.
  (I held my fishing rod as well,)
The vision was of dace and bream,
  A fruitless vision, sooth to tell.
  But round about the sylvan dell
Were other sweet Arcadian shrines;
  Gone now, is all the rural spell,
Arcadia has trolley lines.
                    PAUL LAURENCE DUNBAR

Chapter 5

The Harlem Renaissance:
A Reappraisal

WITH the death of Dunbar and the virtual silence of Chesnutt, the Afro-American short story entered a period of stagnation and decline. Four collections appeared from 1906 to 1922, but none was able to command the imprint of a reputable publisher. George McClellan's *Old Greenbottom Inn and Other Stories* (1906), James McGirt's *The Triumphs of Ephraim* (1907), Joseph Cotter's *Negro Tales* (1912), and William Pickens' *The Vengeance of the Gods* (1922) were the last gasps of a dying Victorian tradition. These books, whose thrust is largely inspirational, embody the prewar consciousness of the black middle class. They belong to the Booker T. Washington era of American Negro cultural expression.

The 1920's witnessed the birth of a new era, known to cultural historians as the Harlem Renaissance. During this period four books of stories appeared: Jean Toomer's *Cane* (1923), Eric Walrond's *Tropic Death* (1926), Claude McKay's *Gingertown* (1932), and Langston Hughes' *The Ways of White Folks* (1934). In addition, three important story writers were at work who never published a collection: Zora Hurston, Rudolph Fisher, and Arna Bontemps.[1] Because these authors functioned in a wider sphere than that of the short story, it will be necessary to enlarge our perspective and to seek an understanding of this complex literary movement as a whole.

It is in the nature of a Renaissance to produce Renaissance men. In the present instance, the principal short-story writers of the age were also its chief poets and novelists. A versatile generation, these black writers worked in a variety of literary forms. It would thus be highly artificial to approach them from the narrow perspective of a single genre. The appropriate unit of study is not the genre but the generation, for the Harlem Renaissance was essentially a generational phenomenon. This cultural revolt, which transformed the premises of Negro art, is best approached through a contrast of the oncoming generation of the 1920's with the literary generation that preceded it.

Booker T. Washington was born in 1858; Charles Chesnutt in the same year; W. E. B. DuBois in 1868; James Weldon Johnson in 1871; Paul Laurence Dunbar in 1872. These were the writers who dominated Afro-American letters from 1885 to 1920.[2] As a generation, these men embodied the "old-fashioned" virtues of a rural and Protestant America. They were formal and dignified in bearing, puritanical in personal habits, and committed to the gospel of success through hard work. In their attitudes toward class and race, they tended to be bourgeois and assimilationist; in the practice of their art, distinctly imitative.

They were supplanted in the 1920's by a generation whose values differed profoundly from their own. This generation was born in the decade 1894 to 1903.[3] Coming to maturity during or soon after World War I, these writers were to dominate the Afro-American literary scene for the better part of two decades. In the arts they espoused modernism; in politics, radicalism; in personal life-styles, bohemianism and cosmopolitanism. Their ethnic stance included pride, militancy, a high degree of race consciousness, the acceptance of one's ties to the folk community, and the firm preservation of one's black identity.

Portrait of a Generation

The postwar generation may be thought of as provincials, seeking fame and fortune in the black metropolis. They came to Harlem, after all, from the boondocks, eager to absorb the sophisticated life-style of the big city. In this they resembled their white counterparts who, ever since the turn of the century, had flocked to Greenwich Village from every corner of the land. This influx of white artists and intellectuals was if anything accelerated by the war. In a literary climate dominated by such authors as Sherwood Anderson, Sinclair Lewis, and H. L. Mencken, "flaming youth" was in headlong flight from Lewis' Main Street and Mencken's booboisie.

Black youth of talent and imagination was no less on the move. Of the leading figures in the Harlem Renaissance, Zora Hurston and Arna Bontemps were products of the rural South, while Claude McKay and Eric Walrond were migrants from the West Indies. Langston Hughes arrived from small-town Kansas, while Wallace Thurman emerged from an equally provincial background in Salt Lake City. Jean Toomer and Sterling Brown were raised in Washington, D.C., which in those days was a Southern city, in terms of its restrictive racial code. Rudolph Fisher grew up in Providence, Rhode Island, a provincial New England town. Only Countee Cullen was a native of New York.

The hunger of these young provincials for sophistication explains not only their migration to New York, but their conduct after their arrival. Instinctively they sought out the most cultivated black men of the older generation: Alain Locke, Charles S. Johnson, W. E. B. DuBois, James Weldon Johnson, and Walter White. These men, most of whom were functionaries of the NAACP or the Urban League, were the mentors of the New Negro movement. They encouraged the

gifted youngsters in a variety of ways: reading their manuscripts, publishing their work in such Negro journals as
Crisis and *Opportunity*, and introducing them to white publishers.

Sophistication also meant a fructifying contact with white
intellectuals. Thus Claude McKay was attracted to Max East-
man and the radicals associated with the *Liberator*, while Jean
Toomer was drawn to Waldo Frank and his circle of esthetes.
Langston Hughes and many others became the protégés of
Carl Van Vechten, while Zora Hurston studied anthropology
with Ruth Benedict and Franz Boas. On a less personal plane,
sophistication meant becoming *au courant* with the major
writers of one's age: reading D. H. Lawrence and Thomas
Mann, James Joyce and Ernest Hemingway. It meant, in
short, mastering the tools of the writer's trade.

For most members of the postwar generation, sophistication implied a college education. Dunbar and Chesnutt were
self-taught men, but Claude McKay attended Tuskegee and
Kansas State; Jean Toomer spent some time at the Univer-
sities of Wisconsin and Massachusetts, NYU and CCNY; Sterling Brown was graduated from Williams and Harvard;
Rudolph Fisher from Brown and Howard; Zora Hurston
from Barnard; and Countee Cullen from NYU and Harvard.
Wallace Thurman was an alumnus of the University of Southern California; Langston Hughes of Lincoln University; and
Arna Bontemps of Pacific Union College and the University
of Chicago.

At the center of the Harlem Renaissance, in short, was a
generation in process of becoming *deprovincialized.* But not to
the extent of being assimilated into the white literary world.
Of all the major figures, only Jean Toomer and Countee
Cullen consciously pursued that course. For the rest, a deep
attachment to parochial or ethnic values provided the necessary resistance to cultural assimilation. A tension thus arises
in their work between the rural and the urban, the primitive

and the sophisticated, the provincial and the cosmopolitan. This is the quintessential subject of the Harlem Renaissance, and its characteristic literary mode is pastoral.

The Primacy of Literary Form

The story of the Harlem Renaissance is by now a twice-told tale.[4] Yet no one has attempted a literary history of the period. We have had intellectual, cultural, and political histories, but not yet a truly literary interpretation. For literary history, if it is anything at all, is a history of literary forms. It must attempt to identify the forms which predominate in a given literary epoch, and to account for the preponderance of those particular forms. A formal history of the Harlem Renaissance, for example, must account for the preponderance of pastoral.

Consider the major authors of the period. Claude McKay was raised in rural Jamaica, and his first two books of verse, *Songs of Jamaica* and *Constab Ballads*, consist of a pointed contrast between the simple virtues to be found in the Jamaican highlands and the corruptions of urban life in Kingston. Nor should we forget that McKay left Jamaica to study agronomy at Tuskegee.[5] Many of his famous poems, like "Flame-Heart," are filled with pastoral nostalgia for Jamaica. His most successful novel, *Banana Bottom*, is pure pastoral, as are the Jamaican tales in *Gingertown*. His autobiographical fragment, "My Green Hills of Jamaica," borrows its title from Hemingway's pastoral, *The Green Hills of Africa*.[6]

Jean Toomer grew up in Washington, D.C., but his family origins, and the deepest roots of his imagination, were in the rural South. Like McKay, his initial academic interest consisted of agronomy. In 1914 he studied agriculture at the University of Wisconsin, transferring in the following year to the Massachusetts College of Agriculture. A teaching post in Georgia in the fall of 1921, and a trip to South Carolina with Waldo Frank in 1922, gave him a firsthand knowledge of the rural South that he would celebrate in *Cane*. Toomer's masterwork, with its striking interplay of countryside and city, folk and bourgeois values, is the classic statement of the Harlem Renaissance.

Zora Hurston was a product of rural Florida, where she settled down for the remainder of her life after spending several years in New York. All of her fiction has a rural setting, and most of it affirms the pastoral ideal. Her finest story, "The Gilded Six-Bits," pits the city slicker against the honest countryman. Her most important novel, *Their Eyes Were Watching God*, celebrates the Negro peasantry, even as it scorns the bourgeois notions of self-improvement and racial progress. Her brilliant allegory, *Moses, Man of the Mountain*, whose theme is the exodus from slavery, and whose form is therefore picaresque, features nonetheless a long pastoral interlude when Moses is a shepherd in Midian.[7]

Langston Hughes grew up in rural Kansas, where his was the only black family in town. He makes use of this pastoral setting in his first novel, *Not Without Laughter*. Much of his early poetry and fiction is pastoral in implication, insofar as it espouses the myth of primitivism. At a later stage of his career, to be sure, he turned to antipastoral, under the provocation of a breach with his white patron. The result was a fiction that stresses satire, and a poetry that features the desecration of the Dream. Yet the Simple sketches, with their Virgilian dialogue between simplicity and sophistication, remind us of Hughes' deep commitment to the pastoral tradition.

So much for the major authors of the Harlem Renaissance. A survey of the major genres would yield a similar result. With few exceptions, the important poems and plays, novels and short stories of the period are pastoral in mode. This should come as no surprise if one recalls the basic facts of Afro-American demographic history. World War I, having opened heavy industry to Negro employment, marked the crest of the first great wave of urban immigration. A black literary movement, arising at such a point in time, was bound to reflect this massive transplantation. With its central contrast of rural and urban values, pastoral became the favored form of the Harlem Renaissance.

It cannot be denied, however, that a number of important works are picaresque in kind. Foremost among them are the three retrospective autobiographies of the Harlem Renaissance: Claude McKay's *A Long Way from Home* (1937), Langston Hughes' *The Big Sea* (1940), and Zora Hurston's *Dust Tracks on a Road* (1942).[8] Certain works of fiction like McKay's *Home to Harlem* (1928) and Hurston's *Moses, Man of the Mountain* (1939) are plainly picaresque in form. And certain poems in the manner of Walt Whitman—notably the celebrations of vagabondage by McKay and Hughes—derive from the tradition of the picaresque.

We seem to have, in short, a mixture of picaresque and pastoral, in which the latter mode predominates. Since these two literary modes are in fundamental opposition, it follows that the era was one of crosscurrents, of simultaneous movement in opposite directions. An effort to account for this paradox will bring us to the heart of the Harlem Renaissance. The key to the period was long ago provided by Alain Locke, who described it as "the mass movement of the urban immigration of Negroes, projected on the plane of an increasingly articulate elite."[9] Let us pursue Locke's suggestive phrase and examine the folk experience on which the Harlem Renaissance was based.

The Folk Experience

The Harlem Renaissance can be approached from many points of view, but without a doubt the basic, underlying phenomenon was demographic. By the end of World War I, American Negroes no longer lived in overwhelming proportions on the land. The Great Migration from the rural South was entering its fourth decade, and a strong beachhead already was established in the Northern cities. This vast population shift, which took place between 1890 and 1920, and which involved some two million Negroes, set the stage for the literary movement that ensued.

The migrating peasant is the key to an understanding of the Harlem Renaissance. For him, the Great Migration was a kind of Exodus, which freed him from the clutches of old Pharaoh, delivered him from the house of bondage, and brought him to the borders of the Promised Land.[10] What motivated him was *opportunity* (the symbolic title of a Renaissance journal). He left the South in pursuit of the American dream. As he emerged into the mainstream of modern industrial life, he experienced a sense of liberation, of expanding horizons, of a wider range of choices and alternatives than had been available to him in the agricultural economy and rigid caste system of the old South.

In a perceptive contribution to Alain Locke's anthology, *The New Negro* (1925), Paul Kellogg calls attention to the Americanizing impact of the Great Migration.[11] He first reminds us that Americans are a nation of pioneers. He then describes the Great Migration as a "belated sharing in the American tradition of pioneering by the black folk from the South." It represents "an induction into the heritage of the national tradition, a baptism of the American spirit that slavery cheated him out of, a maturing experience that Reconstruction delayed." Having experienced for himself the characteristic *mobility* of the American people, the black peasant became less parochial, less of an historical exception, more fully an American.

The Great Migration, moreover, demanded of the black peasant an unprecedented self-reliance. The very act of emigration was an act of spiritual independence. For in leaving the rural South, often over the objections of his former masters, the peasant was dissolving those subtle ties of servility and psychological dependence which had bound him to the land since Emancipation. In the quasi-feudal South, the black man had his "white folks" who functioned both as his oppressor and protector. Now he chose to disengage himself from the snares and nets of white paternalism, and to strike out on his own. The result was that contagious sense of manliness and independence which Locke identifies as the essence of the New Negro.

Once the black migrant had established a foothold in the city, he suffered a severe culture shock. Accustomed to a rural way of life, he now experienced the painful necessity of adjustment and accommodation to the urban scene. As the black community attempted to reconstitute itself in an urban setting, familiar rituals broke down, lines of authority were disrupted, and former values, attitudes, and life-styles became irrelevant. Under the impact of urbanization, the black peasant's moral universe was shattered. Nor did his new surroundings, from a racial point of view, remotely satisfy his expectations of the Promised Land.

On the contrary, the northern migration of the blacks met with a determined, and at times fanatical resistance. The migrants soon discovered that they were an embattled outpost in hostile territory. Resistance in the crucial areas of housing and employment took the form of evasiveness, delaying tactics, and often enough overt violence. The bloody riots that swept through twenty-five industrial centers in the summer and fall of 1919 were the culmination of this resistance. It was in this context that Claude McKay's sonnet, "If We Must Die," became a household word in black communities across the land.

The black migrants were thus the victims of a cruel paradox. Even as the Great Migration broadened their horizons, it forced them back upon themselves. The result was a pronounced upsurge of racial consciousness. The organizational expression of this rising nationalist feeling was the Garvey movement. Garveyism, with its slogan "Back to Africa," was at bottom an emotional rejection of America, a retaliatory gesture by the Southern migrant who was 'buked and scorned. What emerges on the plane of folk experience, in short, is a pattern of expansion and recoil.

The same pattern is duplicated on the literary plane. Most writers of the Harlem Renaissance were themselves migrants from rural areas to the black metropolis. They experienced the same sudden expansion of horizons, the same necessity for self-reliance, the same crisis of adjustment to the urban scene, the same rebuffs and humiliations, and the same emotional recoil as the black masses.[12] Like the inarticulate peasants whose plight they struggled to express, they were propelled by history in contradictory directions. Expansion and recoil were the opposing elements of their experience, and in seeking to endow these antithetical realities with form, they moved tentatively to the picaresque, and then emphatically to pastoral.

Impulse Toward the Picaresque

It was natural enough that such a subject as the Great Migration should find its initial expression in the picaresque. The form consists in essence of a journey, which is not so much a spatial or geographical excursion as a pilgrimage toward possibility, toward experience, toward spiritual freedom. In the course of this symbolic journey, the picaresque hero moves from a static, hierarchical, traditional society to a series of adventures on the open road. Such a literary mode is singularly appropriate to the historical experience of black Americans, as they broke away from the confining racial customs of the feudal South and undertook their northern journey.

Making its first appearance in Renaissance Spain, the picaresque novel reflected the early stirrings of the Spanish bourgeoisie, as they struggled to emancipate themselves from static feudal forms. The new literary mode stressed *mobility*, as opposed to the *stasis* of a closed society. Such a form has particular relevance for black Americans, as they struggle to surmount the barriers of caste. For caste imposes *immobility* upon its victims, freezing them in the social order by teaching them to "know their place." What the picaresque expresses as a literary form is above all freedom of movement. It introduces the revolutionary notion that one's life chances depend primarily on one's personal capacities.

Self-reliance is the central virtue of the *pícaro*, who is typically an orphan or a bastard. He is cut off from the past and from tradition; there is no ancestral fortune to sustain him; he is entirely on his own, and must survive as best he can. He is in short a great *improviser*. On the road he constantly confronts the unexpected, and it is his ability to improvise, to use his wits, and to outmaneuver his opponents that determines his chances of survival. If the rogue-hero of the Spanish Renaissance calls to mind a familiar figure in Afro-American folklore, that should serve to demonstrate once more the natural affinity between the black imagination and the picaresque.

The picaresque journey is at bottom a quest for experience. Hence the importance of the picaresque *adventure*, which is the basic structural unit of the genre, and accounts for its loose and episodic form.[13] The adventure constitutes a personal encounter with experience, as opposed to the vicarious encounter embodied in tradition. A closed society prefers its traditional ways as a guide to human conduct. In effect, it denies its members access to experience. In a caste system— the extreme example—the lives of the untouchables are sharply circumscribed; they are surrounded by prohibitions and taboos. The reclamation of experience is thus a central theme of the Harlem Renaissance.

The authors of the Harlem Renaissance were adventurers, breaking with the fixity of things. A sense of expanding horizons permeates their writing. Images of *far horizon*, for example, dominate the prose of Zora Hurston. The work of Langston Hughes displays the same motif, couched in different terms. The title of his autobiography, *The Big Sea*, is derived from a short poem: "Life is a big sea / full of many fish. / I let down my nets / and pull." Both writers are concerned with the quest for experience, and in this they are representative of their generation. The same spirit of adventure, of openness to new experience, may be found in the vagabond heroes of Claude McKay or the sexually emancipated characters of Jean Toomer.

Outreach is the keynote of the postwar generation. Determined to overleap the barriers of caste, they recognized no prohibition on experience as valid. Like their white contemporaries they were anti-Puritan, anti-Victorian, and anti-Prohibition. To drink bootleg liquor in a Harlem cabaret was symbolic, it would seem, of a deeper thirst. This thirst for experience accounts for their pursuit of sophistication in all its forms. It accounts for their defiant bohemianism, their insistent cosmopolitanism, and their committed interracialism. Having been so long confined in a culture that denied them access to experience, they were not about to imprison themselves in a spiritual ghetto of their own making.

The impulse toward the picaresque was the underlying impulse of the Harlem Renaissance. Manifesting itself primarily in autobiography, autobiographical fiction, and lyric poetry, this form would seem to epitomize the life experience of the postwar generation. What they sought, after all, was an escape from the cramped quarters of American provincial life. The picaresque motif, with its sudden bursting forth from confinement, was the formal equivalent of being deprovincialized. Why, then, was this impulse blunted or aborted; why did it ultimately fail to dominate the age? Because the picaresque, while well suited to portray expansion, was not so well adapted to recoil.

From Picaresque to Pastoral

Resistance to the Great Migration, as we have seen, produced an upsurge of nationalist feeling in the black community. Betrayed in its hope of a Promised Land, the community was driven back upon itself and its own resources. Such a cultural implosion has been called by a young political scientist "the return to beginnings."[14] This phenomenon occurs when an event so shocks or traumatizes a community that a period of self-examination becomes imperative. Spokesmen then arise, both in politics and art, who attempt to elucidate the event and focus or direct the community response. Such was the function of the Harlem Renaissance.

The nationalist temper of the times was reflected in the writings of the black intelligentsia. A case in point is the literary manifesto of the younger generation composed by Langston Hughes.[15] In this famous proclamation, Hughes exhorts his fellow writers to be their dark-skinned selves, to be proud of their ethnicity, and to produce a frankly racial art. He warns them to resist cultural assimilation: ". . . this is the mountain standing in the way of any true Negro art in America—this urge within the race toward whiteness, the desire to pour racial individuality into the mold of American standardization, and to be as little Negro and as much American as possible."

An attentive reader of Hughes' manifesto will discover the emotional dynamics of the Harlem Renaissance. These dynamics may be represented as a series of recoils: (1) from cosmopolitan to parochial values; (2) from cultural assimilation to the celebration of ethnicity; (3) from the norms and standards of the white middle class to the folkways of the black community; and (4) from definition by the white majority to self-definition. The values of the dominant majority were thus turned upside down. This inversion of values, which depreciates the white man's ways, even as it exalts the life-style of the black underclass, found its natural medium in pastoral.

It was the nationalist impulse of the age, in short, that determined its prevailing literary mode. For picaresque, with its invitation to the open road, is cosmopolitan in outlook, but pastoral, with its accent on the local parish, fosters regional and ethnic values. In picaresque, the imagination travels outward toward experience; in pastoral, inward toward the self. The one form is explosive, bursting traditional constraints; the other implosive, exploring the conundrums of identity. Pastoral was the decisive choice of the black imagination in the era of the Harlem Renaissance. An examination of the personal dilemma of these writers will help to clarify their choice.

The young provincials who came to New York in search of sophistication soon drew back from its possible consequences. For they perceived the dangers in too much sophistication, too much higher education, too many white friends, too many bohemian parties, too cosmopolitan a life-style. These dangers were the loss of community, the loosening of ethnic ties, and the ultimate erosion of one's black identity. At the end of the picaresque journey lay the tempting prospect of assimilation. The trick was thus to become deprovincialized without becoming deracinated. That required an acrobatic feat of considerable equipoise.[16]

In the preservation of this psychic equilibrium, pastoral played a decisive role. For as Empson has observed, it is the curious trick of pastoral *to write about the poorest people in a courtly way*, like "those jazz songs which give an intense effect of luxury and silk underwear by pretending to be about slaves naked in the fields."[17] Pastoral was the ideal vehicle for authors of the Harlem Renaissance. By keeping them in touch with their folk origins, it could serve as a check on their cosmopolitan aspirations; assuage their guilt for outdistancing the black community; resolve their ambivalence toward the black masses; and in brief, keep them true to themselves as they faced the temptations of upward mobility.

It is Zora Hurston's distinction to have captured the essence of the Harlem Renaissance in her allegorical novel, *Moses, Man of the Mountain* (1939). Hurston's Moses is a Prince, clearly destined for greatness. Yet at an early stage of his career he spends an interlude of twenty years in Midian with Jethro and his daughter, Zipporah. This pastoral interlude, when Moses is a shepherd, is a period of preparation, during which the hero acquires a certain wisdom and inner strength. Later on, in times of trouble, it functions as an anchor out to windward. It recalls him to the core of his existence; serves him as a touchstone of values; keeps him true to himself and to his moral vision.[18]

This pastoral interlude is a fictional projection of the author's personal relationship to Eatonville, the all-black town in Florida where she was born and raised. Like Moses she aspired to be a spokesman of her people, and in the heat of battle reverted to her folk tradition as a moral touchstone.[19] That is what accounts for her impassioned defense of black folk culture: its pungent language; its flair for storytelling; its hoodoo magic. That is why in all her writing she insists on the vernacular, refusing to forgo the common speech, just because she is a graduate of Barnard. That is why, in short, she curbs her impulse toward the picaresque, and turns instead to pastoral.

Consider now the generation as a whole. Hurston's touchstone of reality was Eatonville, Florida; Toomer's was Sparta, Georgia; McKay's, the highlands of Jamaica; Walrond's, rural Barbados; Hughes', smalltown Kansas; Bontemps', northern Alabama.[20] In terms of actual life histories, we have a mixed pattern. Some of these writers, having reached the black metropolis, rejected it, returning to the parish whence they came. Others remained in cosmopolis to write nostalgic works about the countryside. But the personal parabola hardly matters, for pastoral is a landscape of the mind. Always there was the symbolic return to beginnings, the pastoral interlude, the touchstone of rural life and folk community.

But pastoral was more than a means of attaining psychic equilibrium, establishing continuity with the past, or validating one's black identity. Beyond such personal motives, it was a way of discharging the artist's obligation to the black community. For the mass of black Americans were peasants in the 1920's, albeit in transition to an urban proletariat. A writer who aspired to be a spokesman of his people necessarily addressed himself to this reality. On pain of isolation from the tribe, he was compelled to deal with rural life and to assume a more or less affirmative stance toward rural values. Such was the price of establishing a reputation not only as a personage, but also as a spokesman.[21]

In this respect it is instructive to compare the writers of the Harlem Renaissance with those of the Chicago Liberation.[22] In the prewar years, such figures as Theodore Dreiser and Sherwood Anderson, Edgar Lee Masters and Carl Sandburg, Floyd Dell and Harriet Monroe, flocked to Chicago from small towns throughout the Middle West. Like the New Negroes of the 1920's, they were young provincials in search of big-city sophistication. But for these white authors, the theme of personal liberation was not at odds with any traumatizing historical event. For them, it was all expansion and no recoil: Their provincial origins, far from serving as a touchstone, were largely regarded as a curse.[23]

For authors of the Harlem Renaissance, however, it was not so much a matter of personal as group liberation. They had a stake in the outcome of the Great Migration, and in the fate of the black migrants whose destiny they recognized to be their own. The goal of personal emancipation thus was superseded by their bardic role: that is, their determination to give voice not only to the hopes and aspirations, but also the defeats and disillusionments of black America. In all human cultures, the ancient role of bard cements the ties which bind the artist to his social group. The assumption of this role by writers of the Harlem Renaissance checked their impulse toward a purely personal salvation, and strengthened their proclivities for pastoral.

The Myth of Primitivism

So far we have been discussing indigenous tendencies within the black community that led to pastoral. Now we must consider an external force, emanating from the white community, that served to reinforce the basic trend. This is the force of stereotype, which imposes certain rigid expectations on the black writer. Just as the plantation myth coerced the Afro-American imagination, so the myth of primitivism that superseded it. As in the Age of Washington, certain authors conformed to the requirements of the myth while others sought to undermine it, so in the Harlem Renaissance. And as before, compliance found its formal equivalent in pastoral, while violation was made manifest in antipastoral.

The first decade of the twentieth century witnessed a dramatic alteration in the literary portrait of the black American. The old iconography can be seen at its worst in Thomas Dixon's *The Leopard's Spots* (1902) and *The Clansman* (1905). The latter novel, which inspired D. W. Griffith's film, *The Birth of a Nation,* marks the apex of Negrophobia in American literary history. In 1909, Gertrude Stein's *Three Lives* appeared. Here, in Miss Stein's portrait of Melanctha, the future direction of American letters can be discerned. During the two decades that ensued, such writers as E. E. Cummings, Eugene O'Neill, Sherwood Anderson, and William Faulkner would drastically revise the literary image of the Negro.

The modernist writers who arose in the first three decades of the century introduced a new stereotype into American literature. They abandoned the image of the Negro as contented slave, or as ravisher of white womanhood, replacing these with a subtler, if no less racist caricature. In the writings of the Lost Generation, the Negro was depicted as a primitive. This was the image, for better or worse, that was thrust upon the writers of the Harlem Renaissance. Some black authors embraced the new stereotype, others tried to fend it off, or adapt it to their own ends, but all succumbed in one way or another to its seductive power.

Behind the new iconography stood a major tendency in modern art known as primitivism. This esthetic creed, whose seeds were sown in Paris of the 1890's, but which flowered only in the aftermath of World War I, dominated Western art and letters for a span of several decades. The Harlem Renaissance, in terms of its esthetic, was an offshoot of this larger movement. But primitivism is simply pastoral projected on a global plane. The traditional figure of the shepherd has been replaced by that of the Polynesian, the Mexican Indian, or the American Negro. To the extent, therefore, that writers of the Harlem Renaissance accommodated to the myth of primitivism, to that extent they inherited the forms, conventions, and devices of pastoral.

Primitivism was a dominant tendency in the artistic and literary movements of the 1920's. The origins of this esthetic can be traced to the figure of Gauguin, whose symbolic journey from Paris to Tahiti sums up the central thrust of the movement. Primitivism was a gesture of revulsion from a decadent civilization and an effort to restore the waning vitality of Western art through a return to primitive sources. Like all pastoral, it represents an act of ritual purification, in which the contaminations of the town are purged by renewed contact with the countryside.

Such a myth held obvious attractions for writers of the Lost Generation. Disillusioned by the Great War, and the machine-gun civilization that it symbolized, they were a generation of spiritual exiles. They felt their cultural heritage to be defiled by the torrents of blood spilled on the battlefields of Europe. Their basic impulse, which simply awaited translation into a suitable esthetic, was to avoid the corruption of their fathers at all costs. Western society, in their eyes, was morally bankrupt, and the proof of defalcation was the war. In book after book they turned in disgust from a civilization capable of butchering its own young.

At the heart of primitivism is a recoil from the metropolitan centers of occidental civilization and a quest for simpler, purer, and more elemental modes of life. Thus Hemingway, who is the representative man of his generation, seeks to recapture in Spain or Africa or Cuba the purity and freedom and harmony with nature he has known as a boy in the Michigan woods. Such a quest is the epitome of pastoral.

Writers of the Lost Generation, by their insistence on the corruption of official (that is, court) society, and their location of redeeming values in the underclass, reveal themselves as modern exponents of the pastoral tradition.

The impulse to purify was extended by these artists to include their medium as such. Hemingway, for example, felt that language itself had been corrupted by diplomats and statesmen, public relations and advertising men. His style was an attempt to cut through the false, the pompous, and the manipulative to the clean, unadulterated image. The hallmark of this generation was its accent on technique. In painting and literature, music and the theater, experimentalism went hand in hand with a return to elemental values. The rise of modernism in Western art cannot be understood apart from its pastoral implications.

The discovery of the Negro, and of Negro art, was an inevitable consequence of this esthetic. Here was a primitive, unspoiled people whose natural spontaneity had not been crushed by the forces of modern industrialism. Writers like Gertrude Stein and E. E. Cummings, Sherwood Anderson and Waldo Frank, William Faulkner and Eugene O'Neill, adopted this perspective toward their Negro characters. Their esthetic strategies relied extensively on the inversion of values which, as we have seen, is a central feature of pastoral. Thus Stein's Melanctha, Cummings' Jean le Nègre, and Faulkner's Dilsey are the moral superiors of those who rank above them in the social scale.

The Negro vogue of the 1920's rested, in fact, on pastoral assumptions. It operated, like the fiction of Hemingway and Faulkner, according to the principle of inversion. When white New Yorkers visited the Cotton Club to hear Duke Ellington, they came in search of genuine nobility. When they descended the basement stairs to a funky cabaret, they acted on the precept, common to all pastoral, that a descent in the social scale will be rewarded by a gain in spiritual stature. When white folks danced the Charleston, dug jazz, chewed ribs, and in general tried to pass for colored, they were taking part in an ancient masquerade. By donning shepherd's garb they confessed to their own cultural exhaustion, even as they sought redeeming values in the underclass.

Like all pastoral, the journey from Park to Lenox Avenue represented a symbolic passage from effeteness to vitality. White sophisticates felt the Negro to possess a superior juju. They wanted to touch, literally and figuratively, the magic we have learned to call "soul." Hence the role of the Negro celebrity, who embodied that superior magic. Hence too the integrated parties and interracial love affairs that formed the human backdrop of the Harlem Renaissance. Sympathetic magic, with its principle of contiguity, was at the heart of the Negro vogue. Harlem became, for a time, the Forest of Arden, where jaded courtiers might find a temporary refuge, and by acting out in masquerade some complicated drama of the soul, retrieve their better selves.

Pastoral has always been a means of projecting—and thereby exorcising—the masquerader's antiself. By assuming the guise of a humble forester, the Duke in *As You Like It* discovers what he cannot be, and consequently what he truly is.[24] Burnt cork serves the same purpose in a minstrel show: it helps the masquerader, by the principle of contrast, to discover his essential self. Primitivism may thus be seen as an evolution of the minstrel mask. What the white masquerader would *not* like to be (a comical darky) is now replaced by what he secretly aspires to be (spontaneous and primitive), but is prevented from becoming by the unrelenting discipline of modern industrial society.

The new minstrel mask, by virtue of a subtle and disarming flattery, was far less offensive than the old. The idea, after all, was that primitives were morally *superior*. In consequence, the writers of the Harlem Renaissance were quick to embrace the myth of primitivism. Almost to a man they played the jungle-bunny game. Harlem was transformed in their poetry and fiction to a lush, tropical jungle. Superimposed on images of

Africa, it became the black Arcadia, where fauns and satyrs danced the Charleston, a jazz trumpet substituting for the pipes of Pan. This wholesale capitulation to the new stereotype is by far the least attractive feature of the Harlem Renaissance.

A Negro version of the myth in fact emerged. According to this version, occidental civilization was corrupt, but not beyond redemption. The instrument of white redemption was precisely Negro art. Arcadia, after all, was just uptown. Through a temporary (that is, pastoral) immersion in the primitive—by touring Harlem cabarets, listening to jazz, collecting primitive African sculpture, and buying the books of New Negro authors—the white elite could be redeemed. While authors of the Harlem Renaissance were nationalist in mood, reconciliation with the white majority remained their basic aim. But it was Shakespeare's Duke, *after* his sojourn in the forest, with whom they sought to make their peace.

If the myth of primitivism reinforced the pastoral tendencies of the Harlem Renaissance, disenchantment with the myth was the source of Renaissance antipastoral. By 1930 or thereabout the myth was wearing thin. Satire and social realism began to replace the romantic excesses of the New Negroes. Wallace Thurman was the chief spokesman of this mood of disillusionment with his satirical novel, *Infants of the Spring* (1932). Sterling Brown brought a trenchant realism to bear in his book of poems, *Southern Road* (1932). And Langston Hughes joined the ranks of the debunkers with his caustic antipastoral, *The Ways of White Folks* (1934).

The Harlem Renaissance, it seems, may be divided into two distinct phases. In the early or ascending phase, pastoral predominates, buttressed by the myth of primitivism. In the late or declining phase, the myth exhausts itself and pastoral gives way to antipastoral. "Late Renaissance" may be defined as a phase when the myth of primitivism has been seriously undermined, but not yet replaced by the myth of Marxism. It coincides in time with the early 1930's. One way or another, the pressures of the white man's iconography are ubiquitous in Negro art. Whether in positive or negative terms, the myth of primitivism made a heavy impact on the black imagination.

It would be an error, however, to conclude that the Harlem Renaissance was merely the appendage of a white literary movement. Deriving in part from the myth of primitivism, it sprang as well from the historical traumas and psychological necessities of the black community. Were the outside or inside pressures predominant? That is tantamount to asking if the Harlem Renaissance was a superficial or profound, a specious or authentic cultural phenomenon. Was it simply part of the Negro vogue, promoted and exploited for commercial reasons by white publishers and impresarios, or was it more substantial than the fads and fashions of the Jazz Age?

The answer must be sought in the realm of literary form. The most striking feature of the Harlem Renaissance, from the standpoint of its formal attributes, is the clear preponderance of pastoral. Did these black authors, like Dunbar before them, acquire the form at second hand and employ it blindly, never questioning its relevancy to their own situation? Or did they succeed in adapting a traditional literary form to the spiritual needs of the black community? A responsible judgment will require (1) a closer acquaintance with the form itself, from a theoretical point of view, and (2) a better knowledge of the actual uses to which the form was put by authors of the Harlem Renaissance.

The Possibilities of Pastoral

At the heart of the pastoral tradition, according to a recent commentator, lies "the contrast between two worlds, one identified with rural peace and simplicity, the other with urban power and sophistication."[25] This contrast may be symbolized by shepherd and courtier, rustic and gentleman, or country mouse and city mouse, but always it involves a comparison between the simple rural life and a more complex form of civilization. Pastoral, moreover, affords not merely a contrast but a choice: the simpler world is portrayed as the more intrinsically desirable. The values of the countryside are felt to be deeper and more enduring, its satisfactions more elemental than the shallow pleasures and illusory rewards of the great world.

Idealization of the rural life, if one may judge by the longevity of pastoral, is rooted in a universal impulse of the human mind. That impulse, in its most rudimentary form, is undeniably escapist. Wherever there are cities; wherever the metropolis dominates the provinces; wherever life becomes hectic, artificial, and complex, the pastoral impulse is certain to arise. Former life-modes that have been surpassed—notably those of the herdsman and husbandman—are bound to be revived, if only in the imagination. At its most superficial, pastoral takes the form of an invitation to the jaded urban dweller to lay aside the burdens of a complex culture and seek simplicity and peace among the groves of Arcady.

In its more sophisticated forms, however, pastoral would seem to be less an advocacy of the rural life than a balancing or reconciling force. This is suggested above all by the temporary nature of the sojourn in Arcadia, by the archetypal pattern of withdrawal and return. Insofar as it functions spatially, pastoral seems to be a metaphor of the contemplative life. It involves the momentary retreat of the world-weary from society, their refreshment and invigoration through contact with nature, and their subsequent return, after achieving an inner harmony or reintegration of the self. Pastoral is thus a harmonizing force which mediates between the values of the country and the town, the contemplative and active life.

Because it deals explicitly with social class relations, pastoral has seldom lacked a political dimension. Courtier and peasant, after all, are hardly peers in point of worldly goods and power. Yet pastoral proclaims the countryman the morally superior, in part by virtue of his poverty. Logic then demands that the peasant be protected from the corruptions and temptations of material prosperity. Traditionally, pastoral poetry has urged the lower orders to shun ambition, renounce all claim to wealth and power, and be content with their modest portion and their mean estate. To offer such advice, no matter how high-mindedly, was to employ the pastoral convention as an instrument of social control.

Reconciliation of the classes has always been a crucial aim of pastoral. As William Empson has remarked, "Clearly it is important for a nation with a strong class system to have an art-form that not merely evades but breaks through it, that makes the classes feel part of a larger unity or simply at home with each other."[26] To this end, pastoral functions as an elaborate pretense, or act of ritual masking, in which noblemen don disguises and affect the garb of commoners. Thus employed, pastoral may be understood as a symbolic gesture, an attempt to submerge class differences, like that of a politician who rolls up his sleeves to establish a rapport with the common man.

The significance of pastoral, in any case, does not lie primarily in the social sphere. The town-and-country contrast, or the courtier-and-shepherd contrast, are essentially dramatic vehicles for more fundamental contrasts of a philosophic kind. Under the influence of Platonic thought, pastoral has always had a strong Utopian component. Among the ancients, it was a means of juxtaposing a timeless Golden Age with the tumultuous course of human history. In the hands of Christian poets, it became a means of contrasting God's creation with the fallen and imperfect world of man. But always pastoral performed its harmonizing function, mediating between the realm of actuality and that of the Ideal.

Perhaps at its profoundest level, pastoral deals with the antagonism between the self and the objective world. It copes with this antagonism through the mediating instrument of language. In this sense, pastoral is a state of mind, marked by poise and equilibrium, of which a certain kind of literary work is the outward manifestation. What it offers to mankind is a fresh perspective, a means of criticizing life by identifying with its simplest and purest elements. The pastoral perspective, by a process of reduction, purges the soul of its excrescences. It provides a touchstone, in short, of fundamental values.

Pastoral is a device for coping with a series of antagonisms which otherwise might rend the fabric of society or self. Like paradox, it is essentially a means of reconciling opposites. Within the groves of Arcady—which is a construct of the human mind—the harsh dichotomies of poor and powerful, provincial and metropolitan, simple and complex, innocent and sophisticated, natural and artificial, ideal and actual, timeless and historical, active and contemplative, are momentarily dissolved. The result is a gain in balance and proportion, and a greater complexity of moral vision.

Such have been the customary usages of pastoral. We now must ask: to what effect did authors of the Harlem Renaissance employ the form? Of what, in short, did their originality consist? Zora Hurston, in discussing mimicry as a basic feature of Negro art, makes the point that "What we really mean by originality is the modification of ideas. The most ardent admirer of the great Shakespeare cannot claim first source even for him. It is his treatment of the borrowed material. So if we look at it squarely, the Negro is a very original being. While he lives and moves in the midst of a white civilization, everything he touches is re-interpreted for his own use."[27]

Renaissance pastoral was rooted in the deepest emotional needs of the Negro masses. Nostalgia for the rural South was strong among the black migrants, as the blues tradition will attest. Disenchantment with the Promised Land was equally intense, and it produced a sharp emotional revulsion from city values and city ways. These two moods of longing and disillusionment were given voice in the poetry and fiction of the Harlem Renaissance. The more sentimental side of pastoral served to express a common sense of loss, to enshrine the fading memories of the past, and to provide escapist fantasies from the grim realities of transplantation.

A more tough-minded variant of pastoral acknowledged the necessity of adjustment and accommodation. Most of the black migrants, after all, could not return to a rural way of life, but were compelled to adapt to a complex urban and industrial society. Such an adaptation, however, was no easy matter for the black peasantry. Deracinated, and yet tradition-bound, they were torn between the imperatives of change and a desperate need to preserve some sense of cultural continuity. In confronting this dilemma, black writers turned instinctively to pastoral. By balancing rural and urban, traditional and innovative values, they could mediate between the old and new and reconcile the black community to change.

A second mode of employing pastoral stemmed from the history of social class relations within the black community. Social differentiation had begun during slavery times, when house servants were separated from field hands by virtue of their economic function, special privileges, and degree of cultural and biological assimilation. After emancipation, class lines hardened, and were reinforced by gradations of color and hair texture. The urban immigration, by opening new economic vistas, hastened the process of social stratification. As a professional class formed on the mass base provided by the Great Migration, strains arose which posed a serious threat to racial unity.

At the same time that these centrifugal tendencies appeared, a powerful centripetal force was set in motion. This was the binding and cohesive force of Negro nationalism, whose impact on the younger generation was profound. They saw the necessity of closing ranks, and understood that a precondition of internal unity was a drastic modification of the elitist outlook of the black bourgeoisie. The supercilious posture of the past had to be abandoned and replaced by convincing gestures of racial solidarity. The New Negroes were determined to break down the class barriers erected by their fathers, who had taught them to despise the black masses. They intended to immerse themselves in the common life and serve as spokesmen of the common people.

In this revamping of social class relations, pastoral might play a crucial role. For class and wealth are treated as twin curses in the pastoral tradition. From its inception, the genre has served to consolidate feelings of nationhood by submerging class differences and reminding the people of their common destiny. In Arcadia, class divisions are if not abolished, at least momentarily suspended. Pastoral was thus the ideal instrument of a nascent bourgeois nationalism. Through its mediating power, the separate worlds of the "dickty" Negro and the common folk might be joined and reconciled.[28]

Much of the writing of the Harlem Renaissance is devoted, in Empson's phrase, to "making the classes feel part of a larger unity or simply at home with each other." This is accomplished by the use of such pastoral devices as the double plot and rustic masquerade. The former, which figures prominently in the novels of the period, permits the simultaneous presentation of highlife and lowlife materials.[29] The latter allows the sons of the black elite to pose as commoners. This amiable pretense of folksiness, this claim to a simplicity that one does not in fact possess, this ritual assumption of the shepherd's garb, is the oldest and most persistent stratagem of pastoral.[30]

The dual structure of pastoral, with its contrasting worlds of courtier and swain, might serve as well to dramatize the racial cleavage in American society. The Renaissance writer's aim, however, was not a sentimental reconciliation in the Dunbar vein, but rather a denigration of the white man's world. His end was the affirmation of black superiority; his means, a simple process of inversion. The essential point of pastoral, whether dealing with cleavages of class or caste, is that the "upper" world should be debased, even as the "lower" is exalted. That the peasant led a happier and fuller life than the king was an article of faith in the Harlem Renaissance.

Such is the burden of the novels of "passing" which occupy so prominent a place in the fiction of the age.[31] These dramas of the color line reflect the pastoral belief that happiness does not depend on place or power, or in other words, on being white. Their protagonists, almost always women, are infatuated with the power of the white world. Mistaking appearance for reality, they choose the lesser, though more dazzling way. They are guilty, in short, of a false sense of values. A distinction between Nature and Fortune, crucial in Elizabethan pastoral, would seem germane. To pass for white is to desert the realm of Nature for that of Fortune.

Authors of the Harlem Renaissance shared—or pretended to others and perhaps themselves to share—a crucial sentiment: *Negro life is better.* Armed with that conviction or pretense, they wrote poems, plays, and stories exposing the corruption of the white world and exalting the virtue of the black. The two worlds of pastoral thus served to reinforce the cultural dualism of the Harlem Renaissance. In recoiling from the values of the white middle class, black writers sought an alternative value system in the "lower" world of Negro folk culture. Pastoral, with its characteristic inversion of values, was an ideal instrument for this theme.

The cultural antagonism between the white and Negro worlds expressed itself on the psychological plane as a crisis of identity. Torn between two worlds, the black writer suffered from a sense of doubleness. As a black man living in a racist culture, he knew the spiritual anguish of a soul divided against itself. The burden of a split identity was sometimes more than he could bear. It left him with a restless longing to restore the psychic oneness he had known as a child. Perhaps he could recall a time of inner peace before some racial trauma drove a wedge into his soul. This theme of lost harmony, or disrupted inner peace, is a principal motif in the writings of the Harlem Renaissance.

The pastoral convention offered the black writer a means of coping with his identity crisis without suppressing either half of his divided self. The double vision of pastoral, in which one views the world simultaneously from the perspective of courtier and shepherd, supplied a working model. By cultivating such a double vision, the black writer might hope to harmonize his white and Negro selves. Pastoral, in short, was a means of reconciling the black psyche to its doubleness. For pastoral, like paradox, moves through tension and antithesis to unison and harmony. By a deft balancing of opposites, it invites us to combine the best of two worlds.

Pastoral functions, at its most profound, as a fable of identity. It was thus a means of exploring, dramatizing, and re-integrating the Afro-American's divided self. Such a function is quintessentially poetic, but that should come as no surprise. The major authors of the Harlem Renaissance, while working in a variety of genres, were primarily poets. As such, they were thoroughly acquainted with the main traditions of English verse, including the pastoral tradition. They understood the restorative and integrative capabilities of pastoral and recognized the opportunities that it afforded of achieving psychic harmony and inner peace.

Such were the varieties of pastoral, as cultivated by the authors of the Harlem Renaissance. They ranged from a rather literal response to the problems of urbanization to a more poetic confrontation with the problem of identity. All were rooted in the circumstances and realities of Negro life. It seems fair to conclude that these writers were not so much the captives of a white literary myth as independent agents who assumed a truly bardic role. Their aim was to commemorate in poetry and prose the spiritual crisis of the urban immigration. This effort, despite some excesses and distortions, was largely a success.

It remains to restore the short-story focus and delineate the structure of the next five chapters. The generation of the Harlem Renaissance produced seven important storytellers. Of these, two—Jean Toomer and Langston Hughes—are indisputably major talents. A third, Eric Walrond, is the author of a number of impressive stories which, in the last analysis, are not quite equal to the best work of Toomer and Hughes. The remaining four—Zora Hurston, Rudolph Fisher, Claude McKay, and Arna Bontemps—are distinctly minor figures, so far as the short-story form is concerned.[23]

Our procedure will be to treat the minor figures first, except for Arna Bontemps, whose posthumous collection, published in 1973, had no contemporary impact on the age. Chapter 6 will thus consider the work of Zora Hurston, Rudolph Fisher, and Claude McKay. Chapter 7 will assess the strengths and weaknesses of Eric Walrond, while Chapters 8 and 9, devoted respectively to Jean Toomer and Langston Hughes, will discuss the best short fiction of the Harlem Renaissance. These four chapters, in their alternating rhythm, will serve to reaffirm the pattern of pastoral and antipastoral basic to the book's design. And finally, a short epilogue on Arna Bontemps will provide additional support for the main argument.

Chapter 6

Three Versions of Pastoral

THE Afro-American short story entered an authentic local-color phase in the 1920's. There had been a false dawn in the 1890's, when Dunbar and Chesnutt more or less reluctantly adopted the conventions of the local-color school. But their brand of local color was less ethnic than regional in character. They wrote if not as Southerners at least of Southern themes. Their fiction was an adjunct of the local-color movement insofar as it was closely tied to the literature of the white South.

In the Age of Washington, the celebration of ethnicity remained a muted note, scarcely audible in poetry or prose.[1] One generation from slavery, the Negro writer was too insecure to celebrate his blackness. He was too intent on proving to the whites that he was "just like them," and therefore worthy of acceptance. The local-color concept, in short, was at odds with the racial strategy of the rising Negro middle class. Far from stressing ethnic differences, they strove precisely to obliterate them, in the vain hope that cultural assimilation would permit them to merge and disappear.

It was not until the Harlem Renaissance that Negro writers were able to embrace the local-color concept with genuine enthusiasm. In the aftermath of World War I, a series of physical assaults was visited upon the black community. Under such provocation, the affirmation of one's Negritude became imperative. Abandoning their former hopes of cultural assimilation, black writers began to place a premium on being different. Since white resistance to the Great Migration was based on xenophobia (we reject you on the grounds that you are different from us), it was natural enough that the black writer, in devising a suitable defense, should strive at first to specify, and then to celebrate those differences.

The new emphasis on Negritude found its formal embodiment in local color. Thriving on the exotic and the picturesque, local-color fiction was based on the exploitation of distinctiveness for its own sake. This literary mode had flourished in the post-Civil War era by exploiting the regional variations in American life. Now it was adapted, by authors of the Harlem Renaissance, to the celebration of ethnic singularity. While this made for a commercially successful, and for that matter a psychologically emancipating art, it also fostered what might be called a travel-folder version of Negro life.

From a strictly literary standpoint, the glorification of blackness yielded mixed results. On the positive side, it brought a new subject matter within the purview of the black writer. Since whatever was distinctive was probably of folk origin, the lives of the black masses were accepted as a legitimate subject for the first time. Still more importantly, their speech was perceived as a powerful expression of ethnicity. Heretofore the distinctive qualities of Negro speech had been viewed as a badge of social inferiority. But now the vernacular was rescued from distortion and neglect by such brilliant practitioners as Zora Hurston.[2]

On the negative side, the superficialities of local color took their toll. The appeal of this genre is primarily to the reader's *curiosity*: his anthropological interest, so to speak, in the quaint customs of the natives. Many authors of the Harlem Renaissance, quick to perceive the commercial possibilities inherent in the form, indulged the white man's appetite for the bizarre at the expense of a profounder art.

The fundamental weakness of local-color fiction is a tendency to exploit atmosphere or setting for its own sake. The assumption is that subject matter alone, if sufficiently exotic, will sustain the reader's interest, so that formal considerations need not tax the writer's ingenuity. The local-color movement, however, is not devoid of formal implications. Latent in its focus on the region or the parish or the neighborhood are the devices and resources of the pastoral tradition. The best of local-color fiction strives to transcend the merely picturesque, and when it succeeds, it moves in the direction of pastoral.

What follows, in William Empson's phrase, are some versions of pastoral. The three short-story writers with whom the present chapter is concerned all display a strong tendency toward local color. Zora Hurston, a trained ethnologist, relies extensively on singularity and quaintness in her stories of the Florida lake country. Rudolph Fisher often strikes the pose of tourist-guide, initiating his readers into the mysteries of Harlem. Claude McKay specializes in exotic settings like the Marseilles waterfront, the Arab quarter of a city in North Africa, or a mountain village in Jamaica.

In their best short fiction, however, these authors move within the orbit of the pastoral tradition. Thus Hurston's most impressive tale, "The Gilded Six-Bits," portrays the triumph of rural over urban values. Fisher's most mature stories, "Common Meter" and "Miss Cynthie," are concerned with reconciliation, within a pastoral framework, of the classes or the generations which divide the black community. And McKay's most successful tales, "The Agricultural Show" and "The Strange Burial of Sue," depict rural Jamaica as a touchstone of moral values.

Zora Hurston

The thirst for experience was always strong in Zora Hurston's soul. In her autobiography, *Dust Tracks on a Road*, she writes of herself as a child:

> But no matter whether my probings made me happier or sadder, I kept on probing to know. For instance, I had a stifled longing. I used to climb to the top of one of the huge chinaberry trees which guarded our front gate, and look out over the world. The most interesting thing that I saw was the horizon. Every way I turned, it was there, and the same distance away. Our house, then, was in the center of the world. It grew upon me that I ought to walk out to the horizon and see what the end of the world was like.[3]

Far horizon never ceased to beckon, and the urge to explore it formed the basis of her picaresque adventures. That urge was momentarily suppressed, however, by the stifling atmosphere of a provincial, racist, and male chauvinist society. Everywhere she turned she encountered restrictive boundaries which designated certain areas as "off limits" to a Southern black girl. These limits were enforced no less by the black than the white South; hence the abrasive conflict between this imaginative youngster and the black community. Again and again she was reminded by her elders that, being black, she must settle for a good deal less than far horizon. And she rebelled with every fiber of her being.[4]

To escape from the cramped quarters of her childhood was the central thrust of Hurston's adolescence. This thrust toward freedom, whose literary mode is the picaresque, is dramatized in three early stories, "Drenched in Light," "John Redding Goes to Sea," and "Magnolia Flower." At the same time, a conflicting impulse is apparent in Hurston's early fiction: namely, the urge to celebrate the singularity of Eatonville, the all-black town in Florida where she was born and raised. This local-color strain, which manifests itself in stories such as "Spunk" and "Sweat," flowers ultimately into pastoral.

Zora Neale Hurston (1903-1960) was born and raised in the Florida lake country, not far from the town of Orlando. Her father was a homesteader, carpenter, jack-leg preacher, and three-term mayor of Eatonville. Her mother was an ambitious farm girl who taught her children to "jump at de sun." Never a happy affair, the child's life was thoroughly disrupted at the age of nine by her mother's death. After several years of improvised living arrangements and irregular schooling, she left home as a lady's maid in a traveling Gilbert and Sullivan company. Having been discharged in Baltimore, she completed her secondary schooling at the Morgan College preparatory division, and began her college education at Howard University.

There she joined the undergraduate literary society and published her first story in its journal, the *Stylus*. This maiden effort, "Drenched in Light," attracted the attention of Charles S. Johnson, who reprinted it in *Opportunity* and encouraged her to think of writing as a possible career. In 1925 she left Howard to try her fortunes in New York. Her second story, "Spunk," was awarded a prize at the *Opportunity* Awards Dinner in May. Among those present were Fannie Hurst, who offered her employment as a private secretary, and Annie Nathan Meyer, who arranged a scholarship at Barnard. She completed her degree in 1928, having studied anthropology under Franz Boas and Ruth Benedict.

Soon after Miss Hurston's graduation from Barnard, Franz Boas was instrumental in arranging a post-graduate fellowship for a project in Negro folklore. Subsequent grants permitted her to spend several years of field work in Florida, Louisiana, and the Caribbean islands. In 1932, when her research funds were exhausted, she returned to Eatonville to edit her material. Two books of folklore, *Mules and Men* (1935) and *Tell My Horse* (1938) were the result. In the meantime her interest in fiction was revived. A first novel, *Jonah's Gourd Vine*, appeared in 1934, followed by *Their Eyes Were Watching*

God (1937) and *Moses, Man of the Mountain* (1939). In 1942 she published her autobiography, *Dust Tracks on a Road*, and in 1948 a final novel, *Seraph on the Suwanee.*

Eatonville is the roosting place of Hurston's imagination; it is what she counterposes to the modern world. Founded during Reconstruction by Northern abolitionists, this independent township was the breeding ground of the frontier virtues celebrated in her fiction. Six of Hurston's stories and two of her novels are set in Eatonville, and when she abandons this familiar setting she does so at her peril. Hers is an imagination bound to a specific landscape: its people, its folkways, and its pungent idiom. This deep attachment to the Florida lake country accounts for both the strengths and limitations of her art, since what she gains in density of texture she sometimes dissipates in the depiction of a purely surface world.

The art of storytelling flourished in the town, inspiring its inhabitants to feats of emulation. As Hurston has recalled, "What I really loved to hear was the menfolks holding a 'lying' session. That is, straining against each other in telling folk tales. God, Devil, Brer Rabbit, Brer Fox, Sis Cat, Brer Bear, Lion, Tiger, Buzzard, and all the wood folk walked and talked like natural men."[5] Hurston assimilated this tradition, and worked primarily within its terms. Her standard plot, for instance, pits the weak against the strong. Her tendency toward parabolic or disguised meanings likewise can be traced to the folktales which were omnipresent in her culture and which captivated her imagination even as a child.

In approaching Hurston's short fiction it is well to bear in mind that this was her apprentice work. Six of her eight stories were published from 1924 to 1926, while she was still an undergraduate. Only "The Gilded Six-Bits," which appeared in *Story Magazine* of August 1933, is representative of her mature achievement. Of the apprentice pieces of the 1920's, "Magnolia Flower" and "Muttsy" are hopelessly incompetent. "John Redding Goes to Sea" and "Sweat" hover on the borderline of art and fantasy, while "Drenched in Light" and

"Spunk" display something of the power that is generated by
her best fiction.

"Drenched in Light" (*Opportunity*, December 1924) is a remarkable first story, whose impetus derives from the author's
childhood. Here is the relevant passage from Hurston's autobiography: "I used to take a seat on top of the gate-post and
watch the world go by. One way to Orlando ran past my house,
so the carriages and cars would pass before me. The
movement made me glad to see it. Often the white travelers
would hail me, but more often I hailed them, and asked,
'Don't you want me to go a piece of the way with you?' They
always did."[6]

The story that derives from these materials is a portrait of
the artist as a young girl. The plot depicts a high-spirited
child, full of mischief and invention, in conflict with a
Calvinist, repressive, and experience-prohibiting society. The
white-shell road that beckons to the child's imagination is a
symbol of experience. Her picaresque adventures, undertaken in defiance of adult authority, are emblematic of the
budding artist's unavoidable collision with the narrow outlook
of the folk community. Grandma Potts, who functions like the
Widow Douglas in *Huckleberry Finn*, embodies this restrictive
outlook, while the child-heroine, whose name is Isis, sym-
bolizes joy, laughter, and the pagan attitude toward life.

One day, on the occasion of a village barbecue, Isis makes
off with Grandma's new red tablecloth and wears it as a
Spanish shawl. Thus adorned, she performs a gypsy dance to
the delight of her immediate observers. Among them are two
white men and a lady who befriend the vagrant child, take her
"a piece of the way" in their car, and interpose themselves and
their authority between the malefactor and her grandma's
wrath. In the woman's confession that she is in need of
brightness, while the child is "drenched in light," adum-
brations of the myth of primitivism may be seen.

It is highly significant that the white upper class, in the
person of Lady Bountiful, should support the child in her

imaginative exploits, and her conflict with the folk community. This woman is the fictional projection of a series of white
patrons who encouraged Zora Hurston's art. At a deeper
level, the episode suggests that in Hurston's unconscious
mind, having access to experience was tantamount to being
white. Hurston makes much of the fantasies that she indulged
in as a child, devoting an entire chapter to the subject in her
autobiography.[7] It is clear from "Drenched in Light" that one
of her most potent fantasies—imaged as a princess, wearing
stately robes and riding on a white horse to the far horizon—
was that of being white.

"John Redding Goes to Sea" (*Opportunity*, January 1926) is
essentially a sequel, taking up where "Drenched in Light"
leaves off. The imaginative child—this time a boy—longs to go
to sea and experience something of the world, but his desire is
stubbornly opposed by his mother. Mrs. Redding, like Grandma Potts, embodies the narrow and provincial outlook of the
folk community, which cannot cope with the artistic
temperament. Images of stasis and stagnation dominate the
tale, expressive of the fate awaiting John if he lacks the
courage to be free. Grown to manhood, but still intimidated
by his mother, he is offered a chance to be a hero, when a
bridge is threatened by a hurricane. In an ironic dénouement
he drowns, escaping mediocrity only through a kind of crucifixion.

In his young manhood, John Redding is caught in an agonizing dilemma. To remain in Eatonville is to be trapped
forever in superstitious ignorance, symbolized by his mother.
But to depart is to be disloyal to the folk community where he
was born and bred. This is the central dilemma of Hurston's
life, and a common predicament among black artists. It is
resolved, in Hurston's case, by her assumption of the bardic
role. Guilty for having left the folk community in order to
pursue her personal ambitions, Hurston seeks atonement
through her art. She is determined to avoid stagnation by
transcending her milieu, but equally determined to give voice

to that milieu, to become its spokesman. The result is her bardic fiction, written in the local-color vein.

Two of these local-color stories, "Spunk" and "Sweat," are closely related to the Brer Rabbit tales. In their central polarities between the cruel and powerful and the weak and oppressed, echoes of the master-slave relationship are unmistakable. Like the animal fables from which they are descended, these tales are exercises in the art of masking. The secret theme of "Spunk" is the violation of black womanhood; of "Sweat," the deadly hatred nurtured in the hearts of the oppressed. The racial implications are effectively disguised by an all-black cast of characters, but the emotional marrow of these tales is a sublimated racial anger.

"Spunk" (*Opportunity*, June 1925) is concerned with two varieties of courage or definitions of manhood. Spunk Banks is a giant of a man who carries off his neighbor's wife and defies him to redress the injury. Joe Kanty, the aggrieved husband, hesitates to challenge his tormentor, but taunted by the village men, he attacks him from behind, only to be shot to death. The men function as a chorus, observing and commenting on the action. At the outset Spunk wins their admiration through his fearlessness, while Joe is despised for his apparent cowardice. In the end, however, a villager proclaims that "Joe was a braver man than Spunk." Amid the derisive shouts of his audience he explains that it requires a greater courage for the weaker to attack the stronger man.

Behind the two antagonists loom the archetypal figures of Brer Rabbit and Brer Bear. Joe Kanty, as his name suggests, would be helpless in an open test of strength; his only hope lies in a surprise attack. The story thus endorses the survival values of subterfuge and treachery, up to and including an assault from behind. Two conflicting codes, one "honorable" or Anglo-Saxon, the other "cowardly" or Negro, are juxtaposed. The story repudiates conventional morality and affirms the outlaw code imposed upon the black man by his social subjugation. Hurston thus invokes the ancient wisdom of the folktale to reconcile the frontier virtues of courage and manliness with the brutal facts of caste.

"Sweat" (*Fire*, November 1926) is a less successful tale. The heroine is Delia Jones, a long-suffering laundress whose life is made unbearable by a brutal, tyrannous, and flagrantly philandering husband. Sykes attempts to kill his wife by concealing a rattlesnake in her laundry basket, but in an ironic reversal, he is destroyed by his own villainy. Throughout the story, man and wife are locked in a mutual hatred so intense that it acquires the force of myth. Behind their murderous domestic quarrel we discern the ancient animosities of Brer Rabbit and Brer Wolf. Like the cruellest and most sadistic of the animal fables, this story serves to vent illicit feelings of hatred and revenge.

The story has an ending that can only be described as self-indulgent. In the episode depicting Sykes' ordeal, Hurston loses her composure and rejoices in the torture of her villain. "Sweat" is thus reduced to a revenge fantasy. While such fantasies are a common feature of the animal fables, a more sophisticated medium demands a commensurate advance in emotional control. Nor does the story succeed as a horror tale, for naming the emotion that a reader is supposed to feel is not the same as compelling him to feel it. Hurston is an amateur in horror, and compared to Eric Walrond's "The White Snake," this story is a visit with the children to the Bronx Zoo.

From stories in the local-color vein, Hurston's imagination flowered into pastoral. But not until her disillusionment with urban life was complete. "Muttsy" (*Opportunity*, August 1926) is her story of recoil from the black metropolis, similar in tone and psychological significance to Claude McKay's Harlem tales. "Drenched in Light" and "John Redding Goes to Sea" portray the self setting forth from its place of origin in quest of wider horizons. "Muttsy," Hurston's sole attempt to deal with the urban scene, depicts the self in jeopardy from false, urban values. "The Gilded Six-Bits" brings the theme full circle as the self, reconciled to its provincial origins, returns to its spiritual home in Eatonville.

"The Gilded Six-Bits" (*Story*, August 1933) is Hurston's principal achievement in the short-story form. The tale inaugurates the second and most creative phase of her career, which followed her return to Eatonville in 1932. She now was a mature woman: her ambivalent feelings toward the folk community had been resolved; her adolescent impulse to escape it, mastered. Her curiosity to witness something of the larger world had been appeased, and she was ready to accept her destiny. That destiny, she now perceived, was to embrace her folk experience and give it form. The fruit of self-acceptance was a burst of creativity, beginning with the present story and extending through three novels.

The story is concerned with a crisis in the lives of Joe and Missie May. They have been happily married for a year when Slemmons, an urbanized Negro from Chicago, opens an ice-cream parlor in Eatonville. Dazzled by his fancy clothes and city ways, Missie May forgets herself and takes him as a lover. Joe discovers the deception and drives Slemmons off, but it is many months before he can forgive his thoroughly remorseful wife. Structurally speaking, the woman functions as a pivot between two value systems: the one urban and "sophisticated," the other rural and elemental. At first she chooses falsely, but in the end the deep and abiding values of the countryside prevail.

"The Gilded Six-Bits" is essentially a drama of sin and redemption, a symbolic reenactment of the Fall. As the story opens, Joe and Missie May frolic in prelapsarian innocence. Their pastoral surroundings and simple way of life constitute a Paradise where "all, everything was right." Into this happy Eden comes the Tempter, Slemmons, who proffers not an apple but a ten-dollar gold piece suspended from his watch chain. That the gold should prove to be illusory is Hurston's bitter comment on the Great Migration. Through Slemmons the city is exposed as a repository of false values.

The shallowness of urban culture is conveyed through Slemmons' attitude toward time. In the modern world of progress and improvement, of which the ice-cream parlor is an emblem, time is a commodity. The capitalist ethos, with its obligation to convert time into money, is symbolized by Slemmons' golden watch charm. But the peasant world of Joe and Missie May responds to natural rather than artificial rhythms: "Finally the sun's tide crept upon the shore of night and drowned its hours." In this world, time has a moral and theological rather than economic significance. It is primarily a healing force, repairing the breach that guilt has opened in the human soul.

"The Gilded Six-Bits" thus reveals the central core of Hurston's values. In this story, written in the depths of the Depression, she attacks the acquisitive society from a standpoint not unlike that of the Southern Agrarians. For the first time her social conservatism, inherited from Booker Washington by way of Eatonville, finds in pastoral an appropriate dramatic form. At the same time that her values coalesce, her narrative voice assumes a new authority. A mature style emerges whose metaphors, drawn from folk speech, function as a celebration of agrarian ideals. Having discovered her subject and mastered her idiom, she turns to those longer works of fiction where, for the most part, her achievement as a writer lies.

Rudolph Fisher

In a story called "High Yaller," Rudolph Fisher gives us a brief glimpse of his Harlem boyhood: "Over One Hundred and Thirty-fourth Street's sidewalks between Fifth and Lenox Avenues Jay Martin's roller-skates had rattled and whirred in the days when that was the northern boundary of Negro Harlem. He had grown as the colony grew, and now he could just recall the time when his father, a pioneer preacher, had been forever warning him never to cross Lenox Avenue and never to go beyond One Hundred and Thirty-fifth Street; a time when no Negroes lived on or near Seventh Avenue and when it would have been almost suicidal for one to appear unarmed on Irish Eighth."[8]

This fictional account of Fisher's boyhood encompasses the chief ingredients of his imagination. The notion of a *boundary*, an artificial barrier creating a forbidden territory, and thereby denying access to experience, is basic to the impulse of the picaresque. The taboo, moreover, is enforced by the boy's father, whose paternal authority is associated with the Negro church. Several of Fisher's stories are concerned thematically with the crossing of forbidden boundaries, or in theological terms, with snatching Experience from the jaws of Sin. Their rogue-heroes bear witness to the fact that they derive from the tradition of the picaresque.[9]

At the same time, the passage has profound historical reverberations. All the tensions and hostilities of the Great Migration are embodied in the clash between the Negroes and their Irish neighbors. The exposed position of the blacks, making racial solidarity imperative, is the source of Fisher's pastoral romances. Throughout his work, divisive tendencies within the black community are mollified and harmonized. His primary effort is to bridge the gap between the classes, but differences arising out of regional, generational, or (in the case of West Indians) former national affiliation are likewise subject to the healing qualities of pastoral.

Rudolph Fisher (1897-1934) was born in Washington, D.C., the son of a Baptist minister. In 1903 the family moved to Harlem, and in 1905 to Providence, Rhode Island.[10] Fisher was educated in the public schools of New York and Providence and at Brown University, where he received the BA and MA degrees. He attended Howard University Medical School and interned at Freedman's Hospital. In 1925 he brought his wife and infant son to New York, where he served for two years as a research fellow in biology at the College of Physicians and Surgeons of Columbia University. He established a private practice as an X-ray specialist in 1927, but his career was hampered by a chronic intestinal ailment which took his life in 1934.

Fisher's literary career began auspiciously in 1925. His first story, "The City of Refuge," appeared in the February issue of the *Atlantic Monthly.* "The South Lingers On," a series of Harlem sketches, was published in the March number of *Survey Graphic* and reprinted, together with "The City of Refuge," in Alain Locke's anthology, *The New Negro.*[11] In May a second story, "Ringtail," appeared in the *Atlantic,* while the October and November issues of *Crisis* carried "High Yaller," which had won a prize in the Amy Spingarn literary contest.[12] For a young intern just completing his medical studies, it must have been a gratifying year.

In the course of a decade Fisher was to publish twelve stories: four in the *Atlantic Monthly* and the rest in such journals as *McClure's Magazine,* the *Metropolitan, Crisis,* and *Opportunity.*[13] His most successful effort, "Miss Cynthie," appeared in *Story Magazine* of June 1933, and was reprinted in O'Brien's *Best Short Stories of 1933.* In addition to his work as a short-story writer, Fisher was the author of a novel, *The Walls of Jericho* (1928), and a murder mystery, *The Conjure Man Dies* (1932). The latter was adapted for the stage, after the author's untimely death, by Arna Bontemps and Countee Cullen.[14]

Harlem is the stamping ground of Fisher's imagination; without exception it provides the setting of his tales. His first exposure to the black metropolis occurred when he was six or seven, and his father held a pulpit in New York. His second encounter took place in the summer of 1919, between college and graduate school. This time he explored the cabaret scene, with its postwar atmosphere of gay abandon and illicit pleasure.[15] It was a scene not without spiritual danger for the son of a Baptist preacher. From his fiction, we can surmise that the secular attractions of Harlem life provoked a breach between Bud Fisher and his father.

Fisher's intimate knowledge of the Harlem scene led him to

exploit its possibilities as local color. His stories contain iso-lated passages that are unexcelled in their depiction of the Harlem cabaret, the rent party, the barbershop, the dance casino, and the Sunday promenade on Seventh Avenue. Good social history, however, is not necessarily good literature. If presented for its own sake, such material may detract from the author's larger purposes. In the end Fisher pays a heavy price for his reliance on local color. As the novelty of his Harlem settings wears thin, his imagination falters, and he tends to repeat himself.

Two metaphors convey Fisher's essential relation to the Harlem scene. In several of his stories the protagonist looks down upon the spectacle of Harlem life from an upper box, upper window, or upper balcony. This spatial metaphor em-bodies the social perspective of the black bourgeoisie, which overlooks the Harlem scene from the lofty eminence of Sugar Hill. In other stories Fisher seems to be conducting a guided tour of Harlem for a party of visitors from downtown. The name of the tour is "Adventures in Exotic Harlem," and it includes observations on the quaint customs of the country, helpful hints for fraternizing with the natives, and a Berlitz phrase-book for the comprehension of contemporary Har-lemese.

The psychological setting of Fisher's stories—the interior landscape to which he compulsively returns—is a state of intolerable estrangement from his father. Several of his tales are concerned with dramatizing this estrangement, and effecting a symbolic reconciliation. "The Backslider" and "Fire by Night" (*McClure's*, August and December 1927), for example, are variations on the theme of the Prodigal Son. In these stories a backsliding, ne'er-do-well, and potentially criminal youth is rescued from his self-destructive impulses and restored to middle-class respectability.

In essence there are two Rudolph Fishers: a conforming and rebelling self. The conformist is the middle-class child who obeys his parents when they warn him not to play with roughnecks. He is the brilliant student who is Class Day Orator at Brown, who graduates *summa cum laude* from Howard, and establishes his professional identity as Dr. Fisher. The rebel is Bud Fisher, frequenter of speakeasies and cabarets, who has always envied the bad kids on the block and who writes about them in his fiction. The rebel self, however, is more mischievous than dangerous, and after a period of bohemian adventures settles into middle-class routine. Such is the psychodrama at the heart of Fisher's cruder tales.

In a second group of Fisher tales, the theme of breach and reconciliation is projected outward on the social plane. Here the author strives to repair various divisions that threaten to destroy the black community. Thus "Ringtail" is concerned with the enmity between West Indian and native-born American; "High Yaller," with the potentially disruptive force of a light complexion; "Blades of Steel" and "Common Meter" with the social class division that separates the "rat" from the "dickty." In each of these contexts, Fisher's aim is to exorcise the demons of disruption and cement the ties of racial solidarity.

One of Fisher's stories delineates what might be called the social geography of Harlem:

> Negro Harlem's three broad highways form the letter H, Lenox and Seventh Avenues running parallel northward, united a little above their midpoints by east-and-west 135th Street. Lenox Avenue is for the most part the boulevard of the unperfumed—rats they are often termed. . . . But Seventh Avenue is the promenade of high-toned "dickties" and strivers. . . . These two highways, frontiers of the opposed extremes of dark-skinned social life, are separated by an intermediate any man's land, across which they communicate chiefly by way of 135th Street. Accordingly 135th Street is the heart and soul of black Harlem; it is common

ground, the natural scene of unusual contacts, a
region that disregards class. It neutralizes, equil-
ibrates, binds, rescues union out of diversity.[16]

This is the language of pastoral, and it reveals the central
thrust of Fisher's art. The object of his fiction is precisely to
provide a common ground, to bind the social classes in a racial
confraternity, and thus to rescue union from diversity. A
favorite setting for his fiction is the ballroom scene, where all
of Harlem gathers for the communal rite of the Saturday
night dance. The action of "Common Meter," for example,
takes place in a dance casino symbolically denominated "The
Arcadia."[17] For the ballroom and its ethnic music qualify as
common ground, where the mediating force of pastoral can
work its magic spell.

Fisher's "Arcadia" is modeled on the old Savoy, where two
jazz bands played nightly for the Harlem throng. A lusty
paganism fills the hall: the Pipes of Pan are jazz trumpets, at
whose prompting nymphs and satyrs cavort across the floor.
Metaphorically at least, it is a sylvan scene: "a brace of young
wild birds double-timed through the forest, miraculously
avoiding the trees (77)." Against this background a rivalry
develops between two band leaders for the favors of a lovely
girl. As appropriate to pastoral romance, however, the contest
is contained within a ritual frame. The two musicians and
their bands will compete for "the jazz championship of the
world," with the tacit understanding that the victor wins the
girl.

Two styles of musical performance thus provide the main
dramatic contrast of the tale. Fess Baxter's work is flashy but
inauthentic; his music is full of tonal tricks and false res-
olutions. Bus Williams' stuff, on the other hand, is the genuine
down-home blues. Threatened with defeat in honest competition, Baxter slits his rival's trapdrum with a knife. Our
heroine, however, saves the day, by instructing Williams' band
to beat time with their feet, thus converting the blues per-

formance to a shout. This ancestral form, handed down through generations from the tribal past, so stirs the crowd that opposition fades, abandoning the field to love.

At the center of the story is a pastoral inversion. The smart money hits the canvas; the city slicker is confounded; country music and elemental honesty combine to win the girl. The superiority of blackness is the point: to be possessed of soul is precisely to be capable of improvising, of winning the contest *without* your drums. At bottom, Fisher is warning the black community to guard itself against a certain kind of spiritual loss. Don't abandon your ancestral ways when you move to the big city; don't discard the authentic blues idiom for the shallow, trivial, flashy, meretricious values of the urban world.

A third group of Fisher stories is explicitly concerned with the Great Migration. As the author's imagination reaches out to embrace the historical experience of millions, his art assumes a greater density of texture and complexity of vision. On the plane of history, moreover, Fisher's divided self proves to be an asset: it enables him to project and then to mediate the central value conflict of his age. For the split personality of the Baptist preacher's son mirrors the divided soul of the Southern migrant. Both are torn between a set of standards that are traditional, religious, and puritanical, and a series of temptations that are novel, secular, and hedonistic.

Fisher's strength lies in the fact that he is genuinely torn between these value systems. His very ambivalence allows him to achieve a delicate balance of rural and urban, traditional and modern values. His divided psyche generates a powerful desire to mediate, or reconcile, or find a middle ground, which is the source of pastoral. He is therefore able to encompass the paradoxes of change and continuity, of spiritual loss and gain, which are the essence of the Great Migration. He is able to record the disappointments and defeats of the Southern migrants, and yet to celebrate the hope which survives their disillusionment.

"The City of Refuge" (*Atlantic Monthly*, February 1925) is

Fisher's first attempt to treat the paradoxes of the Great Migration. King Solomon Gillis, a greenhorn from the South, is bamboozled by a Harlem gangster and left to face a twenty-year sentence for peddling dope. His arrest by a black policeman, however, reconciles him to his fate, for he perceives that Harlem, while it may betray the Southern migrant, also offers him the possibility of manhood. The final scene where Gillis stands erect, exulting in his new-born sense of dignity and racial pride, is a powerful epiphany of the New Negro. Unhappily the story as a whole, which is riddled with bad writing, does not match the brilliance of its dénouement.

"The Promised Land" (*Atlantic Monthly*, January 1927) is a more successful treatment of the migratory theme. As the story opens, a spiritual and a blues are contending for supremacy from opposite sides of an airshaft. The words of the spiritual ask, "How low mus' I bow / To enter in de promis' land?" Fisher's subject, then, is the social cost of the Great Migration. Divisiveness is the price the black community must pay to enter in the promised land. Urbanization brings division between the generations; between skilled and unskilled black workers; between established and more recent immigrants; between the partisans of gospel music and the blues.

These divisions are dramatized by the conflicts between Mammy and her grandsons; between the cousins, Sam and Wesley; and between the country cousins and Ellie, the city girl. Mammy is the first of several matriarchal figures who embody the old-fashioned virtues in Fisher's tales. In a memorable scene, she tosses the family Bible through a window of the opposite apartment to restrain her grandsons from fighting over Ellie. She represents the unifying, mediating force of pastoral, and she supplies whatever of cohesiveness and continuity the migratory family is able to achieve. Yet in the end she fails, and one of her grandsons is a sacrificial victim to the gods of racial progress.

"Miss Cynthie" (*Story*, June 1933) is the best of Fisher's stories, by virtue of a crucial technical advance. Having given us a gallery of static characters, he suddenly discovers how to *interiorize* his dramatic conflicts, so that his protagonists have an opportunity to grow. The title character, Miss Cynthie, is thereby able to embody in her own person the spiritual agony of the Great Migration. Painfully, reluctantly, and only after a sharp internal struggle, her old-fashioned morality bends and stretches to accommodate the new. Fisher's theme is the emergence of new moral codes, appropriate to new historical conditions.

As the story opens, Miss Cynthie arrives in New York for a visit with her grandson, David. From the money he has sent back home it is clear that he is a success, but the source of his prosperity remains a mystery. Miss Cynthie hopes that he may be at least an undertaker, but is unprepared to find him a musical-comedy celebrity. David initiates her tactfully by persuading her to witness a performance at the Lafayette. At first she is repelled, and her sense of moral outrage prevents her from acknowledging her grandson's virtuosity. In the end, however, her rigid moral categories are dissolved, and she is reconciled to David's unconventional career.

Art is the solvent that makes this reconciliation possible. As the show unfolds, she recognizes in its central episodes a ritual enactment of the black man's history. As the audience is cleansed and shriven and elevated by these images, she realizes that religion is not the only means of sanctifying experience. The climax of the story comes when David does a song-and-dance routine based on a folksong taught him by Miss Cynthie. Her own folk culture, she suddenly perceives, contains the germ of all that she encounters at the Lafayette. Reassured of an underlying continuity, she accepts the innovations of the younger generation.

The aim of pastoral is reconciliation. In this instance it is not so much a matter of reconciling rural and urban values, or of mediating a conflict between the generations, as of bridging a gap between the black artist and the black middle class. The secret theme of "Miss Cynthie" is the reconciliation of bourgeois success norms with the unconventional and slightly suspect enterprise of art. David is a projection of Fisher's artist-self. The folk material that each employs as the basis of his art is suspect in the eyes of the black elite. To reconcile Miss Cynthie to her grandson's métier is thus to reconcile the black bourgeoisie to a certain kind of "lowlife" art.

Beyond these public meanings, the story serves a private end. The symbolic action indicates that Fisher has resolved the basic conflict of his adolescence and achieved the integration of a perilously fractured self. In the love and mutual respect of David and Miss Cynthie, his rebelling and conforming selves are harmonized. The result is an impressive gain in poise and equilibrium. "Miss Cynthie" constitutes, in short, a psychological as well as an artistic triumph. Published in the shadow of impending death, it testifies to Fisher's inner growth and aggravates our loss of his maturing powers.

Claude McKay

At the climax of D. H. Lawrence's novel, *The Plumed Serpent*, Kate prepares to merge, physically and psychologically, with Ramón, and through him, with the prehistoric consciousness of ancient Mexico. Contemplating her surrender, she imagines a time

> When great plains stretched away to the oceans, like Atlantis and the lost continents of Polynesia, so that seas were only great lakes, and the soft, dark-eyed people of that world could walk around the globe. Then there was a mysterious, hot-blooded, soft-footed humanity with a strange civilization of its own. Till the glaciers melted, and drove the peoples to the high places, like the lofty plateaux of Mexico; separated them into cut-off nations.[18]

This myth of separation and reunion, which is central to the art of D. H. Lawrence, captivated the imagination of Claude McKay.[19] For McKay shared with Lawrence, the great primitivist of twentieth-century letters, a fascination with "the world before the Flood, before the mental-spiritual world came into being."[20] Throughout his career, McKay yearns for that state of Perfect Oneness before the Flood: before, as a child, he was separated from his mother; before, as a youth, he was separated from Jamaica; and before, as a black man in a white man's world, he was separated from himself. He looks in vain for spiritual wholeness in what he comes to call "the pagan isms," but finds it ultimately in the bosom of the Roman Church.

Claude McKay's spiritual journey carries him from oneness to multiplicity and back again. The quest for experience is the basis of his personal peregrinations (recorded in *A Long Way from Home*), his poems of vagabondage, and his picaresque novels, *Home to Harlem* and *Banjo*. Experience, however, leads to chaos and division in the soul, caused not only by the white man's contumely, but the curse of intellect, which sunders men and women from their primitive emotions. Recoiling from racial insult and abuse, and the complexities of consciousness as well, McKay turns for solace to the simple and harmonious strains of pastoral. The fruits of his revulsion from occidental civilization are the novel, *Banana Bottom*, and the book of stories, *Gingertown*.

Claude McKay (1889-1948) was born in Sunny Ville, Jamaica, a small village in the parish of Clarendon.[21] His father was a prosperous peasant whom McKay remembers as a stern man, a hard worker, and "a wonderful teller of African stories." Of his mother he recalls, "Perhaps the quality most prominent in my mother was her goodness; she loved people and believed in being kind to everybody. She was quite different from my father who believed in justice, a kind of Anglo-Saxon justice."[22] McKay's affection for his mother, who died of dropsy while he was still an adolescent, was profound, and he has paid a tribute to her memory in several of his poems and stories.

The most important event of McKay's childhood was his separation from his mother at the age of six. One of eleven children, he was entrusted to the care of an older brother at Montego Bay, where he remained for seven years. This period of estrangement was the central trauma of his life. Not for nothing is the title of his autobiography taken from the spiritual, "Sometimes I feel like a motherless child / A long way from home." McKay's characteristic stance as a writer is that of a wanderer or vagabond. His constant theme is the isolation of modern man, cut off from his emotional roots and deprived of love by the artificial barriers of race or class or nationality.

McKay's intellectual awakening was accomplished by two rather unconventional men. His older brother, U'Theo, was a schoolteacher and freethinker who exposed him during early adolescence to the writings of Huxley, Lecky, and Haeckel. Walter Jekyll was a wealthy Englishman who became the young man's patron. Having discovered that McKay was writing verse, he introduced him to the major English poets. A folklorist and linguist, he encouraged him to write his early poems in Jamaican dialect, and helped him to publish his first two volumes, *Songs of Jamaica* and *Constab Ballads.* He also undertook to finance his college education in the United States.

McKay left Jamaica for America in 1912. After brief attendance at Tuskegee Institute and Kansas State College he settled in New York, where he spent the war years as a porter, janitor, and dining-car waiter on the Pennsylvania Railroad. Meanwhile he was writing verse which began to appear in such publications as the *Seven Arts, Pearson's Magazine,* and the *Liberator.* Two years of radical journalism provided further professional experience. During a year in England he wrote for Sylvia Pankhurst's socialist paper, the *Workers' Dread-*

nought. On his return to the United States he became associate editor of the *Liberator*. In 1922 he published *Harlem Shadows*, a book of poems which helped to launch the Harlem Renaissance.[23]

A twelve-year period of wanderings ensued. After a year in Moscow and another in Berlin and Paris, McKay settled in the south of France, where he led a precarious existence for several years. This was followed by a brief sojourn in Spain and a long residency in North Africa. McKay returned to the United States in 1934 and became an American citizen in 1940. During the depression years he was employed on the Federal Writers Project. After a period of spiritual crisis, he converted to Catholicism in 1944. He spent his final years as a teacher in the parochial schools of Chicago, where he died of a circulatory ailment in 1948.

McKay's literary career may be divided into four phases. The first, or provincial phase, encompasses his first two books of verse, *Songs of Jamaica* (1912) and *Constab Ballads* (1912). The second, or picaresque phase, includes a book of poems, *Harlem Shadows* (1922), and two novels, *Home to Harlem* (1928) and *Banjo* (1929). The third, or pastoral phase, consists of a book of stories, *Gingertown* (1932) and a novel, *Banana Bottom* (1933). The fourth, or retrospective phase, includes an autobiography, *A Long Way from Home* (1937), and a sociological study, *Harlem: Negro Metropolis* (1940).

The stories of *Gingertown* mark a transition from the picaresque to the pastoral phase. The first six tales are concerned with Harlem life. They express McKay's ambivalent feelings toward the black metropolis which, despite its glamor and excitement, he comes to regard as a whited sepulcher. The last six represent the recoil of McKay's imagination from the polluted centers of occidental civilization. Four are set in Jamaica, one on the Marseilles waterfront, and one in North Africa. Their esthetic mode is pastoral; they celebrate the values of simplicity, community, harmony with nature, reconciliation with one's fellow man, and freedom from political or sexual repression.

The two halves of the book were written at different times and under strikingly different circumstances. The Harlem tales were written in France between 1923 and 1926. In the spring of 1926 Louise Bryant, the widow of John Reed and a friend from *Liberator* days, showed the stories to Harper & Brothers, who agreed to publish a collection in the near future. Meanwhile McKay had acquired a Paris agent who urged him rather to attempt an episodic novel of Harlem life, based on the characters of the short stories. The result was *Home to Harlem* (1928), which Harper substituted for the stories. Four of the latter were published in various journals from 1927 to 1931.[24] Subsequently they appeared in the Harlem section of *Gingertown*.

The second half of the collection was written in North Africa in 1930-1931. McKay had left Europe to escape "the white hound of Civilization."[25] He had gone completely native in Morocco, whose landscape, people, and exotic customs reminded him of his Jamaican homeland. In the spring of 1931 he settled in Tangier to work on *Gingertown*. He was joined by an Afro-American woman of bohemian inclinations who was in flight from the stuffiness of bourgeois Harlem. After an idyllic "honeymoon" they quarreled, and she returned to Paris and her white lover. Wounded and resentful, McKay retreated to the mountains of Spanish Morocco, where he completed *Gingertown* and *Banana Bottom*.

This disastrous love affair compounded McKay's bitterness and increased his alienation from occidental values. The figure of his paramour, torn between her black and white lovers, became in his imagination an emblem of the Negro soul, torn between two hostile cultures and antagonistic ways of life.[26] At the same time, his withdrawal to the mountains awakened memories of his Jamaican childhood. In surroundings reminiscent of his native village he made a valiant effort to repossess his peasant heritage. The pastoral impulse which inspired his early poems now became the source of McKay's most enduring fiction.

The Harlem tales of *Gingertown* are concerned with the cultural dilemma of blacks who are compelled to function in a white man's world. These tales reflect McKay's experience as an immigrant to the United States from the West Indies. They express his shock and dismay at being transplanted from a country which is 90 percent black to one where the opposite ratio obtains. The tension that results between the self and its environment, leading in turn to a divisiveness within the self, is McKay's essential theme. He is concerned not so much with the humiliations and inconveniences of segregation as with the breach they open in the black man's soul.

The classic formulation of the black American's dilemma was made by W. E. B. DuBois in *The Souls of Black Folk* (1903): "One ever feels his twoness—an American, a Negro: two souls, two thoughts, two unreconciled strivings; two warring ideals in one dark body, whose dogged strength alone keeps it from being torn asunder."[27] McKay was introduced to *The Souls of Black Folk* by a white English teacher at Kansas State. He recalls in his autobiography that "The book shook me like an earthquake."[28] On the evidence of his Harlem tales, it was this passage concerning the black man's double consciousness that produced the seismic tremors in his soul.

The protagonists of McKay's Harlem stories are men or women divided against themselves. Trying to escape their blackness, and the penalties imposed upon it by the white world, they expose themselves to psychological disaster. They may experience a brief moment of happiness while in pursuit of white ideals, but invariably it proves to be illusory. Sooner or later some racial trauma intervenes to remind them that the barriers of caste are insurmountable. What holds these tales together is the fantasy of playing white. McKay is trying to exorcise a certain kind of psychological infatuation.[29]

The dangers and temptations of "white fever" are the focal

point of these tales. Thus Bess of "Brownskin Blues" mutilates herself in a misguided effort to lighten her complexion. The heroine of "Mattie and Her Sweetman" is vulnerable to social and sexual humiliation by virtue of her passion for "yellow boys." Angie Dove of "Near-White" suffers a disastrous love affair with a white man symbolically named John West. The first half of *Gingertown*, in short, is part of a now familiar literature of extrication, whose aim is to liberate the blacks from psychological enslavement to a false cultural ideal.[30]

Unfortunately the literary quality of McKay's Harlem stories is not high. These early tales, after all, were his first experiments with prose fiction. Their awkwardness of style, which is especially pronounced in the dialogue, suggests that the former poet, in shifting his major emphasis to prose, has not yet mastered his new medium. The widely anthologized "Truant" is hardly free of this defect, but by virtue of its summary position it merits more extensive treatment than the rest. This story, which concludes the Harlem section of *Gingertown*, illustrates McKay's dilemma as he tries to dramatize his disenchantment with the urban scene through the inappropriate conventions of the picaresque.

As the story opens, the hero and his wife are watching a vaudeville show from the "Nigger Heaven" of a Broadway theater. The curtain discloses a domestic scene in which a troupe of Irish actors personifies the happy family of American popular culture. The initial impact of the scene is idyllic, but its ultimate effect is ironic, for the Merry Mulligans possess the warmth, cohesiveness, and cultural integrity conspicuously lacking in the life of the black protagonist.[31] The note of harmony on which the story opens thus serves as an ironic commentary on the disintegrating marriage of the two main characters.

Barclay Oram is an autobiographical creation closely related to the figure of Ray in *Home to Harlem* and *Banjo*. In a long flashback we learn that he has emigrated from the West Indies in pursuit of his dream of attending a Negro university.

At Howard he meets and marries Rhoda, an Afro-American girl of middle-class background and assimilationist outlook. As the tale unfolds, Rhoda emerges as a kind of enchantress who holds her man in thrall to the false values of an artificial civilization. Nor does fatherhood relieve Barclay's feeling of entrapment, for he envisions his daughter marrying a railroad waiter like himself and raising children "to carry on the great tradition of black servitude."

As the present action of the tale begins, Barclay is rousted out of bed at an early hour, in order to report for work on the Pennsylvania Railroad. It is a disastrous trip, and during the layover in Washington he gets drunk, thereby missing the return run. Savoring his truancy, he is not at all disturbed when he is laid off for ten days. Rhoda, however, reproaches him for irresponsibility, and her rebuke precipitates a crisis which is resolved by Barclay's desertion of his wife and child. Through the metaphor of truancy, McKay depicts the black man as a dropout from the Western world, a *pícaro* who is condemned to a life of eternal wandering.

The trouble with "Truant" is a radical divergency of form and content. In his expansionist phase (Jamaica to New York), McKay gravitates instinctively toward the devices and conventions of the picaresque. The phase of recoil, however (New York to Jamaica), cannot be expressed through the same medium. The picaresque is a suitable instrument for the *celebration* of Harlem life (as in *Home to Harlem*), but it cannot be adapted to the theme of urban disenchantment. Pastoral is the appropriate vehicle for the expression of anti-urban sentiments. At this point in his career, McKay has made the emotional transition from expansion to recoil, but has not yet grasped its formal implications. He will do so in his stories of Jamaican peasant life.

Structurally speaking, "Truant" is the hinge of *Gingertown*. The last of the Harlem tales, it provides a logical transition to the counterstatement. For if "Truant" is a myth of disaffiliation, the Jamaican tales are parables of pastoral refreshment and renewal. As McKay's imagination turns from Harlem to Jamaica, a corresponding shift in tone occurs. Feelings of revulsion for the Western world are replaced by a vast affection for the Caribbean island and its people. The source of this tenderness is McKay's memory of his mother. Her presence hovers over the Jamaican tales, imbuing them with a tone of tranquillity and inner peace.

To describe the latter half of *Gingertown* as McKay's "Jamaican tales" is only an approximation. Two of the weaker stories, "Nigger Lover" and "Little Sheik," have Mediterranean rather than Caribbean settings. A third, "When I Pounded the Pavement," is not in fact a story, but an autobiographical account of McKay's experience in the Kingston constabulary. The three remaining tales, which constitute the core of *Gingertown*, are set in the Jamaican highlands. "Crazy Mary" is an undistinguished piece, but "The Agricultural Show" and "The Strange Burial of Sue" are McKay's best stories.

"The Agricultural Show" is a pure specimen of Renaissance pastoral. The central characters are Bennie, an impressionable schoolboy, and his brother Matthew, the village pharmacist. Matthew, who is something of a local booster, undertakes to organize a country fair. There will be prizes for livestock and farm products, handicrafts and the domestic arts. Games and competitions will be held; band concerts and political speeches given; and the Governor himself will address the assembled multitudes. The fair is a communal ritual in which all segments of society participate, and during which all petty barriers of caste or class are momentarily surmounted.

Matthew plays the role of mediator, who orchestrates and harmonizes the great event. Under his direction, lowlander and highlander mingle for a day; Baptist, Methodist, and Anglican rub elbows; village, town, and city folk are represented; black, white, and all shades in between take part. United in a common venture, the peasantry, gentry, and aristocracy transcend their traditional roles. Among the surging throngs, artificial distinctions of rank and status give way to a natural camaraderie, while on the speakers' platform a symbolic reconciliation of the classes and races is effected. The sign and seal of this communal harmony, and a scene that Bennie never will forget, is the presentation of his mother to the Governor.

To a modern sensibility, unacquainted with the pastoral tradition, "The Agricultural Show" will seem a sentimental fantasy. When the lion lies down with the lamb, our cynical century believes, only the lion gets up. We will mistake the author's purpose, however, if we read the story as a realistic social commentary. It is rather a poetic vision, an expression of an inner need. McKay's Jamaican pastoral, with its images of racial harmony and social peace, is an objective correlative of the inner harmony that he so desperately seeks. Split and shredded by his contact with the Western world, he returns in his imagination to Jamaica in order to reconstitute his soul.

What follows is a process of reduction. Tormented by his doubleness, McKay endeavors to achieve a psychic unity by exorcising his Western self. From the complexities of Negro experience in America, he turns to the simplicities of Jamaican peasant life. Intellectuality, which he has come to regard as a burden, is renounced in favor of instinct and emotion. The oneness of spirit that he craves necessitates a stripping away of the false veneer of white civilization and a closer accommodation to his primitive sources. The alien culture must be repudiated, and especially in its oppressive sexual forms. Such are the themes of McKay's most impressive story, "The Strange Burial of Sue."

The plot turns on a sexual triangle involving the title character, her husband, and an adolescent boy. Sue Turner is a peasant woman of free-loving ways, who is nonetheless universally respected and admired in her community. A hardworking field hand, volunteer nurse, and befriender of pregnant village girls, she conducts her private life in such a way as to threaten neither Turner nor the village wives. Her husband is a steady man, amiable, phlegmatic, and totally lacking the proprietary attitude toward sex: "One day an indiscreet relative was trying to broad-hint Turner about Sue's doings, and Turner remarked that he felt proud having a wife that was admired of other men (181)."[32]

Burskin is a shy and awkward youth, still a virgin at the outset of his liaison with Sue. After a passionate affair of several months' duration, she jilts him for a glamorous adventurer recently returned from Panama. Jealous and importunate, Burskin makes a scene at the local grogshop which precipitates a public scandal. Turner, who has thus far been a model of patience and forbearance, now feels compelled to undertake a legal action against the youth who has abused his generosity. Before the case can come to trial, however, it is rendered moot by the sudden death of Sue, perhaps brought on (the facts are never clear) by an unsuccessful effort to abort Burskin's child.

The story gains a new dimension with the introduction of the brown-skinned village parson. A self-righteous busybody, he sees fit at one point to protect the public morals by expelling Sue from church. He represents, in short, the intrusion of Anglo-Saxon values on a world more African than European. Two rival codes of conduct, or concepts of goodness, are thus at issue in the tale. The permissive sexual code of the black peasantry, inherited from slavery times if not from Africa, is weighed against the missionary morals of the Baptist seminarian. As in *Banana Bottom*, McKay employs the metaphor of sexuality to dramatize the sharp divergencies of culture, lifestyle, and moral outlook that separate the colonizer from the colonized.

In "The Strange Burial of Sue," the folk community rallies in defense of its immemorial customs. On the occasion of Sue's funeral, the whole mountain range turns out in tribute to her popularity. The parson makes the error, in his graveside sermon, of denouncing Sue as a backslider and a sinner.

Outraged, Turner drives him off and invites the people to bear witness to his wife's goodness. In effect the folk community defrocks the village parson, rejecting him as the emissary of an alien culture. In defiant tribute to her passion—a value cherished by the black peasants—Turner plants two flaming dragon's bloods on his wife's grave.

Claude McKay's Jamaican pastorals, written in North Africa from 1930 to 1933, mark the outer limits of his flight from the West. The flight was doomed, as we can see in retrospect, because the fugitive was fleeing from himself. Within a year or two of the publication of *Gingertown* and *Banana Bottom*, McKay was back in the United States. In 1940 his last book appeared, a sympathetic portrait of urban life entitled *Harlem: Negro Metropolis*. His pastoral phase therefore must be seen as one polarity in a larger pattern of vacillation and ambivalence. It was a passing phase, expressive of a deep revulsion from the Western world, but incapable of sustaining an integrated moral vision.

McKay achieved this larger vision through conversion to the Catholic faith. Within its unifying framework, the intolerable tensions of duality could be resolved. The reductive strategy employed in the Jamaican pastorals did not prove permanently viable because it entailed a mutilation of the self. What was called for, McKay was later to discover, was not a mutilation but a synthesis. The oneness that he sought in a symbolic fusion with Jamaican peasant life he ultimately found in Roman Catholicism, which combined the simple faith and venerable customs of a peasant culture with the forms and rituals of a highly sophisticated and emphatically Western religion.

Chapter 7

Eric Walrond

ERIC WALROND'S fiction has been described as naturalistic, but nothing could be farther from the mark.[1] His images of horror, especially of horrifying death, his fascination with the supernatural, and his obsession with the dark underside of human consciousness betray the workings of a Gothic imagination. He concerns himself, to be sure, with evolutionary doctrine—often the trademark of scientific naturalism—but not in a mechanistic or reductive way. Rather he employs the primitive or atavistic as a metaphor, a means of exploring the complexities of his black identity.

Gothic is a mode of antipastoral. It represents, in fact, the farthest limits of the countergenre. Satire counters the idyllic attitude with irony; realism.with the sheer weight of actuality; the picaresque tradition with a certain roguish humor. But Gothic turns the idyll inside out; it attacks the pastoral ideal at its very source: the throne of God. To understand the inverted forms of Gothic fiction, we must scrutinize the mode in both its theological and cultural dimensions.

The pastoral ideal is associated in the Christian imagination with the Garden of Eden. In orthodox cosmology, Eden is the earthly Paradise, a reflection of the heavenly Ideal, the most that mankind has been granted as a foretaste of Perfection. The Gothic mode, on the other hand, provides us with a vision

171

of the Garden abandoned by the Gardener, usurped by the powers of darkness. Gothic fiction is to pastoral as night to day, demon to angel, Satan to Divinity, Hell to Paradise. The Castle of Otranto and the House of Usher, with their subterranean crypts and lurid tarns, are images of Hell, inversions of the earthly Paradise.

Gothic fiction made its first appearance in England in the late eighteenth century. Such pre-Romantics as Ann Radcliffe and Matthew Lewis were in revolt against the Age of Reason, and especially its optimistic notions concerning the perfectibility of man. They knew man to be imperfect, not to say Satanic, and scorned prevailing tendencies to deal with the demonic by denying its existence. The cumbersome machinery of their tales—the medieval castles, hidden passageways, vampire bats, instruments of torture, and the rest—was essentially a means of exploring the unconscious self. Their fiction was concerned with what Freud has called the return of the repressed.

Writing in 1800 of the Gothic novel, the Marquis de Sade explains its genesis as a revolt against the tedium of too much goodness in English fiction: "For one who knew all the miseries with which the wicked can afflict humanity the novel became as difficult to create as it was monotonous to read. . . . It was therefore necessary to call Hell to the rescue. . . ."[2] The Gothic novel represented an attack on the Pelagian heresy, as it flourished in the Age of Reason. One can understand a revival of the form in the aftermath of World War II, with its celebrated catalogue of Gothic horrors. But what was its appeal to Eric Walrond, who was writing in a far more innocent and optimistic age?

The sources of Walrond's Gothic strain were both biographical and literary. He was raised by his mother in the Plymouth Brethren, a fundamentalist sect that left no doubt in the minds of its members concerning the reality of hell. As a youth of twenty and a migrant to New York, he suffered at the hands of white Americans a series of humiliations that demonstrated vividly the demonic potentialities of man. During adolescence he was an avid reader of Victorian boys' fiction, whose lurid plots were struck from the Gothic mold.³ And in early manhood, at the outset of his literary career, he was attracted to the Gothic mode by his discovery of the books of Lafcadio Hearn and Pierre Loti.

But above all else, Walrond's penchant for the Gothic may be traced to the anguish of a fragmented self. Born in British Guiana, raised in Barbados and Panama, and growing to maturity in New York, he was beset by the problem of a multiple identity. Was he African or European; Anglo-Saxon or Hispanic; West Indian or North American? His writing is essentially an exploration of the self, moving back in time. It begins with his present circumstances in New York in the early 1920's, and moves inversely to his adolescence in Colón, his boyhood in Barbados, and his infancy in Guiana. The Gothic mode is utilized to express the primitive and atavistic features of his heritage.

Underlying Walrond's whole career is the tragic dilemma of the black Englishman. A British colonial by birth and early education, he remained throughout his life what the French would call an *évolué*. That is the inner logic of his successive moves from British Guiana to Barbados to the Canal Zone to New York and finally to London. These migrations are the outward and visible emblems of a spiritual journey: the black Briton's pilgrimage to Westminster. Walrond's life and work reveal the secret longing of the colonized black for whiteness, enlightenment, gentility, metropolitan sophistication, and similar marks of cultural "salvation."

At the same time, Walrond's traumatic exposure to American racism drove him back upon his blackness. Recoiling from a civilization that was capable of such injustice, he turned in self-defense to the myth of primitivism. Obeah, or black magic, became in his imagination a symbolic antidote to the poisons of racial hatred encountered in the Western world. It was at this point that Walrond discovered the possibilities of Gothic as a literary mode. He employed it to express that part of his personality which remained resistant to the white man's culture: the black, African, pagan, ungovernable, unassimilable, or in a word *demonic* self that stubbornly refused to be "redeemed."

Walrond's excursion into demonism brings him to the brink of the abyss. Like Kurtz he journeys to the heart of darkness only to recoil from the horror. He is fascinated by the possibility of atavism, of lapsing into life-modes more erotic and more indolent than those of European man. But this proves to be an unacceptable alternative because it arouses the fear of psychic dissolution. To go entirely native, to succumb to the lushness of the tropics, would be to slay his European self. It is on the rock of primitivism that Walrond's art eventually founders. In the end his anglicized sensibility prevents him from mounting a convincing demonstration of his chosen myth.

Life and Work

Eric Walrond (1898-1966) was born in Georgetown, British Guiana, of a Barbadian mother and a Guyanese father. Deserted by her husband, Mrs. Walrond returned to Barbados with her young son. There she nursed the wounds of a broken marriage in a small rural settlement owned by Walrond's grandfather, and fictionalized in several of his stories as "the gap," or more formally, "Goddard's Village." It was situated near the town of Black Rock, where Walrond began his education at St. Stephen's Boys' School. His early indoctrination as a black Briton was thus occasioned by his mother's rather desperate gentility. Having married "beneath herself," she was all the more determined to provide her son with a decent education.

The Barbadian phase of Walrond's childhood came to an abrupt end when his mother moved to the Canal Zone in search of her estranged husband.[4] Unsuccessful in effecting a reconciliation, she settled in the city of Colón, where the boy resumed his education in the public schools. He thus became bilingual, and thoroughly exposed to Spanish culture. Between the ages of fifteen and eighteen, he completed his secondary schooling under the supervision of private tutors. Trained as a secretary and stenographer, he found his first employment as a clerk in the Health Department of the Canal Commission at Cristobal. From 1916 to 1918, he worked as a reporter on the *Panama Star and Herald.*

In 1918, at the age of twenty, Walrond migrated to New York, where he spent the next decade of his life. For three years he attended the City College of New York, and for one, Columbia University, where he took extension courses in creative writing. Meanwhile he was employed as a stenographer in the British Recruiting Mission, as secretary to an architect, and to the superintendent of the Broad Street Hospital. In his search for secretarial employment he met with a series of humiliating rejections and rebuffs.[5] As his early fiction indicates, it was these assaults upon his personality that stung him into self-expression.

Toward the end of his college years, he resumed his career as a journalist. From 1921 to 1923, he was co-owner and editor of a Negro weekly called the *Brooklyn and Long Island Informer.* Embittered by his initial encounters with American racism, he was momentarily attracted to the Garvey movement, and in 1923 he joined the staff of the *Negro World* as associate editor. Too anglicized to remain in the Garvey camp, he gravitated toward the Urban League and its monthly publication, *Opportunity.* Serving as business manager of *Opportunity* from 1925 to 1927, he was drawn into the vortex of the New Negro movement.

Walrond's literary career was of brief duration, coinciding with the heyday of the Harlem Renaissance. His essays on historical, political, and racial subjects were published in the early 1920's in such well-known periodicals as the *New Republic,* the *Independent,* and *Current History.* His apprentice fiction appeared from 1923 to 1925 chiefly in the pages of

Opportunity. In 1926 Boni and Liveright brought out a collection of his stories entitled *Tropic Death.* Two years later, according to his publisher's files, he completed a history of the Panama Canal called *The Big Ditch.* Thereafter, he virtually ceased to write. Leaving New York in 1928, he traveled in Europe and lived for several years in France. Eventually he settled down in London, where he stayed until his death in 1966.

"In every artist's life," Walrond has observed, "it is inexorable that environment—early environment—play a determining part."[6] This is manifestly true of his own career. His early manhood in New York, his adolescent years in Panama, his boyhood in Barbados, and even his infancy in British Guiana, provide the places, times, and circumstances of his tales. While it follows that a knowledge of Walrond's life will serve to illuminate his art, it is equally the case that a careful study of his art will illuminate a life about which not too many solid facts are known. Working both from the known facts and the known fictions, let us attempt an imaginative reconstruction of his inner life.

If we examine the interface of Walrond's life and art, four pressure points are evident. First, the underlying pattern of migration: from Guiana to Barbados; from Barbados to Panama; from Panama to New York; and thence to France and England. Second, the agent responsible for the earliest and undoubtedly most painful of these uprootings: an absconding, improvident, and debauched father whose life ended in defeat and failure. Third, the compensatory and somewhat hysterical ambitions of a mother whose overwrought success-drive, transmitted to her son, filled him with rebellion and ambivalence. And fourth, the racial traumas he encountered in New York which precipitated a crisis of identity.

Throughout his life, Walrond found himself in the position of the new boy on the block. He was forever on probation, forever under the necessity of proving, by gesture, style of dress, or appropriate linguistic usages, that he was worthy of admission to "the Club." Conforming to the customs of the country was imperative, for the sooner one conformed the sooner he lost his special vulnerability. The persecuted migrant, who is something like a soft-shelled crab, will pay any price for defensive armor. Hence the protestations of loyalty in Walrond's early work, which sound like Booker Washington, but have their source in the greenhorn's fear of remaining an outsider.

Human transplantation is Walrond's essential theme. Man on the move; man in process of metamorphosis; migratory man, encountering resistance and suffering the agonies of cultural adjustment, constitutes his central vision. Three of his essays are devoted to the subject of the Great Migration, an undertaking that reflects his desire to become a naturalized citizen of black America.[7] Several of his early sketches or vignettes are concerned with the dilemma of the black West Indian who has emigrated to New York.[8] And three of his best stories, "The Black Pin" (British Guiana to Barbados), "Tropic Death" (Barbados to Panama), and "City Love" (West Indies to New York) deal with various dimensions of the migratory theme.

Walrond's feelings toward his missing father are expressed in a series of portraits of ineffectual or sinister father-figures.[9] In "Tropic Death," the fullest statement of this theme, a young boy undertakes the classical quest for a father, consisting of a journey, a series of ordeals, and a descent to the underworld. Unlike Telemachus, however, Gerald Bright discovers in the object of his quest not a hero, but a rum-soaked, skirt-chasing vagabond. This fictive father is about to die of leprosy, a symbol of physical and moral dissolution. Walrond's father, as his son perceives him, is a negative model or antiself: a grim warning of the fate in store for those who succumb to the lushness of the tropics.

Walrond's father, in a word, is a backslider. To his son, he represents *blackness unredeemed* (which is to say, un-English). On the social plane, the father's indolence and irresponsibility threaten to declass his son, forcing him to live in hell (the Bottle Alley of his stories). On the psychological plane, he embodies his son's feelings of inferiority. For Walrond's fear of backsliding is at bottom a fear of failure. His father is an emblem of the worthlessness from which he flees, with the help of his mother, into white-collar respectability.

The mother-son relationship is likewise dramatized in "Tropic Death." At the age of eight—if we may take Gerald Bright as a self-projection—Walrond idolized his mother. But even as a boy, the seeds of future conflict were apparent: "By way of the Sixth Street Mission, his mother rooted religion into his soul. Every night he was marched off to meeting. There, he'd meet the dredge-digging, Zone-building, Lord-loving peasants of the West Indies on sore knees of atonement asking the Lord to bring salvation to their perfidious souls (276)."[10]

Despite the author's mocking tone, it is clear that he absorbed, from early contact with evangelical Christianity, the Protestant ethic of hard work, achievement, and success. Nor should the mission church be underestimated as an agent of acculturation, a transmission belt of Western values. Throughout his life, Walrond tended to equate being British with being saved. While he broke with his religious background during adolescence, it is accurate enough to speak of the theological framework of his art. For his imagination was profoundly shaped by his mother's harsh fundamentalism. His work constitutes, at bottom, a drama of damnation and salvation, worked out simultaneously on the personal, cultural, and theological planes.

Walrond's adolescent conflict with his mother is the basis of a story called "Subjection." In describing a youth whose life circumstances are not unlike his own, he observes, "His mother's constant dwelling on the dearth of family fortunes

produced in him a sundry set of emotions—escape in rebellion and refusal to do, as against a frenzied impulse to die
retrieving things. The impulse to do conquered (147)." The
pressure to succeed exerted by his mother thus drove a wedge
into Walrond's soul. As in the case of Rudolph Fisher, a split
identity ensued. Rebelling and conforming selves were
formed, with the latter momentarily ascendant ("the impulse
to do conquered").

The balance of forces was reversed when Walrond moved
from the Canal Zone to New York. Imagine a personality,
strongly programmed for success, when it collides with the
implacable barriers of caste. Imagine a young man, trained as
a stenographer, and experienced in newspaper work, who
cannot find appropriate employment because of the color of
his skin. Imagine him, with a father's failure rankling in his
heart, as the abyss of menial labor yawns beneath his feet.
Recall, moreover, that this youth, who since early childhood
has been moved about from pillar to post, is obsessed with
gaining admission to "the Club." What would happen to his
psyche on arrival in New York, where the only ticket of admission was a white skin?

He would undergo a major crisis of identity. The conforming self, thwarted by the color bar, would be incapacitated,
while the rebelling self, nourished by a thousand humiliations, would take command. On the ideological plane, a
process of radicalization would occur. Such was the substance
of Walrond's early years in New York. He dabbled briefly in
the Garvey movement, embraced for a time the socialist
alternative, and in the end settled for rebellion of a literary
sort, joining the New Negroes in their unprecedented
celebration of Negritude. The course of his rebellion can be
traced in certain of his essays, but our concern will be with his
apprentice fiction.

Apprentice Fiction
Walrond's total output in the short-story field consists of

twenty tales. Of these, ten are included in *Tropic Death,* while ten may be regarded as apprentice work. These apprentice pieces may in turn be separated into three kinds. First, a series of anecdotes or sketches or vignettes, set in the city of New York, and depicting the author's initial encounters with American racism.[11] Second, a pair of more substantial stories of Negro life in New York.[12] And third, a pair of crude fantasies, set in Panama, which adumbrate the psychological landscape if not the literary power of *Tropic Death.*[13]

The sketches and vignettes may be described as pre-fiction. They represent a halfway house in Walrond's transition from journalism to imaginative literature. Trained as a reporter, he moved in stages from the factual article, buttressed with statistics, to the personal essay; thence to the vignette, and finally, the full-fledged story. His sketches and vignettes are written for the most part in the first person, and some are at first glance indistinguishable from expository prose.[14] Their anecdotal form however, which absorbs increasing proportions of invention, places them in the category of pre-fiction. These pieces are thinly dramatized and crudely written, yet they encompass most of Walrond's major themes.

These early sketches dramatize the "soul pricks" and "spirit wounds" suffered by the author as a black migrant to New York. Behind the narrative voice we discern an ambitious youth whose hopes have been dashed by his exposure to the color bar. At a deeper level, Walrond is concerned with the nature of evil: with the process of initiation into a social order that is evil, and the loss of innocence that this entails. What strikes him most about the racist madness is its irrationality, its capriciousness, its fundamental absurdity. He perceives it correctly as demonic. Philosophically, this leads him to challenge the rationalist view of human nature that derives from the Enlightenment. Esthetically, it prompts him to explore the Gothic mode.

What troubles Walrond most about the racist mentality is its relentless categorization. People are judged, so to speak, by the backs of their necks, rather than their faces.[15] They are threatened psychologically with facelessness—with a humiliating loss of individuality. Depersonalization is the essence of the crime. It is to cope with this phenomenon that Walrond becomes a writer. For if race categorizes, style particularizes. The desire to individuate is the key to Walrond's flamboyant style: "In front of me is a jet black trollop. Her hair is bobbed. I snort at the bumps—barber's itch—I am forced to see on the back of her scraped neck."[16] Art forces us, in other words, to view reality in all of its uniqueness and complexity.

But art alone is not enough. Implicit in Walrond's early fiction are the values of racial consciousness and racial solidarity.[17] These are seen as a defensive armor necessary to protect the self from a fatal innocence and vulnerability. "Vignettes of the Dusk" provides a brilliant image of this vulnerability. The narrator enters an expensive restaurant in the Wall Street area where he orders oyster salad and "a vanilla temptation," only to be brought his food in a paper bag and hustled out. To resist the vanilla temptation—the unconscious desire to be white—is essential to the black man's health and sanity. This theme is given full expression in Walrond's first real story.

"Miss Kenny's Marriage" (*The Smart Set*, September 1923) is the story of a businesswoman of a certain age who invites disaster by marrying a man of twenty-five. She is the owner of a hair parlor on Brooklyn's Atlantic Avenue, where she has amassed a small fortune selling a preparation called Madame Kenny's Tar Hair Grower. Her intended, Mr. Ramsey, is a young lawyer belonging to one of the oldest colored families in Brooklyn, who regard as riffraff anyone who cannot trace his ancestry to the Battle of Long Island. Miss Kenny's social aspirations, however, prove to be her undoing, for Counsellor Ramsey, some three months after the wedding, absconds with his spouse's bank account.

In form, the story is a travesty; its theme, the pretender

brought low. Miss Kenny embodies various forms of pretentiousness: linguistic, cultural, and social. She feels herself superior to other blacks, her pride and bigotry being the antithesis of racial solidarity. Walrond takes an obvious delight in pulling his protagonist down from her empyrean heights, and to this end he employs a wide range of deflationary stratagems. These include a series of reductive metaphors comparing Miss Kenny to a horse, a wolf, a ferret, or a squirrel; a series of descriptive details which undercut her lofty notions by setting forth the grubby facts of her existence; and a series of bathetic devices such as constitute the common arsenal of travesty.[18]

The thrust of this story is similar to that of Claude McKay's Harlem tales. It portrays the assimilationist impulse as a psychological disaster. Miss Kenny maintains a false front for the benefit of whites; hers is a self-disparaging and inauthentic mode of life. By implication, Walrond calls upon his black readers to resist assimilation and cultivate their Negritude. This is the appropriate response to the racial onslaught depicted in his pre-fiction. Miss Kenny is, in short, a negative exemplar or antiself. By means of travesty, which is at bottom a form of ridicule, Walrond hopes to exorcise "the vanilla temptation." Not without a certain awkwardness, this early tale is nonetheless a portent of stronger work to come.

"City Love" (*American Caravan* 1927) is one of Walrond's most effective stories.[19] It is a solidly constructed work consisting of three sections, arranged in the musical progression ABA. The first and third sections (or main plot) are concerned with an extramarital affair between Primus, a married man, and Nicey, his paramour. The middle section (or subplot) depicts Primus in his domestic relations with his wife and son. They are recent migrants from the island of St. Lucia to New York, where Primus is employed as a longshoreman. Harassed and bullied on the docks, he tries to save some vestige of his manhood through his sexual adventures, and through bullying his wife and son.

As the story opens, Primus is trying to seduce Nicey in St. Nicholas Park, but she insists on being taken to a room. At his first attempt to purchase privacy, Primus is turned away because they have no bags. Having returned to his own apartment for a battered suitcase, he tries again, but this time is rebuffed because the lady is without a hat. "Why don't you people come right?" the black landlord demands. Angry and embarrassed, Nicey takes flight, but is persuaded to return after Primus buys her a bonnet. In the final scene, they are escorted down a moldy corridor and warned by the proprietor, "Don't forget . . . that if you want hot water in the morning, it'll be fifty cents extra."

The exacting nature of society (represented by the Harlem landlord) is Walrond's theme. Its demands on the greenhorn are relentless, even down to the pettiest detail. These demands reflect the iron law of metamorphosis by which an immigrant becomes a naturalized citizen. Nor is society erroneous in imposing such harsh terms. For the newcomer represents a threat to social order. His blunders tend to undermine the commonly accepted fictions on which society depends for its stability. Everyone understands that Primus and Nicey are not married, but the amenities, or outward forms, must be preserved. Nicey's hatlessness is an affront because it lacks verisimilitude: "Don't they know that folks don't travel that-a-way?"

It is only on second reading that the close articulation of subplot and main plot becomes apparent. The structure of the story invites us to compare two kinds of bullying. Thus the father's abusive treatment of his infant son in Section Two is an ironic echo of the treatment he himself receives at the hands of the host society. Immigrants,like children, are often bullied by those more knowledgeable, and hence more powerful than themselves. Walrond embodies this perception in a metaphor, portraying the migrant as an orphan child, naked and defenseless. In this impressive tale, he universalizes the migratory theme, removes it from the realm of racial melodrama, and invests it with an unanticipated poignancy.

In the early phase of his apprenticeship, Walrond's imagination was primarily engaged with the racial situation in the city of New York. Commencing in 1924 and 1925, however, he turned increasingly for his material to the Caribbean countries of his youth. This major shift of focus was accompanied, on the esthetic plane, by a corresponding shift from realism to romanticism, and more precisely to the Gothic mode. For Walrond was in process of embracing the myth of primitivism, whose fundamental movement was away from the metropolitan centers of occidental civilization, and toward a tropical environment such as he inhabited for the first twenty years of his life.

Walrond's first attempt in this direction was a pair of tales entitled "A Cholo Romance" and "The Voodoo's Revenge." From their titles it would seem that he intended to explore the Indian and African features of his Caribbean heritage. But in moving from his early manhood in New York to his adolescent years in Colón, something went awry. Repressed emotions were released, associated with his parents and his adolescent sexuality, with which his art was not prepared to cope. The result is raw fantasy. These tales are flat failures, yet they adumbrate the Gothic atmosphere of mystery and horror that permeates the pages of *Tropic Death*.

"A Cholo Romance" (*Opportunity*, June 1924) is a drama of backsliding and redemption, stemming from that period in Walrond's life when he was poised on the edge of the abyss. The possibility of atavism, or reversion to savagery, is embodied in Maria, a Cholo girl threatened with white slavery by Baxter, her putative father. She is saved from degradation in the nick of time by a clean-cut hero named Enrique Martin. This lurid melodrama contains the seeds of one of Walrond's finest stories, "Tropic Death." They share a common setting (a shabby boardinghouse in Bottle Alley), overlapping characters, and the crucial presence of an evil and corrupting father-figure. In "Tropic Death," however, Walrond masters these materials artistically.

In an essay called "Imperator Africanus," Walrond describes the rise of Garveyism after World War I:

> Fresh from the war, from the bloodstained fields of France and Mesopotamia, the black troops, bitter, broken, disillusioned, stormed at the gates of the whites—pleaded for a share of that liberty and democracy which they were led to believe were the things for which they had fought. And it was of course a futile knocking. Hardened by the experience of the conflict, the negroes . . . rose in all their might to create for themselves those spoils of war and peace which they knew they could not hope for from the ruling whites.[20]

"The Voodoo's Revenge" (*Opportunity*, July 1925) may be read as a parable of Garveyism, whose psychological foundation was loyalty betrayed. A Panamanian editor, Nestor Villaine, is treacherously jailed by a politician he has helped to place in office. In revenge, he hires a young St. Lucian to kill the Governor by poisoning. The youth is then disposed of in order to conceal the crime. The repressed emotions at the heart of this crude fantasy are revolt and rebelliousness. Villaine is Walrond's Bigger Thomas—a "baad nigger," as his name implies. The clash between the author's conforming and rebelling selves is nowhere more apparent than in this embittered loyalist, practitioner of voodoo, and emissary of revenge.

Lafcadio Hearn and Pierre Loti

In an early essay called "El Africano," Walrond eulogizes an Afro-Hispanic painter born in the Canary Islands whose full name is Nestor Martin Fernandez de la Torré. It is clear from his laudatory tone that he identifies deeply, if perhaps sub-consciously, with de la Torré, and adopts him as a model for his own art.[21] Thus he writes, ". . . de la Torré is a genius of the rarest water who looks out on the boulevard of life from the romantic point of view of a Negro. Were he a literary artist he would be a combination of Balzac, Pierre Loti, Lafcadio Hearn, Joseph Conrad, and de Maupassant."[22]

In this composite portrait of the ideal literary man, Walrond gives himself away. He reveals his own esthetic by acknowledging his major influences. Balzac was the source of his close observation and unflinching realism; Maupassant of his clinical detachment and cosmic irony. Conrad's "Heart of Darkness" helped to shape the atavistic implications of his art. But Lafcadio Hearn and Pierre Loti were the writers who supplied him with an animating myth.

Something of a Hearn revival was in progress during Walrond's apprentice years. From 1915 onward, a number of evaluative essays had appeared.[23] In 1922, Houghton Mifflin brought out a uniform edition of sixteen volumes called *The Writings of Lafcadio Hearn*. In 1923, Albert Mordell edited a volume of newspaper pieces entitled *Essays in European and Oriental Literature by Lafcadio Hearn*. In 1924, Edward Tinker published *Lafcadio Hearn's American Days*. Hearn's place in American letters was thus in process of assessment just as Walrond began to write. The force that he exerted on the young West Indian's imagination will be better understood if we examine his remarkable career.

Lafcadio Hearn (1850-1904) was born on the ancient island of Leucadia, or in modern Greek, Lafcada, whence derives his given name.[24] His father was a British Army officer of Anglo-Irish antecedents; his mother, a Greek of Maltese extraction. When the marriage foundered, Hearn was adopted by his father's wealthy aunt, and he passed his early childhood in the British Isles. He was educated by private tutors in Ireland and Wales, at a Jesuit college in northern France, and at Ushan, the Roman Catholic college of Durham. He lost the sight of one eye in an accident at school, and since the other was myopic, he suffered throughout his life from a partial blindness.

When his great-aunt died without providing for his future, Hearn migrated to New York, arriving in 1869 at the age of nineteen. After an initial period of menial jobs and bitter poverty, he found employment on a Cincinnati newspaper. In 1874 he married a black woman from whom he separated after three years. In 1877 he moved to New Orleans, where he worked as a reporter, editor, and feature writer on the *Times-Democrat*. For two years (1887-1889) he lived on the island of Martinique, returning briefly to the United States before his permanent departure for Japan in 1890. There he married a Japanese woman who bore him several children, became a naturalized citizen, taught English in government schools, and achieved a considerable reputation as an orientalist before his death in 1904.

The similarity of Hearn's life to his own must have been a source of wonderment to Eric Walrond. Like himself, Hearn had been a cosmopolitan, belonging to no one nation or cultural tradition, but suffering the pain and bafflement of multiple identities. Like himself, he had arrived in New York as a penniless youth and then, after a period of struggle, had climbed the ladder of journalism to the literary heights. Hearn, too, had been an outcast in his adopted land by virtue of its racist attitudes.[25] Above all, Hearn had cultivated a taste for the exotic that drew him to the West Indies. Was it any wonder that a young apprentice should eagerly devour the writings of a man whose life made so many points of contact with his own?

Hearn's literary work may be divided into three phases. First a journalistic phase, consisting of the feature articles and editorials, book reviews and critical essays, sketches and translations written for the Cincinnati and New Orleans newspapers. Next a West Indian phase, consisting of a book of sketches, *Two Years in the French West Indies* (1890), and a romantic novella, *Youma: the Story of a West Indian Slave* (1890). Finally, a Japanese phase, consisting of such titles as *Kokoro* (1896), *A Japanese Miscellany* (1901), and *Japan: an Attempt at Interpretation* (1904). For our purposes, it will suffice to examine certain literary essays of the 1880's, together with his chef d'oeuvre, *Two Years in the French West Indies.*

Lafcadio Hearn was a lover of the French language and the French *douceur de vivre* from his student days in northern France. Hence his predilection for New Orleans and the French Antilles. He was also an assiduous student of French letters, who believed that Paris was the literary center of the Western world. While employed on the staff of the New Orleans *Times-Democrat,* his work consisted mainly of translations from the French and criticism of contemporary French writing. His translations included fiction by Guy de Maupassant, Théophile Gautier, and Pierre Loti, while his criticism centered on Loti, whom he regarded as the *dernier cri* of modern prose.

Among Hearn's essays in the *Times-Democrat* were three devoted to the art of Pierre Loti.[26] These essays were written in the 1880's, not long before Hearn left New Orleans for Martinique. It seems clear that the primitivistic effusions of Loti had a major impact on the life and art of Hearn, playing no small part in his decision to live in and write about the West Indies. Since the Hearn essays on Loti were reprinted in 1923, it seems likely that Walrond, who was already captivated by the life and work of Hearn, discovered the writings of Loti through these essays. In any case, we have a chain of influence linking the careers of the three men.

"Pierre Loti" was the *nom de plume* of a French naval officer whose real name was Julien Viaud. He was born in Brittany in 1850, and was thus the exact contemporary of Lafcadio Hearn. His naval career took him to every corner of the

French empire, including the Levant, North Africa, South America, Polynesia, and the Orient. To relieve the boredom of military life, he wrote a series of romantic novels, utilizing as their settings the exotic lands that he had seen. Of his first four books, all of which are discussed by Hearn, one was set in Tahiti (*Le Mariage de Loti*, 1878); one in Turkey (*Aziyadé*, 1879); one in Senegal (*Le Roman d'un Spahi*, 1881); and one (a book of stories) in Montenegro, Algeria, and China (*Fleurs d'Ennui*, 1883).

Loti's imagination characteristically rejected European subjects, turning instead to the exotic cultures of Asia, Africa, and Polynesia. The myth of primitivism may thus be said to constitute the framework of his art. Loti was a late romantic, looking backward to Rousseau and Byron, and forward to Gauguin and the modern primitivists. Lafcadio Hearn became a part of this tradition when, in imitation of Loti, he abandoned his American materials in order to exploit the exotic cultures of the French Antilles and Japan. A generation later, Eric Walrond moved within the same orbit when he shifted the setting of his fiction from New York to the West Indies.

In addition to a flair for the exotic, Loti's imagination was marked by a taste for the macabre and grotesque. Hearn found this Gothic strain appealing, for his own imagination was distinctly of a morbid cast.[27] Thus he writes of *Le Mariage de Loti* that "The last chapter is not only an agony of pathos, but an agony made awful by contrasts so weird and supernatural fancies so ghastly that no idea could be formed of it by those who have not read the book."[28] Of *Le Roman d'un Spahi*, he notes that it is full of "monstrous landscapes and fantastic incidents." And of *Fleurs d'Ennui* he remarks, "In his last book a certain strange horror of death is manifested. . . ."

The word "eldritch" best describes the quality of imagination shared by Loti and Hearn. It is marked by a preference for the mysteries of night to the lucidities of day. James

Huneker writes of Hearn that "He was Goth, not Greek; he suffered from the mystic fear of the Goth, while he yearned for the great day flame of the classics."[29] One manifestation of this eldritch quality in Hearn was his fascination with the supernatural, and more precisely with the voodoo mysteries that he encountered in the city of New Orleans.[30] This side of Hearn must have kindled Walrond's imagination, since obeah, the West Indian variety of voodoo, plays so prominent a part in *Tropic Death.*

If Loti's subject matter and cast of mind were Romantic, his stylistic bent was Impressionist. His method of literary composition, according to Hearn, was to keep a notebook of his sense impressions of exotic lands, to which "he subjoined notes of the thoughts and fancies also which such impressions of sight, sound, or smell produced in the mind; and thus his work is as much introspective as it is retrospective."[31] This is the procedure employed by Hearn in *Two Years in the French West Indies,* a book which had a major impact on Eric Walrond's *Tropic Death.* Walrond's esthetic may thus be said to derive in part from the French Impressionists, by way of Pierre Loti and Lafcadio Hearn.

Loti was an artist of the pencil and the brush as well as the pen, which accounts both for his painterly style and his close links with French Impressionism. Writing of Loti's stylistic influence on Hearn, James Huneker observes, "You can't read a page of Loti aloud; hearing is never the final court of appeal for him. Nor is the ear regarded in Hearn's prose. He is not 'auditive'; like Loti and the Goncourts, he writes for the eye."[32] This eye-orientation produces a prose in which hue and texture matter more than clarity and precision. Loti, Hearn, and Walrond all employ a brilliant palette, but their evanescent prose sometimes sacrifices sharpness of outline to verbal chromatics and emotional nuance.

In 1887, Hearn left New Orleans and settled in St. Pierre,

Martinique. Having chafed for years under the insistent deadlines and artistic limitations of newspaper work, he hoped to achieve a more leisurely pace and to find a wider scope for his art. In formal terms, this entailed the abandonment of translation and criticism, and a more venturesome attempt at travel books and fiction. After the success of *Chita: a Memory of Last Island* (1888), a novella depicting the destructive fury of a hurricane in the Mississippi delta region, he was commissioned by *Harper's Magazine* to write a series of sketches on the West Indies. The result was perhaps the finest work of his career, *Two Years in the French West Indies* (1890).

The book is an amalgam of personal anecdote, travel sketch, and atmospheric rendering. It belongs to that category of pre-fiction, lying between journalism and imaginative literature, which was the dominant form of Eric Walrond's apprentice period. Such a book was plainly of the liveliest interest to a young West Indian, trained in journalism, and about to embark on a literary career. The work consists of two parts: an introduction called "A Midsummer Trip to the Tropics," and a series of "Martinique Sketches." The latter are with one exception not directly relevant to our present line of inquiry.[33] But the long introductory section will tell us all we need to know about the genesis of *Tropic Death.*

"A Midsummer Trip to the Tropics" is a journalistic account of the voyage made by Hearn in the summer of 1887 from New York to British Guiana and back to Martinique. Among the islands visited en route were Nevis, Barbados, Grenada, and Trinidad. Written in an age dominated by evolutionary doctrine, Hearn's essay is a metaphor of human evolution in reverse. The movement of his journey is farther and farther from New York and closer and closer to the primitive, the savage, and the sensual; the fermenting and decaying jungle, and the blinding tropic sun. In Guiana, the southernmost extent of his travels, Hearn encounters the essence of the tropics: the primeval, equatorial swampland where life on earth might have begun.

If we recall that this same Guiana was the birthplace of Eric Walrond, we can readily appreciate the strong appeal of Hearn's book to his imagination. He was fascinated by the atavistic implications of the work. For Guiana was associated with his "backsliding" father, and more precisely with his father's moral and physical decay. Embedded in the structure of Hearn's book he found a controlling myth that might give form to his own most intimate experience. And so we find in *Tropic Death* a sharp polarity between the Panama Canal, a symbol of modern, industrial technology, and the basin of the Essequibo River in Guiana where nature, as in Hearn's account, has resisted every effort to civilize, tame, or subdue her.

As the antelope's flank is carved by the leopard's tooth, Hearn's style is shaped by the tropic sun. It is a style of astonishing chromatic force, which dissolves land- or seascape into the shimmering surfaces of French Impressionism. This atmospheric tinting is Hearn's stylistic legacy to Walrond: "The sun is high up now, almost overhead: there are a few thin clouds in the tender-colored sky—flossy, long-drawn-out, white things. The horizon has lost its greenish glow; it is spectral blue. Mast, spars, rigging—the white boats and the orange chimney—the bright deck lines and the snowy rail—cut against the colored light in almost dazzling relief."[34]

The book's imagery is lush, like the tropical vegetation it describes. Hearn stresses the ambivalence of nature in the tropics, where her great fecundity is equaled by her powers of decay. Thus he acknowledges the sense of awe and mystic fear inspired by a tropical rain forest, even as he dwells upon its dangers: the *fer-de-lance*, a deadly viper found on Martinique whose venom putrifies the living flesh, or the manchineel apple of Grenada, whose merest touch is fatal, and whose milky juice supplied the Carib Indians with poison for their darts. It is evident, in short, that the gruesome images of "tropic death" set forth by Hearn provided Walrond with the unifying concept for a book of Gothic tales.

Complementing the images of death are those of decomposition, dilapidation, and decay. Their function is to support the theme of atavism by suggesting that in the tropics the physical foundations of human culture are in constant danger of reverting to the jungle. ". . . Nature consumes the results of human endeavor so swiftly, buries memories so profoundly, distorts the labors of generations so grotesquely, that one feels here, as nowhere else, how ephemeral man is, how intense and how tireless the effort necessary to preserve his frail creations even a little while. . . ."[35] Add to this sense of cultural fragility Walrond's personal fear of backsliding, and what emerges is the central theme of *Tropic Death.*

Hearn is aware of the social and historical decay of the West Indies as well. He perceives that with emancipation of the slaves and a subsequent decline in the sugar trade, many of the islands were left with abandoned plantations, empty warehouses, rotting wharves, and restless populations. Walrond's black peasants were of course the chief victims of this tortured history. Writing of their fate in the early 1900's, during the construction of the Panama Canal, Walrond takes up the history of the region where Hearn left off. In *Tropic Death* he measures not only the human costs of economic dislocation, mass migration, and the rest, but still more poignantly the split identities and fractured selves that were the legacy of three centuries of colonial rule.

Hearn's view of Caribbean history was derived from the principles of social Darwinism. A disciple of Herbert Spencer, he believed that human history was a struggle between the races of mankind for the survival of the fittest. In a Caribbean context, this meant that "the slave races of the past must become the masters of the future."[36] Not only were the white populations fated to succumb, but the mixed races too were doomed to extinction: "the future tendency must be to universal blackness . . . perhaps to universal savagery." Such was the historical perspective that Walrond inherited from Hearn; the controlling myth that gave both form and substance to his Caribbean tales.

Tropic Death

Tropic Death consists of ten stories, set for the most part in Barbados or in Panama. The settings are symbolic of a vast upheaval in the lives of the Caribbean peoples. The village of Black Rock represents the dying vestiges of the plantation economy established by the British, while the city of Colón embodies the forces of industrialization set in motion by the building of the Panama Canal. Awakened from their ancient, rural way of life by the promise of greater economic opportunity, the black peasants of *Tropic Death* are flocking to the crowded cities of the Canal Zone. Walrond has contrived, in short, a Caribbean version of the Great Migration.

In addition to their common historical setting, the tales are linked by the motif of sudden death. Existence is precarious in Walrond's fictive world, and he employs the lethal dangers of the tropics to undermine our faith in Western rationalism. He is concerned with those dimensions of reality—accident, disease, and natural disaster—which Western man is under the illusion of having conquered through machine technology. From the depths of his Gothic sensibility, Walrond challenges the notion that man has won his freedom from physical nature by means of the machine. His snakes and sharks and vampire bats, his droughts and fires and tropical diseases, serve as grim reminders of mankind's tenuous position in the universe.

Technological optimism having been discredited, Walrond proceeds to explore the realm of the demonic. Always a hazardous enterprise, such a course traditionally involves a descent to the underworld. The movement of *Tropic Death* is perpetually downward into turbulence and chaos. Typically we descend from the deck to the bowels of a ship, from the sparkling surface to the murky depths of the sea, from civilized to primitive codes of conduct, or from the human to the reptilian plane of being. Only in the final story, "Tropic Death," does the self complete the cycle of descent and return, and having visited the lower depths, emerge triumphant.

The quality of the collection is uneven. Certain of the stories contain lumpy autobiographical ingredients inadequately metamorphosed into art. Others, while more successfully distanced, are lacking in coherence and design. As Robert Herrick writes of Walrond in the *New Republic*, "He is careless of composition, as the younger writers of the day often are, disdaining unity and coherence in their effort to seize a deep reality."[37] Yet the stronger tales in *Tropic Death* must be counted among the most effective of the Harlem Renaissance. Five of these stories, discussed in some detail, will serve to illustrate the range and power of Walrond's art.

"Drought" is the story of a natural disaster and its impact on the lives of a Barbadian peasant family. Leading at best a marginal existence, the family of Coggins Rum is reduced by the drought to a state of near-starvation. Despite repeated warnings from her parents, the six-year-old Beryl persists in eating marl to relieve her hunger pangs. Like some imp of the perverse she refuses to be disciplined and subsequently dies, her stomach bloated by the coral dust she has ingested. Her blighted life, which mirrors on the human plane the devastated landscape, is emblematic of the cramped, impoverished, and desperate circumstances of the Caribbean peasantry.

Walrond's theme is the intractability of nature and human nature. The drought no more responds to the peasants' prayers than the child to the parents' pleas or imprecations. Coggins Rum, his "brow wrinkled in cogitation," is a symbol of human reason. But the universe that he inhabits is envisioned as a jagged rock and human life a stubbed toe. "Yo' dam vagabond yo'!" Rum exclaims as he lacerates his naked toe. Yet the child is no more to be governed than the wayward toe. Sexual waywardness in fact produced her: yellow Beryl, "the only one of the Rum children who wasn't black as sin." The tale is concerned, in short, with those elements of human experience which defy reason.

"Hard-ears," the child is called, and the fruit of her stubbornness is a hard belly. The story is dominated by images of stones and rocks and petrifaction. Coggins Rum works in a quarry where throat and lungs are filled with stone dust. His children kill birds with "touch-bams," hollow pipes rammed with stones and gunpowder. Beryl rams herself with marl until she bursts, and an autopsy reveals the calcium deposits in her stomach. If the story has a villain it is Rum's wife, whose heart is hardened against her daughter's suffering. The spiritual danger of these peasant folk, the imagery suggests, is coming to resemble inwardly the hard, unyielding qualities of their environment.

Migration and resistance to migration is the subject of "The Black Pin." It is a subject deeply embedded in Walrond's life experience. Moving from British Guiana to Barbados, he was called a "mud-head"; from Barbados to Colón, a "chumbo"; from Colón to New York, a "nigger" or a "monkey-chaser." His recognition that xenophobia is a universal human trait enables him to elevate his personal humiliations to the plane of myth. He understands only too well what it means to be resented as a trespasser on the territory of another, to be treated as an untouchable, to be the innocent victim of un-provoked assault. In the confrontation between April Emptage and Zink Diggs, he creates an archetypal image of the immigrant's ordeal.

April and her four children have fled from British Guiana to Barbados in quest of a better life. They buy an old shack and settle on a tiny plot of land where they begin subsistence farming. Their nearest neighbor, Zink Diggs, is not long in opening hostilities. She strikes a child, takes a goat hostage, and in the course of a boundary dispute, levels April's crops to the ground. Her poisonous hatred is symbolized by a black pin, soaked in "some demon chemical," and employed as a voodoo fetish. When the pin threatens to ignite April's shack, she redirects the poisonous smoke toward the house of her tormentor and Zink Diggs—in a brilliant image of retaliatory hatred—is destroyed by her own malice.

Structurally speaking, the story possesses an admirable symmetry. Each woman has a favorite song: in April's case, a hymn of universal love, "An' crown Him Lahd av ahl"; in Zink's, a folk-song, "Donkey wahn de watah, hole 'im Joe," which in context means "hold back the immigrant." One woman represents constructive; the other, destructive energy. April's name is suggestive of her spring plantings, while Zink's is associated with the "buzzing and zimming of a saw." Poison is balanced by counterpoison, as Zink's murderous intentions boomerang. Her determination to burn out the migrants is countered by April's peasant tenacity, her strongest weapon in the struggle to survive.

The title story, "Tropic Death," is a parable of lost innocence. The story opens with the image of a boy, standing on a dock in Barbados, and dressed in the fashion of the Victorian middle class. Unlike the ragged street urchins with whom he is contrasted, the boy has obviously led a sheltered life. He is about to embark with his mother on a quest for her missing husband. At the end of his voyage to Colón, Gerald finds himself installed in Bottle Alley, the slum and red-light district of a booming harbor town. There is no protection from its noise and dirt, poverty and disease, violence and sensuality. The boy's migration from Barbados to Colón is thus a rite of passage from boyhood into manhood, an abrupt transition from the state of innocence to that of fallen man.

The fate in store for Gerald and his mother is adumbrated by a shipboard incident. The Bishop of the West Indies, a red-jowled Scotsman, deserts the comfort of the upper deck to bring the Word of God to the black deckers. Piously avoiding grime and filth, he is the accidental victim of an ill-timed gob of spit. Like the Bishop's perilous descent into chaos, Gerald and his mother are about to descend to a lower level of the social scale. Declassed by the weakness and ineffectuality of his father, the boy must learn to live amid the grime and filth of Bottle Alley. At the same time, compensating factors are at work in the form of a new resiliency, a greater maturity, and a wider experience of life. The story thus is a recapitulation of the Fortunate Fall.

In its central image of the Garden, the story illuminates the dynamics of inversion that link the pastoral and Gothic modes. As the boy observes the sordid life of Bottle Alley, the sun, striking a galvanized roof, reflects the brilliant colors of a tropical garden: "It created a Garden of the roof. It recaptured the essence of that first jungle scene (267)." This image of *reflected glory*, as in Milton's description of the fallen angels, vividly conveys the boy's sense of loss. For the main burden of "Tropic Death" is the loss of Eden (or childhood in rural Barbados), and its replacement by the Gothic horrors of Bottle Alley in the city of Colón.

Following her husband's deportation to a leper colony, Sarah Bright takes refuge in the English Plymouth Brethren, a dissenting sect which promises redemption from the world of Bottle Alley. She attempts to impose a rigid fundamentalism on her son, but he is moving to the rhythm of a different drum. Transformed by his father's sufferings, the boy develops greater insight and sensitivity. Increasingly he withdraws into a brooding isolation. A protective detachment becomes his defense against the world. Out of unendurable catastrophe, the artistic temperament is born. Compassion will be the instrument of Gerald Bright's redemption, but compassion expressed not through religious but esthetic forms.

In "A Midsummer Trip to the Tropics," Lafcadio Hearn envisages a bitter struggle for survival in the Caribbean:

> But with the disappearance of the white populations the ethnical problem would still be unsettled. Between the black and mixed peoples prevail

hatreds more enduring and more intense than any
race prejudices between whites and freedmen in the
past; a new struggle for supremacy could not fail to
begin, with the perpetual augmentation of numbers,
the ever-increasing competition for existence. And
the true black element, more numerically powerful,
more fertile, more cunning, better adapted to pyrogenic climate and tropical environment would
surely win. All these mixed races, all these beautiful
fruit-colored populations, seem doomed to extinction. . . .[38]

This passage forms the conceptual basis of Eric Walrond's
widely anthologized story, "The Yellow One." His heroine,
"La Madurita," is a symbol of those beautiful fruit-colored
populations which the Europeans left behind them in the
Spanish Main: "She was lovely to behold. Her skin was the ripe
red gold of the Honduras half-breed (68)." She meets her
doom on a voyage from Honduras to Jamaica, when caught
up in the deadly hatreds of a coal-black Negro from the
Florida coast and a Cuban who is a mestizo like herself. Their
savage brawl, in the course of which she is trampled to death,
takes place in the sizzling ship's galley, whose heat is emblematic of that "pyrogenic climate" which so impressed itself on
Hearn.

"The Yellow One" reverberates with echoes of Caribbean
history. La Madurita's husband, for example, is a Jamaican
mulatto named Alfred St. Xavier Mendez. His middle name
reminds us of the sixteenth-century Jesuit who missionized
the Spanish Main. Walrond's point is that the vaccination
didn't really take. Christianity remains a thin veneer among
the Caribbean peoples, while just "below decks," sex and
violence tempt the psyche to resume its pagan ways. When La
Madurita goes below, she is descending into the Caribbean
past, into the cauldron of hatreds which are the chief legacy of
white colonialism. The brawl that she unwittingly provokes is

rendered in images that stress the atavistic tendencies in Caribbean life.

Alfred, who lies lethargically on deck while his wife is being killed below, adds a new dimension to the theme of atavism. A delinquent father and husband, he represents the indolence and irresponsibility that Walrond associates with his own father. Not for nothing is Alfred from Jamaica, which has been described by Walrond as "a land with as many color distinctions as there are eggs in a shad's roe." In his essay on Marcus Garvey, Walrond writes that "In Jamaica, as elsewhere in the United Kingdom, England differentiates between the full bloods and the half bloods. In Garvey's Jamaica, the mulattoes were next in power to the whites. The blacks, who outnumber them three to one, have actually no voice politically or economically."[39]

This background will help to explain the central image of the tale: "The sea was calm, gulls scuttled low, seizing and ecstatically devouring some reckless, sky-drunk sprat (69)." For a sprat (or herring) to be "sky-drunk" is to aspire to an alien element, the air. The penalty for such presumption is to be devoured by a gull. So with the mestizo class, created by miscegenation, who are intoxicated by the social layer just above them. Oriented toward whiteness, holding themselves aloof from ordinary blacks, and forever putting on airs, they expose themselves through their anti-black bias to the risk of psychic death.

"The White Snake," which is Walrond's most impressive tale, displays his talents at their most Gothic. We are plunged at once into the world of nightmare, as a black Guyanese servant-girl cries out in her sleep that "a white snake [is] crawlin' up me foots (186)." The tale that follows amounts to an objectification of her dream. Seenie, who has been seduced and impregnated by a mulatto adventurer named Jack Captain, takes refuge on the sparsely populated isle of Waakenham near the delta of the Essequibo River. There she finds employment in the household of a Negro constable. And there, in a primitive hut deep in the Guiana woods, she fulfills her motherhood by rearing Water Spout, her illegitimate child.

One night, returning to her hut after work, Seenie drops off into an exhausted sleep beside her infant son. Awakened by his hunger cries, she nurses him—half asleep, and surrendering to the sublime mammalian passivity of breast feeding. Later on she reawakens, feels a reassuring presence at her breast, but puzzled, hears her son crying on the floor: "Was he a dual being? Here he was at her breast, gnawing away at it. And there he was down on the floor, howling (206-7)." The cold head at her breast suddenly recedes, and she jumps up, screaming out in horror. Next morning, one of the constable's men drags in "the fresh dead body of a bloaty milk-fed snake the sheen of a moon in May (208)."

It is crucial that the episode takes place at night, in a twilight zone between sleep and waking: "Cycles of the day sped through Seenie's head. There was a fugitive line between them and the half-realized happenings in a dream (203)." That thin and fragile line is basically what interests Eric Walrond. Psychologically, it is the boundary between the conscious and unconscious mind; culturally, between civilization and savagery; morally, between angelic and demonic tendencies in man. The story is concerned, in short, with the precarious nature of the human enterprise. Seenie's hut, located in an isolated clearing on the edge of the jungle, is emblematic of the constant danger of declining to a lower plane of being.

Civilization remains in jeopardy because nature, including human nature, is recalcitrant to human will and purpose. On the Essequibo Coast, river timbers buried in the mud overturn the boats of miners returning from the gold fields. Sheep dogs mutiny at night, devouring their own charges. And the omnipresent snakes, abandoning the coral road to man only during daylight hours, reassert their immemorial dominion after dark. Human nature is no less intractable: Seenie has been missionized, but gives birth to an illegitimate child; she is tyrannized by her employers, but subtly resists their authority. The White Snake may thus be seen as the embodiment of those ungovernable cosmic forces which lie beyond the reach of progress or policemen.

Walrond's White Snake, like Melville's White Whale, is an emblem of the dual nature of the cosmos. Thus the *White Snake* and *Water Spout* are manifestations of the same reality: "Was he a dual being?" This image of the child-serpent, with its Melvillean blend of innocence and terror, is fundamental to Walrond's cosmology. Jack Captain, who sired Water Spout in a moment of "dismal oversight," is described as hermaphroditic. His sexual ambivalence, projected on the cosmic plane, becomes a symbol of Divine Ambiguity. For the cosmos confronts us principally with mystery, so that groping in the dark toward the child-serpent, we can only scream with Seenie, "Oh, me Gawd, me Gawd (207)."

Tropic Death was a remarkable achievement for a man of twenty-eight. It remains to inquire why, after so promising a start, Walrond was reduced to silence. We know very little of his private life, and nothing that might account for the disconcerting fact that shortly after *Tropic Death* appeared, and at the height of his literary fame, he left New York for Europe, never to return. Of his writing, we know only that he labored unsuccessfully on a history of the Panama Canal which he planned to call *The Big Ditch.* Perhaps one day letters, diaries, or manuscripts will come to light which will dispel the mystery. In the meantime, we must rely on the internal evidence provided by his stories.

A survey of Walrond's fiction reveals a fundamental contradiction in his art. On the one hand, he adopts the myth of primitivism and works within its terms. Influenced by the writings of Loti and Hearn, and encouraged by the climate of the times, he explores the theme of atavism in its various ramifications. On the other hand, in his secret heart he endorses the missionary point of view. He believes in racial progress up the evolutionary ladder into some ineffable White Heaven. In consequence, he cannot really bring himself to celebrate the primitive. *Tropic Death* is in fact the veiled confession of a colonized black that he cannot return to his primitive sources.

In terms of Walrond's artistic development, *Tropic Death* turned out to be a dead end. Like Toomer's *Cane*, the book was essentially a backward glance, whose aim was the consolidation of identity. As a "return to beginnings," both personal and cultural, it generated a considerable power. But it failed to lead anywhere, leaving its author bereft of an artistic future. Yet despite its limitations, *Tropic Death* will be remembered as a notable achievement of the Harlem Renaissance. And it will be particularly treasured, by American Negroes of West Indian descent, as a pioneer attempt to grapple with the complex fate of hailing from the Spanish Main.

Chapter 8

Jean Toomer

A vast body of Toomer criticism has appeared since the Harper and Row paperbound edition of *Cane* was published in 1969. Most of it has been restricted to the book itself, which no one will deny is still in need of explication.[1] But there is a great danger of distortion in isolating this enigmatic masterpiece from the full body of Toomer manuscripts now available in the Fisk University Library. While an exclusively exegetical approach may have been justifiable prior to 1967, when the Toomer papers were deposited at Fisk, now no one who has not made his pilgrimage to Nashville can expect to be taken seriously as a Toomer critic. That is known, in the world of scholarship, as paying your dues.

A prime example of critical myopia is a recent essay by Clifford Mason called "Jean Toomer's Black Authenticity." After assuring us that "Toomer, unlike almost any other writer, really talks to Black people about themselves, giving white reality very little play indeed," Mason concludes his essay by praising Toomer for "creating a Black world of reality that lived for itself, by itself, . . . strictly of itself, and that treated whiteness with the indifference or the hate or the tolerance that it may or may not have deserved. . . ."[2]

Doubtless an accurate enough rendition of Mason's personal philosophy, such a statement simply has no bearing on the historical personage of Jean Toomer. It is Mason, and not Toomer, who desires to partition the social world, and even the realm of metaphysics, into black and white compartments. While Mason strives to harden these racial categories, it was Toomer's lifelong aim to decrystallize them. At no point in his career was Toomer's concept of reality racially exclusive. On the contrary, he insisted repeatedly and emphatically on a noumenal reality that existed beyond the phenomenal world, and specifically beyond the categories of race.

But let Toomer speak for himself in this regard. In *The Crock of Problems*, one of the unending versions of his autobiography preserved at Fisk, Toomer writes: "Damn labels if they enslave human beings. Enough of race and nationality and labels. Above race and nationality there is Mankind. Beyond labels there is reality."[3] Toomer was concerned in everything he ever wrote, including *Cane*, with this transcendent reality. This fact will be readily apparent to anyone who cares to peruse "Bona and Paul," one of the more finely crafted stories to be found in *Cane*.

Unless we grasp Toomer's neo-Platonism, with its basic commitment to noumenal reality, we cannot comprehend his attitude toward race. As early as 1914, on the eve of his departure for the university, Toomer formulated a racial stance that would remain essentially unchanged throughout his life:

> Going to Wisconsin, I would again be entering a white world; and, though I personally had experienced no prejudice or exclusion either from the whites or the colored people, I had seen enough to know that America viewed life as if it were divided into white and black. Having lived with colored people for the past five years, at Wisconsin the question might come up. What was I? I thought about it independently, and, on the basis of fact, concluded

that I was neither white nor black, but simply an American.[4]

In the 1930's, Toomer elaborated his racial views at considerable length, both in poetry and prose.[5] He wrote, for example, in *A Fiction and Some Facts*, an autobiography published privately in 1931, "As for being a Negro, this of course I am not—neither biologically nor socially. . . . In biological fact I am, as are all Americans, a member of a new people that is forming in this country. If we call this people the Americans, then biologically and racially I am an American. . . . As long as I have been conscious of the issues involved, I have never identified myself with any single racial or social group."[6]

The crucial point concerning Toomer's racial stance is, in Darwin Turner's pithy phrase, that "he is not merely denying that he is black; he is also denying that he is white."[7] In other words, Toomer is challenging the philosophical validity of these racial categories. He maintains that in America the older races—Indian, African, and European—have fused and blended so as to produce a new race that transcends its historic origins. Any man is free to agree or disagree with this position (personally I find it quixotic, and of disastrous consequence for Toomer's art). But no critic, in the light of his repeated and unequivocal assertions to the contrary, can write responsibly of Toomer's "black authenticity."

Anyone who reads the many versions of Toomer's autobiography will readily acknowledge that his blackness, far from being a pillar of psychological stability, was a source of unending agony and consternation. As for his resolution of this bitter conflict, the facts speak for themselves. In the course of a lifetime, Toomer was deeply in love with three women, all of whom were white. For most of his life he lived exclusively among white people. The overwhelming bulk of his writing was not concerned with blacks in any way. There was no black writer, in short, with a lower ethnicity quotient. The norm and standard of his life and work, from which *Cane* constitutes a momentary deviation, was emphatically non-ethnic.

If this be so, and if Toomer maintained his transcendent view of race consistently throughout his life, how can we account for *Cane*, which is, or seems to be, a celebration of ethnicity? The apparent contradiction is readily resolved by sundering the future from the past, or in other words, by stressing the vatic nature of Toomer's art. He is essentially a poet, and a poet in the prophetic tradition of Blake and Whitman. His characteristic stance is that of an Old Testament prophet. And a prophet is by definition one who lives more intensely in the future than the past.

Cane is Toomer's tribute to the past; his reconciliation to the painful history of the black man in America. It is a celebration of the Negro folk-spirit, which Toomer sees as being rapidly obliterated by the forces of modern industrialism. To lament that loss is the aim of his magnificent lyric, "Song of the Son," which stands at the spiritual center of *Cane*. When Toomer writes of "a song-lit race of slaves," whose plaintive soul is "leaving, soon gone," he employs the language and the form of pastoral elegy. For *Cane* is in essence a pastoral interlude, like Thoreau's trip to the woods, through which the author seeks to achieve a consolidation of the self, in order to move forward to the fundamental task of prophecy.

Cane was Jean Toomer's hail-and-farewell to his blackness. Springing from a sojourn of several months in Sparta, Georgia, the impulse that gave birth to *Cane* was soon exhausted. Toomer was never to touch on these materials again. "The folk-spirit," as he explains in the *Outline of an Autobiography*, "was walking in to die on the modern desert. That spirit was so beautiful. Its death was so tragic. Just this seemed to sum up life for me. And this was the feeling I put into 'Cane.' 'Cane' was a swan song. It was a song of an end. And why no one has seen and felt that, why people have expected me to write a second and a third and a fourth book like 'Cane' is one of the queer misunderstandings of my life."[8]

Life and Work

Jean Toomer inherited the problem of racial ambiguity at birth. His maternal grandfather, P. B. S. Pinchback, was born in Macon, Georgia, of a white father and mulatto mother. Caucasian in appearance, he lived in the deep South sometimes as a Negro and sometimes as a white. Before the Civil War he married Nina Hethorn, a woman of Anglo-French and perhaps Creole extraction. During the war, he served as captain of a Negro company in the Union Army. At the conclusion of hostilities he declared himself a Negro, and having entered politics, became at the height of his career the Acting Governor of Louisiana.

In the 1890's Toomer's grandparents moved to Washington, D.C., where they settled in a white neighborhood. There his mother, Nina Pinchback, married a man considerably older than herself. The illegitimate son of a Georgia plantation owner, Nathan Toomer had lived in the South as a white man, although he was known in Washington as a Negro. Jean Toomer (1894-1967), christened Nathan Eugene, was born in Washington on December 26, 1894. His parents, who were mismated, soon divorced, and Toomer was to see his father only once in his lifetime. He was raised in his grandparents' household, and during his early years bore their name, Eugene Pinchback.

In 1906 Toomer's mother married a white man and moved to Brooklyn, then to New Rochelle, New York. Toomer thus spent three years of his life (age twelve to fourteen) as a white person. When his mother died in 1909, of complications resulting from an appendectomy, he returned to his grandparents in Washington. The family fortunes, however, had fallen into disrepair, and the Pinchbacks now were living in a shabby-genteel, predominantly Negro neighborhood. "For the first time," Toomer writes of this period, "I lived in a colored world."⁹ There he spent his high school years, graduating from Dunbar High in 1914.

As Toomer left Washington for Madison, Wisconsin, where he would be living once again in a white world, he gave sober thought to the question of his racial identity. Two of his grandparents were probably white.¹⁰ His maternal grandfather, his father, his mother, and he himself had lived on either side of the color line. The family saga, with its truth-is-stranger-than-fiction quality, struck him as being peculiarly American. It was logical enough that he should conclude, "I was neither white nor black, but simply an American." Whether this conclusion brought him peace of mind is something else again.

In the fall of 1914, Toomer embarked on a university career which soon became a shambles of dropouts and false starts. After four years of chaos and indecision, he was unable to establish a foundation on which to build his life. He studied agriculture briefly at the University of Wisconsin and the Massachusetts College of Agriculture; physical education at Chicago's American College of Physical Training; history at CCNY and anthropology at NYU. After each defeat, his grandfather made life miserable for him in Washington. This pressure to succeed gave Toomer one of his major themes: the place of the artist in bourgeois society. It also left him with a predisposition to failure that threatened to become a self-fulfilling prophecy.

Toomer's intellectual gropings began in 1916, during his first sojourn in Chicago. Under the influence of Clarence Darrow and Carl Sandburg, he became an agnostic and a socialist. On moving to New York in 1917, he read intensively in Shaw and Ibsen, Santayana and Goethe. Brief employment in a Jersey shipyard cured him of his socialism, while a reading of Goethe's *Wilhelm Meister* made him an esthete.¹¹ His esthetic tendencies were reinforced by a meeting with Waldo Frank in 1919. Back in Washington in the summer of 1920, he read "all of Waldo Frank, most of Dostoievsky, much of Tolstoi, Flaubert, Baudelaire, Sinclair Lewis, Dreiser, most all of the American poets, Coleridge, Blake, Pater—in fine, a good portion of the modern writers of all western countries."[12]

From 1920 to 1923 Toomer lived in Washington, caring for his aging grandparents and serving his literary apprenticeship. Setting the most exacting standards, he accumulated a trunkful of manuscripts before he was satisfied with their quality: "I wrote and wrote and put each thing aside, regarding it as simply one of the exercises of my apprenticeship."[13] For three months in the fall of 1921 he served as Acting Principal of a Negro school in Sparta, Georgia. This pilgrimage to his sources inspired Toomer's first book. *Cane* was written in approximately thirteen months, from November 1921 to December 1922.

With the publication of *Cane*, Toomer became a personage among the avant-garde: "In New York I stepped into the literary world. Frank, Gorham Munson, Kenneth Burke, Hart Crane, Josephson, Cowley, Paul Rosenfeld, Van Wyck Brooks, Robert Littell—*Broom, The Dial, The New Republic*, and many more."[14] Waldo Frank became his mentor. He criticized his manuscripts, introduced him to his circle, which included many influential editors, found him a publisher, wrote the Introduction to *Cane*, and in a word, launched his career. In addition he proffered his friendship and extended the hospitality of his home. Toomer reciprocated these kindnesses by bedding his friend's wife.

The Franks' marriage was admittedly rather unconventional. Frank himself was notorious for his erotic adventures,[15] and Margaret Naumburg, who had studied with Montessori and founded the progressive Walden School in New York, was one of those emancipated women who arrived in Greenwich Village armed with the collected works of Sigmund Freud. On her part, the affair was serious enough to precipitate divorce proceedings, despite the existence of a small child. On Toomer's side, it seems to have been something less than definitive. He accompanied Margaret to Reno in the spring of 1924, but withheld himself from the ultimate commitment. In the summer of that year he left America for the Gurdjieff Institute at Fontainebleau, France.

Toomer's interest in the teachings of George Gurdjieff was aroused primarily by Gorham Munson. Gurdjieff was a Caucasian Greek who, after spending many years in Asia, became the guru of a worldwide movement in the 1920's. Several members of the Frank circle attended meetings in New York led by A. R. Orage, Gurdjieff's representative in America. Toomer's interest was reinforced by his reading of P. D. Ouspensky's *Tertium Organum*, to which he was intro- duced by Gorham Munson and Hart Crane. In 1924 he embraced the Gurdjieff teachings, announcing in a letter to Gorham Munson, "I have given up art—as we have practiced it. And I am about (have already imperfectly commenced) to undertake the Gurdjieff discipline."[16]

Toomer's active involvement in the Gurdjieff movement lasted from 1924 to 1931. On his return from France in 1925, he formed a group in Harlem. The following year he was commissioned by Gurdjieff to organize a group in Chicago, where he remained for the better part of five years. It was during this period that he wrote most of the short stories assembled for publication under the title *Lost and Dominant*.[17] He also finished two novels (*The Gallonwerps* and *Transatlan- tic*), a novella ("York Beach"), a version of the autobiography (*Earth-Being*), and a book of aphorisms (*Essentials*). It was a period of intense literary activity which, however, bore little fruit in terms of publication.

In 1931 Toomer married Margery Latimer, who was her- self an accomplished short-story writer. Within a year, she died in childbirth. In 1934 he married Marjorie Content, a friend of Alfred Stieglitz and Georgia O'Keeffe, and the daughter of a wealthy stockbroker. The Toomers settled in Doylestown, Pennsylvania, in 1936, among the Bucks County Quakers. Toomer joined the Society of Friends in 1940, and wrote from time to time thereafter for Quaker publications. Forgotten by the literary world, and estranged from the black community, he died on March 30, 1967, after having been an invalid for the last fifteen years of his life.

Waldo Frank and His Milieu

It would be difficult to overstate the influence of Waldo Frank on Jean Toomer. The younger was quite simply a disciple of the older man. It follows that an adequate conception of Toomer's art is impossible without a detailed knowledge of the work of Waldo Frank. To understand the genesis of *Cane*, we must familiarize ourselves with the intellectual milieu in which Frank functioned, and of which Toomer soon became a part. We must examine Toomer's professional relationship with Frank; assess the influence of particular Frank works on *Cane*; and trace the esthetic which Toomer derived from Waldo Frank to its source in the poetry and fiction of Jules Romains.

Our point of embarkation is the brilliant, if short-lived periodical, the *Seven Arts*.[18] This review, which flourished for about a year in 1916-1917, until it was silenced on account of its opposition to the war, was the most distinguished literary journal of its day. The editors and chief contributors regarded themselves as the spiritual heirs of Walt Whitman. Speaking in prophetic tones, and dedicated to a kind of mystic nationalism, they called upon the nation to renounce its vulgar moneygrubbing and fulfill its highest destiny. Under the leadership of men like Van Wyck Brooks, Randolph Bourne, and Waldo Frank, they called for a cultural revolution in America.

Waldo Frank was associate editor of the *Seven Arts*, while among its regular contributors were Alfred Kreymborg, Paul Rosenfeld, and Sherwood Anderson. These men, together with Gorham Munson and Hart Crane, were to shape the literary destiny of Jean Toomer. They were his peers, his intimates, and his true audience. These writers understood the politics of culture and played the game with considerable skill. They occupied strategic posts in the little magazines, reviewed each other's books, exchanged manuscripts, conducted correspondence, and signed one another's manifestos. Each was a center of energy in his own right, and together they generated lines of force that radiated in all directions.

It was Alfred Kreymborg who introduced Jean Toomer to Waldo Frank. A poet, critic, and editor, Kreymborg lectured at the Rand School, where he encountered Toomer in the winter of 1919-1920. He invited the young neophyte to a literary gathering at Lola Ridge's (then editor of *Broom*), where he presented him to Frank. Some years later Kreymborg, together with Paul Rosenfeld, Van Wyck Brooks, and Lewis Mumford, edited a five-volume series called *The American Caravan*.[19] In its pages Toomer was to publish "Winter on Earth," "York Beach," and "Blue Meridian," a long poem written under the influence of Hart Crane.

Paul Rosenfeld, whose articles on music, painting, and literature appeared in the *Seven Arts*, the *Dial*, and the *New Republic*, befriended Toomer and sought to promote his career. His book of criticism, *Men Seen* (1925), contained essays on Toomer, Kreymborg, and Frank. In 1925 Rosenfeld accompanied Toomer on a visit to Stieglitz at Lake George, and as editor of a testimonial volume devoted to Stieglitz solicited an article from Toomer commemorating that event.[20] In 1928 Rosenfeld invited Toomer to spend the month of August with him on the coast of Maine. The result was "York Beach," in which Rosenfeld provides the model for a major character.

Gorham Munson was the editor of *Secession* when, at the behest of Waldo Frank, Toomer submitted a story. The piece was rejected, but the incident initiated a correspondence that soon would ripen into friendship. In 1923 Munson published *Waldo Frank: a Study*, and arranged for Toomer to review the book in S4N.[21] Toomer's essay, "The Critic of Waldo Frank," appeared in a special number entitled "Homage to Waldo

Frank," edited by Gorham Munson and with frontispiece by Hart Crane. In 1928 Munson published *Destinations*, "a convass of American literature since 1900," which included chapters on Jean Toomer and Hart Crane.

Sherwood Anderson was introduced to his American audience in the pages of the *Seven Arts*. In the first issue of the journal (November 1916) Frank published an essay on Anderson, whose novel, *Windy McPherson's Son*, had just appeared in England. The title of the piece, "Emerging Greatness," was flattering enough. Anderson responded by submitting to Frank a number of his Winesburg sketches, several of which were published in the *Seven Arts*. In *Our America* (1919), Frank paid a moving tribute to the work of Anderson. Inspired by the good opinion of his mentor, Jean Toomer read most of Anderson's short stories and tried to assimilate his fictional technique.

Toward the end of 1922, in a letter to Sherwood Anderson, Toomer made a generous acknowledgment of this influence:

> Just before I went down to Georgia I read *Winesburg, Ohio*. And while there, living in a cabin whose floorboards permitted the soil to come up between them, listening to the old folk melodies that Negro women sang at sundown, *The Triumph of the Egg* came to me. The beauty, and the full sense of life that these books contain are natural elements, like the rain and sunshine, of my own sprouting. . . . I sprang up in Washington. *Winesburg, Ohio* and *The Triumph of the Egg* are elements of my growing. It is hard to think of myself as maturing without them."[22]

Through his ties with Waldo Frank, Toomer joined forces with a group of writers who for a decade or more exercised an important influence on the course of American letters. From them he derived not only his major publication outlets, but his visionary strain, his respect for craft, and his notions of high seriousness where the art of writing was concerned. The impulse that originated with the *Seven Arts* was perpetuated by a group of young idealists whose aim was no less than to spiritualize, and thereby to rejuvenate America. And for a period of perhaps five years, Jean Toomer was a member of that happy band.

Toomer's personal relationship with Frank began in 1920. At first it was a question of hero worship from afar. Toomer was content to absorb the Frank canon, and to serve his apprenticeship with Frank's books in mind. Late in 1921, however, he initiated what would soon become a steady correspondence. In the spring of 1922 he invited Frank, who was working on a novel with a Southern setting, to join him in a journey to the deep South. The implication was that they would travel and live together among the Negroes as if they both were black. They made such a journey to Spartanburg, South Carolina, in September and October of 1922.[23]

Two books were born of this joint venture, both in 1923: Waldo Frank's *Holiday* and Jean Toomer's *Cane*. Several critics have attempted to establish the influence of *Holiday* on *Cane*, especially in matters of style and technique. But it was not so much a question of influence as of simultaneous gestation. Both books were delivered, so to speak, at the same lying-in hospital. Frank sent Toomer his criticisms of *Cane*, and Toomer reciprocated by correcting the dialogue of *Holiday* to make it conform more realistically to Negro speech. If the two books resemble one another stylistically, it is because Toomer had already absorbed the principal elements of Frank's technique from his earlier publications.

So pronounced was the Frank influence that about this time Gorham Munson warned Toomer of the dangers of discipleship. He replied, "I cannot *will* out of Waldo. With the exception of Sherwood Anderson some years ago (and to a less extent, Frost and Sandburg) Waldo is the only modern writer who has immediately influenced me. He is so powerful and close, he has so many elements that I need, that I would be afraid of downright imitation if I were not so sure of myself. But I know my own rhythm (it has come out fairly pure in a formative way, in some of my southern sketches. It is when I attempt a more essentialized and complex pattern that Waldo comes in.) and I feel with you that I will 'eventually make a successful amalgamation with (my) own special contribution.' I must *grow* out of him."[24]

On December 12, 1922, Toomer wrote triumphantly to Frank, "*Cane* is on its way to you!" By the spring of 1923, Frank's publisher, Boni and Liveright, had accepted the book and arranged for Frank to write the Introduction. In a letter to Frank, Toomer responded enthusiastically to this suggestion: "You not only understand CANE; you are *in* it; specifically here and there, mystically because of the spiritual bond there is between us. When you write, you will express me, and in a very true way you will express yourself."[25] In the event, Toomer was upset by Frank's introduction, which stressed his black identity too insistently for Toomer's taste. This was the beginning of the breach in their friendship.

In the spring of 1923, a few months before they published *Cane*, Boni and Liveright brought out Gorham Munson's *Waldo Frank: a Study*. Early in 1924 an essay-review by Jean Toomer appeared in S4N.[26] "The Critic of Waldo Frank" establishes the fact that Toomer was thoroughly acquainted with everything that Frank had written prior to 1924. It is clear from this essay that three of Frank's books, *The Unwelcome Man* (1917), *The Dark Mother* (1920), and *Rahab* (1922) made a deep impression on Toomer during his formative years. But for our purposes, it will suffice to trace the influence of *Our America* (1919) and *City Block* (1922).

Our America *and* City Block

The *Seven Arts*, as we have seen, was silenced in 1917 because of its opposition to the war. The cultural impulse it embodied, however, was very far from dead. It was revived in Waldo Frank's *Our America* (1919), a book that soon became the manifesto of the postwar generation. Synthesizing and extending the work of Van Wyck Brooks and Randolph Bourne, Frank drew up a sweeping indictment of the puritan-industrial order, ransacked the past for a viable American tradition, and called upon the young to assume the role of spiritual pioneers. This is the stuff of which proselytes are made. The book attracted a host of young admirers, among them Gorham Munson, Hart Crane, and Jean Toomer.

Our America was Toomer's guidebook to American civilization. It rooted him in his American tradition (Romantic, Transcendentalist, and Whitmanesque), and offered him a cogent analysis of contemporary American reality. It formed, in short, the programmatic basis of *Cane.* The essence of the Frank position was a firm repudiation of the extroverted tendencies characteristic of a pioneer-puritan-industrial society, and a countervailing emphasis on inwardness and spirituality. The task of the artist was to fashion counterforms, or antibodies, to the Machine. *Cane* was projected as precisely such a counterform.

Crucial to the influence of *Our America* on Toomer are the pastoral assumptions that underlie the work. Waldo Frank was a dedicated modernist, and as we have seen, the rise of modernism in the arts was closely linked to the primitivistic perspective. Frank's lifelong interest in Hispanic culture, of which *Virgin Spain* (1926) and *America Hispana* (1931) were the first fruits, reflects this perspective. To the decadent machine civilization of the West, Frank counterposed primitive and pastoral alternatives. The destruction of the false gods of modern industrialism was to be accompanied by the creation of new gods rooted in the soil. Hence the redemptive role of such Machine-resistant peoples as the Indian, the Mexican, and the Negro.

Of particular pertinence to *Cane* is a chapter in *Our America* entitled "The Land of Buried Cultures." Here Frank describes the interment of Indian, African, and traditional European cultures beneath the puritan-industrial juggernaut: "Some day some one who is fitted for the task will take the subject of this Chapter and make a book of it. He will study the cultures of the German, the Latin, the Celt, the Slav, the Anglo-Saxon, and the African on the American continent: plot their reactions one upon the other, and their disappearance as integral worlds. . . ."[27]

The conviction that Negro folk culture was about to disappear, to be destroyed as an integral world, lies at the heart of *Cane*. Writing to Frank in the spring of 1923, Toomer observes:

> There is one thing about the Negro in America which most thoughtful persons seem to ignore: the Negro is in solution, in the process of solution. . . . The fact is, that if anything comes up now, pure Negro, it will be a swan-song. Don't let us fool ourselves, brother: the Negro of the folk-song has all but passed away; the Negro of the emotional church is fading. . . . In my own stuff, in those pieces that come nearest to the old Negro, to the spirit saturate with folk-song: Karintha, and Fern, the dominant emotion is sadness derived from a sense of fading, from a knowledge of my futility to check solution.[28]

Cane was conceived as a cultural swan-song; it sprang from Toomer's wish to commemorate the Negro past, before it disappeared forever. Hence the tone of sadness that suffuses *Cane*, transforming it from simple pastoral to pastoral elegy. Hence also the images of evening, of dusk, and of the setting sun that proliferate throughout the book. From Virgil to Thomas Gray, vespertinal imagery has been employed to create the distinctive mood of pastoral elegy. *Plaintive* is the crucial word:

> . . . for though the sun is setting on
> A song-lit race of slaves, it has not set;

Though late, O soil, it is not too late yet
To catch thy plaintive soul, leaving, soon gone.[29]

In the light of *Our America*, we must be wary of misreading Toomer's commitment to the Negro past. Just as Waldo Frank was reconciled to his Jewishness on the basis of the Jew's spiritual rather than ethnic qualities, so Jean Toomer was attracted to the folk Negro's spirituality, rather than ethnicity as such. Just as Frank perceived his Jewish past as one of many eroding traditions in the Land of Buried Cultures, so Toomer made a truce with his black ancestors on the basis of a fading memory. In effect, he *distances* himself from his blackness by locating it essentially in the past. A still more potent distancing device was to be transmitted from Frank to Toomer through the former's book of stories, *City Block.*

Waldo Frank was nothing if not a cosmopolitan. To a literary man of his time and place, that meant at least a casual affair, if not a permanent liaison with Paris. He lived on the Rive Gauche for several months in 1913, and again in 1921, fraternizing on the second occasion with most of the French literary establishment. During the war years, he became acquainted in New York with Jacques Copeau, director of the Théâtre du Vieux Colombier and editor of the *Nouvelle Revue Française.* From this encounter came a book, *The Art of the Vieux Colombier* (1918). It was Copeau and his associates of the *NRF*, in fact, who commissioned Frank to write *Our America.* But his interest in French letters antedated these events.

In 1906-1907, Frank spent a year at a preparatory school in Lausanne, where he not only mastered the language, but began a rather precocious study of French literature. As a freshman at Yale in 1908, he submitted a prize essay on Zola to the *Lit*, which attracted the attention of William Lyon Phelps. While still an undergraduate, he began a book called *The Spirit of Modern French Letters*, which was accepted in incomplete form by the Yale Press, but never brought to a conclusion. After graduation, however, he worked on the manuscript in Greenwich Village, at a time when he was also experimenting with short fiction that remained unpublished, but that eventually led to the story cycle entitled *City Block.*[30]

An essay called "A Prophet in France," which appeared in the *Seven Arts* of April 1917, reveals the link between Waldo Frank's French studies and the composition of *City Block.* Here Frank discusses the esthetic philosophy of Jules Romains, whose career he had been following since its inception in 1909. Jules Romains (1885-1972), whose real name was Louis Farigoule, was the founder of an esthetic theory known as *unanimisme.* In his first book of verse, *La Vie Unanime* (1909), and in such early novels as *Mort de Quelqu'un* (1911), *Les Copains* (1913), and *Sur les Quais de LaVillette* (1914), Romains develops an esthetic which exalts the group above the individual, and is technically concerned with devising a means of rendering group rather than individual consciousness.

"The striking feature of the art of Jules Romains," according to Frank, "is that his characters are not individuals, but collective groups: complex and dynamic units created out of the stress and passion of society. He pictures the soul, not of the occupants of a room, but of the room itself; not of a soldier but of a regiment; not of travellers but of their railway carriage; not of rebels, but of the riot." In French fiction of the nineteenth century, Frank continues, "The group is either passive, a thing to be transcended; or it is destructive, a thing to be avoided. With Jules Romains, it becomes, for the first time, the Hero."[31]

Group portraiture is thus the animating principle of *City Block* (1922). Frank is interested not so much in the individual lives of its inhabitants as in rendering the collective soul of the street.[32] He wishes to portray the unity-in-diversity of a polyglot community on Manhattan's East Side. He insists that the Block, despite its mixed population of Irish, Italians, and Jews, remains on a deeper level compact and one. He therefore abandons the conventional form of the novel, which was designed to accommodate the individual hero, and creates a new form whose collective hero is the social group. This is the form of the story cycle, consisting of separate stories which nonetheless comprise a unified whole.

City Block was printed privately in 1922 on the advice of Boni and Liveright, who felt that its public appearance might entail a jail sentence under the obscenity laws. Frank therefore solicited the help of his friends in promoting sales. Jean Toomer responded enthusiastically, acting in effect as an agent for the book: "Aside from the broadly cultural, I have a strictly personal interest in the sale of *City Block*: It will pioneer and set a high standard for those who read it—they will the better absorb my own."[33] On July 31, 1922, Toomer mailed an advertising circular to his friends in which he comments, "I believe *City Block* to be one of the most significant contributions of our age to what is best and most enduring in American letters."

A chain of influence may thus be traced from Jules Romains to Jean Toomer, by way of Waldo Frank. The emotional appeal of *unanimisme* to men like Frank and Toomer is obvious enough. Both were members of minority groups toward which they felt ambivalent. They were in conflict over their Jewish and Negro identities, torn between their personal vision and the imperious demands of an ethnic group. Drawn as artists to explore their group heritage, they were yet resistant to the claims of tribal consciousness, and fearful lest their singularity be overwhelmed by the mass. Unanimist theory offered them a distancing device, by which they might portray the ego in its social dimension, without making a permanent commitment to ethnicity.

In the light of *unanimisme*, a new interpretation of the form of *Cane* is possible. As *City Block* attempts to render the collective soul of a street, so *Cane* of a race. Part I represents the group soul in its native habitat in rural Georgia. The anonymous group culture of the black South is evoked through the hovering presence of the spirituals. Part II portrays the group soul transplanted to the city pavements, and in conflict with the white world that surrounds it. Part III depicts the relation of the black artist to the group soul. For this composite portrait, the appropriate form is the mosaic or collage.

Three Stories from Cane

The genre of *Cane* has been the subject of considerable speculation and debate. Some critics have viewed the book as an experimental novel; others as a miscellany, composed of poetic, dramatic, and narrative elements; still others as a work *sui generis*, which deliberately violates the standard categories. The problem is complicated by the fact that parts of *Cane* were published independently as poems, sketches, and stories.[34] This would suggest that Toomer thought of them as separate entities, whatever their subsequent function in the overall design. Without attempting to resolve the larger issue, let us reduce the book to its constituent parts, in order to determine which may be legitimately classified as short stories.

Of the twenty-nine units of which *Cane* is composed, fifteen are plainly poems, written for the most part in free verse. "Kabnis" is a free-form play, complete with stage directions. Six of the less substantial pieces are sketches, or vignettes, or prose poems, too slender to afford much narrative development.[35] The seven that remain may reasonably be regarded as short stories.[36] Of these seven stories, we have chosen to discuss three: "Fern," "Theater," and "Bona and Paul." They will serve to illustrate the tendency of Toomer's art to move beyond mere surfaces to a realm of transcendent reality.

"Fern," which first appeared in the *Little Review* of Autumn 1922, has been as widely anthologized as it has been misconstrued. Restricting their vision to the psychological plane, critics have variously regarded Fern as a victim of sexual repression, a promiscuous, castrating female, and an emblem of the mystery of Negro womanhood. The bafflement of the young narrator, in short, has been shared by most commentators, who have failed to perceive that the story functions primarily on a philosophical or religious plane. The heroine's sexual passivity is evoked merely to accentuate her other-worldly qualities. The story's theme, which may be traced to Vachel Lindsay's poem, "The Congo," is the spirituality of the Negro race.

Fern spiritualizes everything and everyone with whom she comes in contact. The story opens with the sentence: "Face flowed into her eyes." The eyes, in Toomer, are windows to the soul, and in Fern's countenance they dominate, and even obliterate, the surrounding flesh. They seem to focus on some vague spot above the horizon, seeking always to transcend, or rise above, the Georgia landscape. The movement of the imagery is upward, and it defines Fern's relation to the world. Her domain is the unseen and intangible: the noumenal world that exists beyond the senses. The men that she encounters, including the narrator, are uplifted and ennobled by the contact, and struggle subsequently to transcend their selfishness.

Fern's spiritual force is redoubled by virtue of her mixed ancestry. The daughter of a Jewish father and a Negro mother, she is the inheritor of two sets of sorrow songs. At his first sight of her, the narrator recalls, "I felt as if I heard a Jewish cantor sing. As if his singing rose above the unheard chorus of a folk-song (28)."[37] Fernie May Rosen possesses the Jewish genius for suffering. She takes upon herself the agony of others, including the sexual torment of her lovers. She is the eternal scapegoat who must suffer in order that others (specifically the narrator) may be born. That is why, in the minds of the townspeople, she remains a virgin, and why she is associated, in Toomer's iconography, with the Virgin Mary.[38]

Fern embodies not only the Negro of the folksongs, but also of the revival meeting and the emotional church. That is the point of the climactic episode in which the narrator—half curious concerning Fern, and half in love with her—escorts her through a canebrake. Vaguely conscious of her spiritual power, but acting from force of habit, he takes her in his arms.

She responds by running off, sinking to her knees, swaying back and forth, and uttering convulsive sounds, "mingled with calls to Christ Jesus." She thus performs a priestly, if not a sexual office. Her body, although he doesn't recognize the gift, has been offered as the instrument of his salvation.

Fern is a symbol, in short, of the Negro folk-spirit. As such, she is the repository of a doomed spirituality. The quality of soul that she embodies, and whose cultural expression is folksong and revivalist religion, is about to disappear. It will not survive the Great Migration: "Besides, picture if you can, this cream-colored solitary girl sitting at a tenement window and looking down on the indifferent throngs of Harlem (28)." Fern could not exist apart from her pastoral milieu, and yet this rural folk-culture is fading into memory. The elegiac note is unmistakable. It is in the Georgia dusk that Fern weaves her most potent spell. Images of evening suffuse the story, producing that peculiar blend of sadness and tranquillity which is the hallmark of pastoral elegy.

"Theater" was inspired by a two-week stint that Toomer served as assistant manager of the Howard Theater in Washington, D.C. It was long enough to absorb the atmosphere of a Negro vaudeville house and to fashion out of this milieu a complex symbol. In the opening paragraph, the walls of the theater are described as a kind of semipermeable membrane through which a complicated process of osmosis takes place. The "nigger life" of alleys, poolrooms, restaurants, and cabarets nourishes the shows that are presented within these walls, and conversely, the shows exert a shaping influence on the life-style that gave them birth. The theater thus emerges as an emblem of the two-way, reciprocal relationship of life and art.

The walls of the theater press in upon the human world until they become symbolic of the prison of the flesh, from which imagination alone can offer an escape. In the translucent glow of the lighted theater, human flesh seems to dissolve: "Stage lights, soft, as if they shine through clear pink fingers (92)." The theater is a place of shadowy forms, of artificial contrivances, of elaborate mirrorings of life. Throughout the story, Toomer never lets us forget the paraphernalia of illusion: the scenery and costumes and lighting effects that function to transform reality. His theme is precisely the relationship between the image and the life it represents, or, in Ralph Ellison's illuminating phrase, between the shadow and the act.

Toomer's theater is a place where magical transformations occur. The throbbing life of Washington's black belt is translated by the black musicians into jazz forms. The raw sexuality of brown and beige chorus girls is converted before our very eyes into dance forms. Dorris, the most talented among them, is transfigured into a woman of surpassing loveliness by the writer-hero's dream. The instrument of all these metamorphoses is the human imagination, symbolized by the shaft of light that streaks down from a window to illuminate the afternoon rehearsal.

On this symbolic stage the plot unfolds. John, the manager's brother, and a writer, watches Dorris dance. He entertains erotic fantasies, but finally dismisses them, not because of the obvious barrier of background and education, but rather on complicated philosophic grounds. While he is dedicated, in a priestly vein, to contemplation of the noumenal, she represents precisely the attractions of the phenomenal world. Putting it another way, John is torn between the higher and lower functions of his being. Dorris, on her part, does her best to win him through the only art at her command: the dance. Failing to ignite his passion, she mistakenly concludes that he has rejected her on the grounds of social class.

Momentarily the philosophic gulf between them is bridged in the imagery of John's dream. This climactic episode, where daydream shades off into fiction, is emblematic of the transforming power of imagination. In it the raw materials of John's experience are transfigured by the writer's art. Dorris becomes a woman of surpassing beauty; their imagined union, disembodied and ideal: "But his feet feel as though they step on autumn leaves whose rustle has been pressed out of them by the passing of a million satin slippers (98)." In this image of nature *dematerialized* by art, Toomer reveals the heart of his esthetic. John's dream is a vision of the union of flesh and spirit, of the phenomenal and noumenal worlds.

Art-as-transfiguration is Toomer's theme. He is concerned in "Theater" with the death of experience and its rebirth as art. Thus John's renunciation of a love affair with Dorris, and his distillation of their encounter into poetry. John is to Dorris as an artist to his material: she represents *untransformed* experience. But the artist, by definition, is a man who cannot tolerate the untransformed world. Through his imagination, he must remove the rustle from the autumn leaves. Paradoxically, the artist must renounce the phenomenal world, even as he celebrates it. The result is a tragic alienation, whose subjective mood is melancholy.

"Bona and Paul" derives from Toomer's undergraduate experience at the American College of Physical Training in Chicago. The hero of the story is a near-white college boy, studying to be a gym director. He becomes romantically involved with Bona, a Southern girl who is attracted not so much to Paul as to the idea of a Negro lover. Bona has the courage to defy convention to a point, but only by inverting, rather than transcending racial categories. Paul, who wishes to be loved for himself alone, struggles to escape the burden of exoticism. Ironically, he loses the girl by being overly intellectual: that is, by refusing to conform to Bona's preconceived idea of blackness.

The kernel of the story is contained in the opening tableau. On the floor of a gymnasium, students are engaged in precision drilling. Paul, out of step with the rest, is dressed in nonregulation blue trousers. It is precisely this nonconformity that Bona finds appealing. The precision drilling is symbolic of a regimented society that not only marches, but thinks in rigid line formation. Paul's white companions, as the story unfolds, are alternately fascinated and repelled by his ambiguous exoticism. Tormented by uncertainty, and desirous of reassuring absolutes, they press him to declare his race. They remain, in short, *unawakened* to the possibilities of life, to the individual reality that lies beyond the social category.

The theme of the story is epistemological. Verbs of cognition predominate, as Paul and Bona grope across the color line for a deeper knowledge of each other. Toomer's central metaphor, which compares the lovers to opaque windows, is drawn from St. Paul's first epistle to the Corinthians: "For now we see through a glass darkly; but then face to face: now I know in part; but then shall I know even as I am known."[39] The color line, symbolized by the South-Side L track that divides the city, constitutes an artificial barrier to human understanding. Based on *a priori* rather than *a posteriori* knowledge, it serves to blind rather than illuminate.

The story moves to a climax in the episode of the Crimson Gardens. As he enters the nightclub with Bona, Paul feels inclined to cheer, for the Crimson Gardens represents a yea-saying, an affirmation of life. With its white patrons and Negro music, the club is a symbol of cultural amalgamation. It is also the Garden of Eden, where Paul loses Bona by eating of the Tree of Knowledge. As the young couple whirl around the floor, "The dance takes blood from their minds and packs it, tingling, in the torsos of their swaying bodies (151)." Intoxicated with passion, they head for the exit, but their progress is interrupted by a leering Negro doorman. Paul steps back to assure the man that something beautiful is about to happen, but when he returns for his companion, Bona has disappeared.

The resolution of the story is conveyed entirely through the imagery. The style becomes intensely lyrical, as it attempts to shape the moment of epiphany: "I came back to tell you, brother, that white faces are petals of roses. That dark faces are petals of dusk. That I am going out and gather petals. That I am going out and know her whom I brought here with me to these Gardens which are purple like a bed of roses would be at dusk (153)." Reality, in other words, is not categorical, but contingent. A flower that is red in daylight is purple in the dusk. And dusk is the point in time when day and night mingle and become one.

What Paul has mastered, in short, is a new epistemology, a new way of knowing. He has discovered the imagination as a mode of knowledge. He has learned that while thought divides (categorizes), imagination synthesizes. Through metaphor, the language of poetry, the imagination transcends categories and frees the human mind for a genuine encounter with reality. At the same time, Toomer's hero pays an awesome price for his new knowledge. Intent on philosophic clarity, he loses the girl. It is Toomer's characteristic gesture of renunciation: the eternal paradox of earthly values lost, even as transcendent aims are realized.

"Bona and Paul" is a model of artistic economy and symbolic compression. In its density of texture and profundity of theme, it is one of Toomer's richest stories. On the face of it, the story seems to undermine the central thrust of *Cane*. Once we take account of its strategic position at the end of Part II, however, this difficulty is resolved. The urbanization of the Negro, Toomer feels, will lead inexorably to his assimilation. In the process, America will be transformed. Like Toomer's hero, we will one day discover within ourselves the courage to transcend our racial categories. Then we will see not through a glass darkly, but face to face at last.

The Gurdjieff Phase

The year that followed on the heels of *Cane* (1923-1924) was the turning point of Toomer's life. His career was launched, but within a matter of months he abandoned the artistic vocation as the Frank circle understood it and embraced the teachings of George Gurdjieff. This year of crisis and decision, as we have noted, coincided with the time of his deepest involvement with Margaret Naumburg. It is clear that

Toomer's love affair with Mrs. Frank shook him to the foundations of his being. He entered a period of chaos and disorder, withdrawal and seclusion, guilt and self-recrimination which culminated in the virtual abandonment of his paramour and his commitment to the Gurdjieff cause.

The inevitable consequence of Toomer's love affair was the loss of his spiritual home. His breach with Frank implied the loss of a milieu—the only world in which he had been thoroughly at ease. But homelessness was an intolerable state, and he promptly found a substitute in the Gurdjieff movement. At a deeper level, Toomer had experienced a frightening loss of control, an emotional skid that threatened devastation to himself and others. His response was to recoil from the flesh: from sensuality, spontaneous emotion, waywardness—the very qualities he celebrates in *Cane*. He turned instead to an all-embracing system which stressed the qualities of order, discipline, and self-control.

Toomer's emotional revulsion from the flesh was reinforced by his reading of Ouspensky. *Tertium Organum* swam into his ken after the composition but before the publication of *Cane*. Writing in the tradition of Plato and Plotinus, Ouspensky stresses the illusory nature of the phenomenal, and the ultimate reality of the noumenal world. The book is a systematic attack on positivism, and a summons to mankind to attain a cosmic consciousness. According to Ouspensky, a higher race is emerging among humanity, a clairvoyant few who represent the vanguard of the evolutionary process. These and similar ideas, deriving from the neo-Platonist tradition, formed the theoretical foundations of the Gurdjieff movement.

Under the Gurdjieff discipline, self-perfection was more important than career goals. Nonutilitarian values were uppermost, so that books, in Toomer's case, became a mere by-product: a validation of his inner growth. This is what accounts for his persistent efforts in the face of literary failure. At the same time, his new emphasis on inwardness—

on personal and spiritual growth—forced him to revise his esthetic views. For man in the mass, according to the Gurdjieff teachings, was incapable of inner growth. The attainment of a higher plane of consciousness lay within the purview of the individual alone. It followed that the group esthetic of his early phase had to be discarded.

As the influence of Waldo Frank and *unanimisme* waned, Toomer began to think once more in individual, rather than ethnic terms. After *Cane*, his fiction is virtually devoid of any reference to race. In the poem "Blue Meridian," however, he celebrates the emergence of an American race, composed of Indian, African, and European elements, whose living embodiment he feels himself to be. The complexities of Toomer's racial views are set forth in an early version of "York Beach": "He knows that everyone is necessarily connected with, and indebted to the Past; and he respects it. But at the same time he feels and knows . . . that he is an ancestor, a beginner. That he is a Builder of the Future. A creator and projector of new symbols."[40]

In furtherance of this prophetic role, Toomer turns from pastoral to satire. The objects of his satire are the spiritual corpulence, amiable hedonism, limited horizons, and sheer indifference of a generation dedicated to materialistic goals. Such is the burden of Toomer's later fiction. If pastoral elements survive, the Arcadian ideal is implicit in the Gurdjieff teachings. On this account, the tone of Toomer's later prose becomes insufferably condescending. Feeling himself to be the bearer of a cosmic consciousness, he has little patience with the foibles of mere earthlings. Self-righteousness, however, only serves to isolate him from his audience. The writings of his Gurdjieff phase display the bitterness of a spurned prophet.

In November 1926, Toomer was commissioned to Chicago as a professional organizer and fund-raiser for the Gurdjieff cause. As he rode the Twentieth Century Limited to the heart of industrial America, he contemplated the resistance he was certain to encounter: "I would have to work against the huge double wall formed, in part, by the domination of business in the affairs of men, in part, by the domination of factualism in the views of men."[41] The word *domination* is the clue to Toomer's mood. He was about to confront a technological Goliath—a society of Philistines who were externally powerful but spiritually lost. Hence the title of his projected volume of short stories: *Lost and Dominant.*

Toomer expected to find in Chicago "A separation from reality; a tendency to see things upside down, so that, e.g., the nonessential was mistaken for the essential, the unimportant was valued higher than the important; a twisting of energies, so that energies tended to flow into and be misused for trivial or harmful behavior, rather than be rightly used for significant constructive behavior."[42] These were the themes that would preoccupy him during his Chicago years. *The Gallonwerps*, a satirical novel, was to lampoon the business and commercial classes, together with their artistic and intellectual sycophants and hangers-on. *Lost and Dominant*, a collection of shorter fiction, would address itself to particular instances of vice or folly.

Lost and Dominant was assembled in 1929 and dedicated to Margaret Naumburg. The book was to contain ten prose pieces, three of which had been previously published.[43] Within a year Toomer revised the volume, dropping several of the weaker pieces, substituting others, and changing the title to *Winter on Earth.* No amount of repackaging, however, would suffice. Most of Toomer's later tales are flat failures. The exceptions are "Drackman" and "Love on a Train," which ought to be rescued from oblivion, and "Mr. Costyve Duditch," the one story of Toomer's Gurdjieff phase that compares in quality to the best of *Cane.*

"Drackman" is a fantasy concerned with the perverted values of modern man. The protagonist is a successful businessman who owns a New York skyscraper. On his way to work one morning, he experiences a sudden premonition: his building seems to resemble a tombstone. Later in the day, the tower seems to melt and assume his own shape. Terrified by this metamorphosis, Drackman abandons his former life goals. His behavior becomes increasingly bizarre, as intimations of a better way of life fight for entry to his consciousness. In the end, he devotes himself to sounding the alarm, warning his friends that their souls are in danger of being absorbed by their own vision of power, as embodied in the skyscraper.

The central symbol of the story is the Drackman Tower. Like John Marin, whose paintings of New York skyscrapers he had viewed at the Stieglitz gallery, and Hart Crane, with whose early drafts of "The Bridge" he was familiar, Toomer regarded the skyscraper as an emblem of the modern age. To him it was a product of neurosis, an attempt to compensate through outward forms for inner emptiness and boredom. In "Drackman" it comes to represent a grotesque extension of the human ego, a perversion of the vital energies in a monumental quest for dominion over time. It dominates the story as a terrifying force which threatens to transform its victims into pillars of iron and steel.

"Love on a Train" dramatizes the conflict between career and self-perfection. Dr. Coville is a young neurologist en route from Chicago to a European sabbatical. Mindful of the dangers of overspecialization, he plans to divide his time between his medical pursuits and the study of art history. On the train to New York, he meets an attractive woman whose independent outlook fascinates him, even as it challenges his deepest convictions. If he has a career, she tells him, he cannot possibly understand her. For "career" is just a name for the sum of habits that impede inner growth. The very notion, she insists, is symptomatic of a rampant utilitarianism, and by embracing it he capitulates in advance to the Enemy.

Behind this strikingly contemporary argument lies a very ancient philosophical dichotomy. Dr. Coville inhabits the world of becoming. A modern man, he is unresponsive to the present moment because of his preoccupation with causes and futurities. His traveling companion represents the world of being. Through her spontaneous enjoyment of the passing moment, she escapes the tyranny of time. Dr. Coville experiences such a moment of transcendence when they kiss. This climactic scene, however, is followed by a decrescendo of panic, futile quest, inexorable loss. For the pure moment cannot be possessed; the world of being may be glimpsed but never violated. The most that can be hoped for is a brief angelic visitation from the realm of the Ideal.

"Mr. Costyve Duditch" was published in the *Dial* of December 1928, and subsequently chosen for inclusion in O'Brien's *Best Short Stories of 1928*. Like "Mr. Limph Krok's Famous 'L' Ride," its companion piece in *Lost and Dominant*, the story is closely related to *The Gallonwerps*, the major undertaking of Toomer's Chicago years. All three are concerned with the state of culture in Chicago, and more precisely with the role of the Chicago bourgeoisie as patrons of the arts: "Chicago had given rise to a class of modern barons, those associated with industry, public utilities, big business, and finance. . . . The trouble was that as yet Chicago had failed to give rise to a class of modern priests: men needed by society to productively engage in art, literature, pure science, and philosophy."[44]

Costyve Duditch is such a modern priest. Without family ties or recognized career, he is an incorrigible rover who comes to roost on rare occasions in his native city of Chicago. A bit eccentric, while in town he tends to avoid his friends, partly in order to work on a book tentatively titled "How Travel Grooms the Person." When cornered, however, he greets them with an air of delighted apology which is his characteristic tone. For the truth is that he feels inferior to "settled people," and is convinced that they regard him as an aimless globe-trotter. He is a type, in short, of the artist, who is misunderstood by his society, but who wants nothing more than social recognition for his indispensable services in "grooming the person."

The story is encapsulated in the opening scene. It is a blustery day in the Chicago Loop. Costyve Duditch sweeps down Michigan Boulevard with the velocity of a racing car, passing his friend Coleeb without recognition, and leaving him "shocked out of balance by Costyve's glancing impact." The wind is a symbol both of the artist's vagrant and erratic life-style and the hostile environment through which he moves. The skyscraper world of the Loop is the milieu of the American artist, but unlike the cathedral world of El Greco, which is evoked later in the story, it does not nourish or sustain. Nonetheless, the artist generates considerable force, and exerts at least a glancing impact on his culture.

Costyve's progress brings him into Marshall Field's, where he is attracted by an exquisitely wrought cut-glass bowl. Turning it over and admiring the design, he drops it to the floor, "sending glittering splinters in all directions." Overwhelmed with embarrassment, he resolves to leave Chicago at once: "The city suddenly seemed to be in the same condition as the bowl." This episode is emblematic of the artist's dual function: to destroy as well as to create. Costyve Duditch is forever shattering complacencies, breaking taboos, shocking conventional opinion. At the same time, as the ensuing scene reveals, he is the great Mender, whose function in a splintered culture is to make it whole again.

At Constance Hanover's tea, Costyve charms the guests with stories of his travels. Compelling their attention with his vivid anecdotes, he wins a kind of recognition and a place in their esteem. At one point, however, a timorous woman inquires what would happen to his body if he were to die in some outlandish place. He answers in a matter-of-fact tone, "It would be disposed of according to the custom of the place." Sobered by the thought of death, and offended by his unconventional reply, the guests depart. By transcending their tribal prejudices and revealing his own cosmopolitan tendencies, Costyve has shattered the crystal bowl.

"Mr. Costyve Duditch" culminates in a chilling image of alienation: death in a foreign land, discovery by a stranger, and burial according to the custom of the place. For Toomer's theme is the alienation of the American artist from his cultural milieu—a particularly poignant theme for a deracinated black. Toomer is concerned in this story with the peculiarly *disembodied* nature of American art. He sees this tendency toward abstraction as a defensive gesture, provoked by the indifference and suspicion with which a Philistine society regards the creative act. The story thus amounts to a confession, and it sheds considerable light on the ultimate failure of Toomer as an artist, which it now becomes our business to explore.

The Angelic Imagination

In an essay on Edgar Allan Poe entitled "The Angelic Imagination," Allen Tate accuses Poe of seeking to evade the human condition. He finds in Poe a tendency, deriving from his neo-Platonism, to deny the reality of the physical world. Lacking a commitment to the order of nature, Poe's imagination soars off into the Beyond, where it tries to create a transcendental order of its own. This thrust of the imagination beyond the human scale Tate denominates "the angelic fallacy." For it leads to a grandiose presumption on the part of man: "When neither intellect nor will is bound to the human scale, their projection becomes godlike, and man becomes an angel."[45]

The angelic tendency of Toomer's imagination is everywhere apparent in the fiction of his Gurdjieff phase. Several of his stories, including "Love on a Train," "Mr. Costyve Duditch," and "Winter on Earth"; his two novellas, "York Beach" and "The Angel Begori"; and his novel, *The Gallonwerps*, are based on the concept of angelic visitation. The White Island fable which comprises the core of "Winter on

Earth" is perhaps his most explicit statement of the theme.[46] Here he depicts a band of angels "commissioned to teach and aid the men of Earth to improve their way of living." The truth is that Jean Toomer, under the influence of Gurdjieff and Ouspensky, cast himself in the angelic role, and displayed in his writing a sense of mission whose grandiose pretensions stem from the angelic fallacy.

It is in his sketch of Alfred Stieglitz, however, that the metaphor is most revealingly employed. Ostensibly describing Stieglitz, Toomer might be speaking of himself:

> He will sometimes tell you that he feels uprooted. From one point of view this is true. He has not had a fixed establishment. What is more to the point, he is not a tree. The human nostalgia to revert to the vegetable may occasionally move him, but with him, as with so many of us, it has come to nothing. Yet I do not feel he is suspended or unplaced. Always I feel he is rooted *in himself* and to the *spirit* of the place. Not rooted to things; rooted to spirit. Not rooted to earth; rooted to air."[47]

"Rooted to air." There in his own phrase is the essential tragedy of Jean Toomer. His urge to transcendence leads him to project a world above the body, above the solid earth, in the element of air: thin, etherial, appropriate to birds or angels. But the task of the imagination, as a master-craftsman has instructed us, is to "give to airy nothing / A local habitation and a name." What, in Toomer's case, does such a dwelling place for the imagination mean? What if not the Southern soil? But under the spell of Gurdjieff, his sense of soil has eroded. He prefers Utopia (literally, no place) to a Georgia canefield. As for the name, let it remain unspoken: he would rather be etherial than black.

No one familiar with Toomer's life history will fail to grasp the connection between that history and his neo-Platonism.

To question the reality of matter was natural enough for a man whose very existence challenged the reality of race. To such a man the world of nature was only skin-deep. Toomer's Platonism was at bottom a projection of his impulse to escape his fate. He resented being earth-bound as much as being race-bound. In rebelling against the artificial boundaries of race, however, he tried to overleap the immutable boundaries of human existence. He denied, in short, the limitations of the flesh. The result was a disembodied art.

Throughout his Gurdjieff phase, Toomer's style becomes increasingly abstract. The vivid images that were its crowning glory give way to windy generalities. The pungency of *Cane* is nowhere to be found. We are served a drab and tasteless gruel and told that it is rich in vitamins. Toomer's later fiction, which suffers from his grandiose intentions, is at once over-wrought and underimagined. Dramatization is thin, and incessant sermonizing takes the place of narrative. As imagination falters, the dry rot of abstraction sets in. The rich concreteness of experience is sacrificed to the pursuit of philosophic Absolutes.

"I call that imagination angelic," writes Allen Tate, "which tries to disintegrate or circumvent the image in the illusory pursuit of essence." That is the crux of Toomer's failure as an artist. He abandons the image for precept and idea. Concreteness and transformation, the primary laws of the imagination, are violated by abstraction and exposition. Toomer's first allegiance in the Gurdjieff years is to some other than the esemplastic power. But Imagination is a jealous god, and will not be supplanted without exacting a terrible revenge.

There is something heroic in Jean Toomer's lifelong effort to transcend the arbitrary bounds of race and establish his existence as an individual. His stubborn insistence that social reality is not the ultimate reality will not fail to touch a responsive chord in thoughtful men. Nonetheless, the fiction of his Gurdjieff phase must be counted for the most part as a devastating failure. It is primarily a failure of imagination, but behind that lies a moral failure, whose essence is that pride has conquered love. For it is pride that tempts man to usurp the role of angels, and love, as Richard Wilbur has observed, that recalls us to the things of this world.

Chapter 9

Langston Hughes

THE impulse toward the picaresque, as the two volumes of his autobiography attest, was strong in Langston Hughes.[1] His quest for experience took him to Africa, Europe, and the Caribbean in his twenties, and through Moscow to Soviet Asia and the Far East in his early thirties. These years of vaga-bondage are reflected in his poems, plays, and stories. Yet still more basic to his art was the bardic impulse that tied him to the Negro folk experience and led him at the age of forty to settle down in Harlem. For it was Hughes' ambition from the first to play the role of bard, singing the joys and sorrows of his people, and establishing himself, in his own phrase, as the Shakespeare of Harlem.

The performance of this bardic role required of him that he curb his impulse toward sophistication and remain in close rapport with his folk origins. To this end, he donned the Mask of Simplicity that is the hallmark of pastoral. An early poem called "Disillusion" contains the central metaphor of his career:

> I would be simple again
> Simple and clean
> Like the earth,
> Like the air.[2]

Hughes loved to pretend to less sophistication than in fact he possessed. Hence the famous Hughes persona, Jess' B. Semple. The Simple sketches, which first appeared in the *Chicago Defender* in 1943, and were subsequently published in several volumes, attest to the persistence of the pastoral mode throughout his long career. Their form, consisting of a dialogue between a shrewd countryman (transplanted in this case to the streets of Harlem) and his urbane interlocutor, derives from the *Eclogues* of Virgil. By splitting his consciousness in two, the artist gains access to the folk wisdom of his race without relinquishing the insights of sophistication and urbanity.

Pastoral elements are particularly prominent in the early phase of Hughes' career. While still an undergraduate at Lincoln, he published two books of verse, *The Weary Blues* (1926) and *Fine Clothes to the Jew* (1927). He also placed his first stories in the *Messenger,* and completed several preliminary drafts of his first novel, *Not Without Laughter* (1930). This early poetry and prose moves to the tom-tom rhythms of primitivism, which as we have seen is a version of pastoral. The setting of his first novel, which reflects his smalltown, Midwestern origins, is further evidence of Hughes' affinity for the pastoral mode.

Pastoral, whose source is disillusionment with courtly life, contains within itself the seeds of satire. The higher the degree of alienation from the life-style of courtiers and kings, the greater the tendency toward satire. Langston Hughes is essentially a satirist, at least in the short-story form. His first book of stories, *The Ways of White Folks* (1934), might well have been subtitled "In Dispraise of Courtly Life." The pride and pretentiousness, arrogance and hypocrisy, boorishness and inhumanity of white folks are the targets of his caustic prose. The genius of Langston Hughes, which is a gift for comedy and satire, is thus displayed within the broad outlines of the pastoral tradition.

Within the context of its times, however, *The Ways of White Folks* functioned as antipastoral. The early, or ascending phase of the Harlem Renaissance was dominated by the myth of primitivism. Hughes himself, during what may be described as the undergraduate phase of his career, conformed substantially to the requirements of the myth. The late, or declining phase of the Renaissance, however, was increasingly antagonistic to the stereotype of the Negro as primitive. Finely tuned as always to the climate of the times, Hughes joined forces with such authors as Wallace Thurman and Sterling Brown to discredit the myth and challenge its pastoral assumptions.

Life and Work

Langston Hughes (1902-1967) was born in Joplin, Missouri, but he spent his crucial boyhood years in Lawrence, Kansas, in the care of his maternal grandmother. His father, chafing under the restraints and humiliations of black life in America, abandoned wife and child to pursue his fortunes in Mexico. His mother, left alone with her infant son, struggled to survive. Educated briefly at the University of Kansas, she was now reduced to a life of poverty and insecurity, working at whatever she could find, chiefly in the domestic line. Unable in the end to hold a job and care for Langston too, she left him at the age of seven with her mother.

Mary Langston was a woman of seventy, who earned a meager living by renting rooms to students at the university. Born free during slavery times, she migrated to Ohio, where she was the first black woman to attend Oberlin College. She was married twice: first to Sheridan Leary, who was killed in John Brown's raid at Harper's Ferry, and then to Charles Langston, who owned a farm and grocery store in Lawrence. A proud woman, she introduced her grandson to Negro history, to copies of the newly founded *Crisis*, and to the writings of W. E. B. DuBois. She was a gifted *raconteuse*, regaling the boy on summer evenings with an inexhaustible supply of freedom tales. Of such cultural antecedents are "natural" storytellers made.

His mother's second marriage, when Hughes was fourteen, supplied the backdrop of his high-school years. He attended Central High in Cleveland, where he graduated in the class of 1920, having been editor of the school paper, editor of his yearbook, contributor to the literary magazine, and class poet. At Central he discovered the poetry of Carl Sandburg, whom he was to call his "guiding star," and the stories of de Maupassant, which awakened his desire to write short fiction. Jewish classmates introduced him to the world of radical politics, supplying him with copies of the *Liberator* and the *Socialist Call*, and inviting him to hear an antiwar address by Gene Debs.

In the summer of his junior year, he visited his father's ranch in Mexico. It was a disastrous trip, for father and son discovered that they had next to nothing in common. The elder Hughes was interested exclusively in making money, and wanted his son to become a bookkeeper or a mining engineer. Because of their alleged improvidence, he hated American Negroes, and according to Hughes, hated himself for being one.[3] A fanatical devotee of the Protestant ethic, "Hurry up!" was his constant injunction to his son. At one point in the summer, after being told once too often to hurry up, Langston became violently ill with suppressed rage and hatred for his father.[4]

Many of Hughes' deepest convictions may be understood as an inversion of his father's values. Thus his celebration of blackness, his affirmation of joy, his political radicalism, and his lifelong commitment to art may be seen as the obverse of his father's self-hatred, self-denial, conservatism, and Philistine approach to life. It was little wonder, when his father reluctantly agreed to send him to Columbia, that Hughes deserted Morningside Heights for livelier precincts to the north and east. After a year of exploring Harlem, he quit college to ship out on a freighter bound for Africa. Passing Sandy Hook, he consigned his textbooks, a symbol of his father's way of life, to the bottom of the sea.

Two years of vagabondage followed, in the course of which he tested his identity in Africa and Europe. Meanwhile, his reputation as a poet grew. His first poems were published in *Crisis* and *Opportunity* in the early 1920's. In March of 1925, the "Harlem" issue of *Survey Graphic* appeared, edited by Alain Locke, and featuring more of Hughes' work than that of any other poet. Soon thereafter he won first prize for poetry in *Opportunity*'s literary contest. Meeting him at the awards dinner, Carl Van Vechten took a sheaf of his poems to Alfred Knopf, who published them in 1926 under the title of *The Weary Blues.*

The first fruit of fame was an offer from Amy Spingarn to pay his expenses at Lincoln University. He entered the all-male college at Oxford, Pennsylvania, in February 1926, and graduated in the class of 1929. For a year or so after graduation, he was supported by a white patron. Strains appeared in the relationship, however, his health was affected, and a bitter breach ensued. After a recuperative period of several months in Cuba and Haiti, Hughes decided to stave off the Depression by making a tour of Southern Negro colleges, giving poetry readings. On his way through Alabama he visited the deathhouse at Kilby Prison, where he read his poems to the Scottsboro boys.

In May of 1932, Hughes accompanied a group of blacks to Moscow, where he was to write the English dialogue for a Soviet film on American Negro life. The venture soon collapsed, but he remained in Russia for several months. Winter found him in the New Moscow Hotel, writing an account of his travels to Tashkent. Having borrowed a book of stories by D. H. Lawrence, he was seized with a determination to apply the same techniques to American Negro materials. The result was a group of five stories, written in Moscow during the spring of 1933, four of which were promptly sold by his agent to the *American Mercury, Scribner's Magazine,* and *Esquire.*

Meanwhile he was occupied with cumbersome procedures that might enable him to leave the Soviet Union by way of the Far East. In the summer of 1933 he took the Trans-Siberian Express to Vladivostok, and after spending several weeks in China, Japan, and Hawaii, disembarked in San Francisco. There he visited a second patron, Noel Sullivan, who offered him the use of his cottage at Carmel-by-the-Sea for a year. This generous offer enabled Hughes, working steadily throughout the fall and winter, to complete some of his best stories. These tales, together with the Moscow group, formed the basis of his first collection, *The Ways of White Folks.*

During the spring and summer of 1934, Hughes remained at Noel Sullivan's retreat at Carmel-by-the-Sea writing stories. In the fall he made a trip of several weeks' duration to Reno, Nevada, where he witnessed at first hand the hobo jungles, relief lines, and jobless desperation of the Great Depression. Learning there of his father's death, he journeyed to Mexico City, only to find himself disinherited by the terms of his father's will. He stayed in Mexico throughout the winter and spring of 1935, returning to California in June. After a brief sojourn in Watts with Arna Bontemps, he left for Oberlin, Ohio—and later Cleveland— to be near his mother during the course of a fatal illness which would take her life in 1938.

A new career opened for Hughes in 1935 with the successful Broadway production of his play, *Mulatto.* For the next five or six years, he turned to drama and the theater for his main creative outlet. In 1936-1937, half a dozen of his plays were staged at Karamu House, a center for the arts founded by a white couple in the Cleveland ghetto. After a six-month interval in Spain, during which he served as a war correspondent for the *Baltimore Afro-American,* he returned to the United States, where he organized three separate theatrical ventures: the Harlem Suitcase Theater (1938), the

Negro Art Theater of Los Angeles (1939), and the Skyloft
Players of Chicago (1941).

Hughes spent most of 1939 in Los Angeles, working on the
first volume of his autobiography, *The Big Sea*. In 1940, after
receiving a Rosenwald Fellowship, he retired to Noel Sullivan's Hollow Hills Farm in Monterey, where he passed a
quiet year writing poems, stories, and historical dramas. In
the fall of 1941 he moved to Chicago, where he launched the
Skyloft Players and became a frequent contributor to the
Chicago Defender. The summer of 1942 found him in New
York, where the rolling stone came to rest at last. For a quarter
of a century, until his death in 1967, Hughes made Harlem
U.S.A. the center of his life and art.

Since Hughes wrote steadily from 1925 or 1926 until his
death in 1967, it is essential to establish an overview of his
career. We cannot expect tidy compartments in the case of an
author who is so prolific, but allowing for some overlap we
may discern four distinct phases. Hughes' early period (1926
to 1934) encompasses his first four books: *The Weary Blues*
(1926), *Fine Clothes to the Jew* (1927), *Not Without Laughter*
(1930), and *The Ways of White Folks* (1934). Roughly co-
extensive with the Harlem Renaissance, this period is dominated by the vogue of the Negro and the myth of primitivism.
Hughes establishes himself as a romantic poet and a satirist—a
not uncommon breed if we bear in mind the Byron of *Childe
Harold* and *Don Juan*.

His second, or fellow-traveling, period (1930 to 1939), over-
laps with his late Renaissance phase. As early as 1930-1931,
Hughes was a frequent contributor to the *New Masses*. In 1932
he published a verse pamphlet in defense of the Scottsboro
boys, and was promptly rewarded with a trip to Russia. From
1935 to 1937 he placed several stories in such Party-oriented
journals as *Anvil, Fight Against War and Fascism,* and *New
Theater*. The climax of his proletarian phase came in 1938
with the staging of an historical pageant, *Don't You Want to Be
Free?*, and the publication of a verse pamphlet, *A New Song*

(International Workers Order, introduction by Michael Gold). Both display the revolutionary sloganeering characteristic of the times.

In 1935 Hughes, along with Richard Wright, signed the convention call to the first American Writers' Congress. In 1937, on his way to Spain, he attended the International Writers' Congress in Paris, returning the following year as a full-fledged delegate, together with Theodore Dreiser. The point of this recital is not to lend aid or comfort to the McCarthy committee which subpoenaed and harassed Hughes in 1953,[5] but to set the record straight and account for a serious creative slump in the midst of his career. For Harold Cruse's strictures against a black intelligentsia which allowed itself to be disoriented by the Stalinists certainly apply to Langston Hughes.

The Big Sea marks the onset of Hughes' mature phase (1940 to 1955). The book appeared when he was thirty-eight: both parents were dead, and he was able to confront his filial emotions. Liberated from the past by the act of composing an autobiography, Hughes proceeded to accomplish his mature work. This includes, above all, the creation of Simple, who first appeared in the *Chicago Defender* columns of 1943, and Alberta K. Johnson, his female counterpart in *One Way Ticket* (1949). The mature period further encompasses three books of verse (*Shakespeare in Harlem*, 1942; *Fields of Wonder*, 1947; and *Montage of a Dream Deferred*, 1951), and two of prose (*Laughing to Keep from Crying*, 1952; and *The Sweet Flypaper of Life*, 1955).

I Wonder As I Wander (1956) marks the beginning of Hughes' decline. Inferior to *The Big Sea,* this rambling and evasive work betrays the author's inability to cope in retrospect with his fellow-traveling phase. Symptomatic of Hughes' waning imaginative power is a corresponding increase in his editorial activities. In the last decade of his life, he is more enterprising as an editor, anthologist, or folklorist than as a creative writer. Increasingly he repeats himself, or simply reprints old material. Among the books of Hughes' decline are *Tambourines to Glory* (1958), *Something in Common* (1963), and *The Panther and the Lash* (1967). These books are distinctly inferior, in their respective genres, to earlier achievements.

It is against this background that we must seek to comprehend Hughes' career as a short-story writer. After a brief experimental period in 1927-1928, he turned to serious professional work in 1933. During that year he wrote fourteen stories, all of which were published in *The Ways of White Folks* (1934). Retaining this momentum, in 1934 he wrote eleven more, most of which were collected some years later in *Laughing to Keep from Crying* (1952). From 1935 to 1939 there was a tapering off (only five stories), as he turned from fiction to drama. A year at Hollow Hills Farm in 1941 produced a cluster of four stories. In 1943 the first Simple sketch appeared, and from that date until his death in 1967 Hughes wrote only seven tales.[6]

The point is that Hughes never remotely matched the productivity of 1933 and 1934. More than half of his stories, and nearly all of his best stories, were written in a period of two years, marked by an exclusive concentration on the short-story form. Apart from a flurry of activity in 1941, he never made a sustained effort in the genre again. He published two collections, to be sure, in 1952 and 1963, but these publication dates are misleading, since both volumes draw substantially on stories written in the 1930's. In point of fact, most of Hughes' significant production in the short-story form falls within the chronological limits of the Harlem Renaissance.

The Making of a Satirist

Hughes' first published stories appeared in the *Messenger*, a little magazine of the Harlem Renaissance edited by Wallace Thurman and George Schuyler. "Bodies in the Moonlight," "The Young Glory of Him," and "The Little Virgin" (April, June, and November 1927) reflect the author's personal experience as a mess boy in 1923 on the S.S. *Malone*.[7] Together with "Luani of the Jungle" (*Harlem*, November 1928), these tales comprise what James Emanuel has called the West Illana Series.[8] Their common setting is a freighter, the *West Illana*, making various ports of call along the West Coast of Africa.

These early tales are lushly romantic: their dominating image is a tropic moon. They express an adolescent eroticism not quite certain of its object, but focusing tentatively on dusky maidens with names like Nunuma or Luani. Imitative of Conrad and O'Neill, they reflect the atavistic yearnings and primitivistic posturings of the postwar generation. Yet they sound a deeper note which reveals the central thrust of Hughes' career. This is the outreach toward experience, and its inevitable price, the loss of innocence. In one way or another, these stories are concerned with the wound or trauma or symbolic scar which marks the rite of passage from the innocence of childhood to the bittersweet enchantments of adult sexuality.

When Hughes returned to short fiction after a lapse of several years, it was not to write romantic idyls, but caustic satires. What had happened in the interval? A clue is provided by his account of the winter of 1933, when he was stranded in a Moscow hotel. After reading a copy of D. H. Lawrence's *The Lovely Lady*, he remarks: "I had never read anything of Lawrence's before, and was particularly taken with the title story, and with 'The Rocking Horse Winner.' Both tales made my hair stand on end. The possessive, terrifying elderly woman in 'The Lovely Lady' seemed in some ways so much like my former Park Avenue patron that I could hardly bear to read the story. . . ."[9]

The Park Avenue dowager that Hughes will never name was Mrs. R. Osgood Mason. The widow of a prominent physician, she thought of herself as godmother of the New Negro movement, and adopted several of its luminaries as her protégés. Hughes had met her when he was an undergraduate at Lincoln, and she not only offered to support him during the summers of 1928 and 1929, when he was working on his first novel, but provided him with a year of economic freedom following his graduation. Her emotional support was equally important to the young author. It is not too much to say that Mrs. Mason became a surrogate parent, supplying Hughes with the love and admiration and affectionate concern that he had never known as a child.

The breach in their relationship was shattering in its effect on Hughes. It precipitated what can only be described as a nervous breakdown.[10] As he recounts the story of this crisis in *The Big Sea*, he cites three factors that contributed to their estrangement. First was Mrs. Mason's demand for constant productivity, which interfered with his desire to rest between projects. He was enjoined, in short, to "hurry up." Second was the painful contrast between his patron's wealth and the growing misery of the Great Depression. This was a goad to Hughes' social conscience, filling him with guilt for accepting her largesse. Third was her conception of the Negro as a primitive, which she attempted to impose on her protégé:

"She wanted me to be primitive and know and feel the intuitions of the primitive. But, unfortunately, I did not feel the rhythms of the primitive surging through me, and so I could not live and write as though I did. I was only an American Negro—who had loved the surface of Africa and the rhythms of Africa—but I was not Africa. I was Chicago and Kansas City and Broadway and Harlem. . . ."[11] This passage from Hughes' autobiography tends to minimize his collaboration with the myth of primitivism, and place the responsibility for it outside the self. But the disillusionment is genuine enough, and from it sprang his caustic antipastoral, *The Ways of White Folks*.

The breach with Mrs. Mason brought about a psychosomatic illness reminiscent of a boyhood episode in Mexico. Hughes himself is well aware of this connection when recounting matters in *The Big Sea*. Through a series of allusions to his father, he invites us to perceive the two events as manifestations of a single psychological reality. What we have, in short, is the reenactment of a primal drama, in which his patron is assigned the father's role. Nor is there anything mysterious about this drama. Hughes resented his father's domineering ways almost as much as he coveted his love. The result was a deep emotional conflict, in which a strong desire for independence clashed with infantile dependency needs.

Transpose this conflict to the cultural plane, and we touch a sensitive nerve of the Harlem Renaissance. For an end to white paternalism was one of the things that the Renaissance was all about. Hughes' literary manifesto in the *Nation* was nothing if not a declaration of independence.[12] Yet paradoxically, it was promulgated by a writer who depended on a series of white patrons for his daily bread. The stark reality of the New Negro movement was that Hughes and his contemporaries were dependent in many ways on white patrons, impresarios, editors, agents, critics, and ordinary members of the reading public. It was an agonizing dilemma, which neither Hughes nor the generation of which he was a leading spokesman was able to resolve.

The Ways of White Folks was at bottom an attempt to come to grips with this dilemma. Hughes' solution was to strike a satirical stance toward his former patron and the world that she represents. In this way, he was able to preserve an essential dignity and self-respect, even while living rent-free in Noel Sullivan's cottage at Carmel. His experience with Mrs. Mason had left him in a satirical frame of mind. He was more than ready for a caustic treatment of white folks, rich folks, or pompous and pretentious folks of any hue. This turn to satire, moreover, involved a momentary shift from poetry to prose. For a brief period, the short-story form became the growing edge of his career.

The unmasking of hypocrisy became his central theme. The emotional source of this impulse was of course his father, who made a show of fatherly concern which in fact he didn't feel. By a process of transference, Hughes attributed the sins of his delinquent father to the patrons of the Harlem Renaissance. They too, he had come to feel, were lacking in a genuine commitment to the cause that they espoused. This is the burden of several stories in *The Ways of White Folks*. Before approaching the book itself, however, let us scrutinize the art of satire and familiarize ourselves with the principal devices which the skilled practitioner must have at his command.

All commentators seem to agree that the indispensable feature of satire is attack. Its ancient source in magic spells, incantations, maledictions, imprecations, and the like, is evidence of its aggressive properties. The metaphors in which we represent the genre—cutting or dissecting, lashing or scourging, blistering or biting—expose it as an act of animosity. The satirical impulse, which springs from a sense of personal injury, is at bottom a form of personal revenge. But such is our abhorrence of vindictiveness that the satirist is forced, if he would cultivate the good opinion of mankind, to cool his anger, simulate detachment, and universalize his theme.

To this end the satirist assumes a mask, or creates a public persona, whose chief characteristic is an ingratiating sense of humor. He poses as an amiable fellow: a man of good humor, easy laughter, and ready wit. In point of fact, his laughter is invariably tinged with malice. Its function is to humanize the satirist, but never his intended victim. The object of attack is held in moral isolation by the satirist's derisive laughter. The purpose of this ridicule is to forestall audience identification. For the mask of geniality and warm humanity must never be allowed to render the satire ineffective.

Satire is in short a double game. Its linguistic mode is therefore irony, whose indirection coincides with that of the satirical attack. The words do not mean what they seem to mean, and may indeed be lost on an imperceptive audience. They constitute a verbal mask which serves, like humor, to disguise the satirist's hostility. Irony functions also as a distancing device, helping to establish a necessary psychological remoteness between the satirist and his intended victim. It is irony that accounts for the coolness at the center of the art. For satire is a cool medium which, in order to persuade, must make a show of detachment and impersonality.

"For effective attack," as Northrop Frye has observed, "we must reach some kind of impersonal level, and that commits the attacker, if only by implication, to a moral standard."[13] The satirist confronts us with a universe whose moral outlines are clear and unambiguous. Good and evil are readily distinguished; standards of judgment, firm and dependable. Moral indignation is the conscious motivation of the satirist, who approaches his material in a spirit of corrective zeal. He sees himself as an instrument of castigation, a sanative agent whose task is to cleanse the body politic and restore society to moral health.

The Manichean universe of satire dictates its bipartite structure. Satire has an A-B form, with A representing the arraignment of vice or folly, and B the delineation of a moral norm against which A is judged. This moral norm, in Frye's terminology, is a *low* norm, which is to say that the satirist tends to view society from outside or below. Typically the satiric persona is an *ingénu:* "he has no dogmatic views of his own, but he grants none of the premises which make the absurdities of society look logical to those accustomed to them. He is really a pastoral figure, and like the pastoral, a form congenial to satire, he contrasts a set of simple standards with the complex rationalizations of society."[14]

The Ways of White Folks (1934) is a textbook illustration of these principles. Eleven of its fourteen tales are satires, and the rest contain satiric elements. The book was born in a sense of personal affront. Wounded by his former patron, Hughes lashes back at white paternalism in all its forms. His objects of attack include delinquent parents, domineering patrons, unscrupulous employers, and self-appointed missionaries in whatever guise. In the caustic language of H. L. Mencken (it is no accident that two of these stories first appeared in the *American Mercury*), Hughes excoriates the guile and mendacity, self-deception and equivocation, insincerity and sanctimoniousness, sham, humbug, and sheer fakery of white America in all its dealings with the black minority.

The author's personal pique is obvious enough, and to lift the curse of his vindictiveness toward Mrs. Mason, Hughes assumes a mask of genial humor. His comic muse is most apparent in such light satires as "Slave on the Block," "A Good Job Gone," and "Rejuvenation Through Joy." Hughes is a gifted humorist, but it would be an error to construe this gift in narrow literary terms. Rather it constitutes a lusty adaptation to his life circumstances. Nourished by the boundless absurdities of American racism, this humor is, by the author's own account, a matter of "laughing to keep from crying." But "laughing to keep from hating" may be closer to the mark. In any case, a humor of diverse tonalities is an essential feature of Hughes' satiric mask.

Irony, as we have noted, is the satirist's linguistic mode. Hughes is a resourceful ironist whose verbal indirections often saturate his tales. Among his favorite rhetorical devices are ironic understatement (to intensify, while seeming to diminish, the satirical attack); ironic inversion (to apportion praise or blame by indirection); ironic reversal (to add an element of shock or surprise to the attack); and ironic repetition or refrain (to create a cumulative tension that is finally discharged against the satiric victim). These are but a few of the devices by which Hughes is able to control his anger and simulate the coolness and detachment of effective satire.

Two standards of morality are juxtaposed in Hughes' satiric fiction: a white and Negro code. This division is the basis of the bipartite structure of his tales. He begins with the arraignment of a white society which constantly betrays its own professed ideals. But at some point a Negro character is introduced who embodies a different and more authentic moral code. This character—whether maid-of-all-work, kitchen boy, janitor, or jazz musician—provides the low norm by which the conduct of the whites is judged and found wanting. For the whites, despite their wealth and power, are failures as human beings, while the blacks, despite their poverty and vulnerability, are tough and resourceful and certain to survive.

The Ways of White Folks

Hughes' achievement as a satirist is clearly of a high order. Yet literary men may fruitfully debate the degree of consistency with which he attains his top form. In a recent study, critic James Emanuel compiles a list of the author's twelve best stories. Eight of the twelve titles were selected from *The Ways of White Folks*.[15] I cannot concur in this generous estimate of Hughes' first collection. I find only four stories—"Cora Unashamed," "The Blues I'm Playing," "Little Dog," and "Red-Headed Baby"—to be vintage Hughes. This tally suggests that the book is rather a promising beginning than the mature achievement that Emanuel's judgment would imply.

"Cora Unashamed" is one of Hughes' most bitter, as well as most successful satires. Written in Moscow, it was published in the *American Mercury* of September 1933; and chosen by Edward O'Brien as one of the best short stories of the year. It is the lead story in *The Ways of White Folks*, where it serves to establish the book's basic operational mode: satire of the low norm with close affinities to pastoral. Cora is the first of several Negro servants who provide Hughes with a base from which to satirize their white employers. Simple, natural, and unpretentious, these folk Negroes are forerunners of Jess' B. Semple and his signifying ways.

Cora is employed by the Studevants as maid-of all-work in a small Midwestern town. Lonely and isolated (hers is the only black family in town), she has an illegitimate child, who dies in infancy of whooping cough. All of her maternal love is thus transferred to Jessie Studevant, a "backward" child born at the same time as her own daughter. At the age of nineteen,

Jessie is impregnated by a high-school classmate of "unacceptable" social stock. Mrs. Studevant rushes her daughter off to Kansas City "for an Easter shopping trip." Jessie dies as a result of the abortion, and at her funeral the outraged and bereaved Cora speaks the truth, scandalizing the entire community.

The Studevants, who in effect have murdered their own daughter, are the targets of Hughes' most devastating satire. They are guilty, at bottom, of a spiritual crime: a false and artificial isolation, both socially and morally, from the human community. Obsessed with their own purity, they fail to respond to their daughter's predicament with love, yielding instead to a ruthless puritanic impulse to expel evil from their midst. Hypocrisy compounds the sin of pride and issues forth in tragedy. Hughes' satiric portrait of the Studevants constitutes a blistering attack on Middle America, and a crushing indictment of the value-system and life-style of the white middle class.

Beyond its power as a satire, "Cora Unashamed" affords a crucial insight into Hughes' career, whose inner dialectic manifests itself in the clash of pastoral and antipastoral. Among the elements of pastoral are Cora's simplicity; her natural (or unashamed) attitude toward pregnancy and childbirth; and the way of life that she adopts at the story's end: "Now she and Ma live from the little garden they raise (18) . . . ."[16] Among the antipastoral elements are the opening description of Melton, a rural seat of no charm whatsoever; Cora's rebellious and even blasphemous moods, which make a mockery of pastoral humility; and her disruption of the idyllic funeral service, which opens with a hymn, "He Feedeth His Flocks Like a Shepherd."

The interplay of genre and counter-genre is best revealed in a refrain concerning "green fields and sweet meadows" which appears three times in the course of the tale.[17] The first occasion is the summer night when Cora gives herself to a white lover; the second, the burial of her child, when she curses God; the third, the pregnancy of Jessie, which revives her memory of love as well as loss. These passages reflect three successive spiritual states: an initial period of youthful innocence and happiness; a time of disillusionment, when hopes are buried and the heart becomes embittered; and a retrospective phase of complicated double vision, when both attitudes are simultaneously present in the mind.

This dialectic of the soul, which constitutes the irreducible core of Hughes' art, derives in form and spirit from the blues. For the complex vision of the blues, even as it balances the claims of hope and disillusionment, absorbs both attitudes in a higher synthesis. The blues, as Richard Kostelanetz has remarked, is a "tightly organized lyric form in which the singer narrates the reasons for his sadness, usually attributed to his failure to attain the ideal role he conceives for himself."[18] The blues are born, in short, out of the inexorable tension of dream and actuality. By mediating poetically between the two, the form itself makes possible a bittersweet and retrospective triumph over pain.

The centerpiece of the collection is "The Blues I'm Playing." This story is a fictional account of Hughes' relationship with Mrs. Mason. The black heroine, Oceola Jones, is a gifted young pianist equally at home in the jazz or classical tradition. Her white antagonist, Mrs. Dora Ellsworth, is a rich and aging patron of the arts. The plot traces the successive stages of their relationship: discovery and sponsorship; increasing efforts to dominate not only the musical career, but the private life of her protégée; a crisis following the girl's announcement of her impending marriage; and eventual estrangement, after a painful, parting interview.

The dramatic conflict centers on the girl's stubborn effort to preserve her black identity in the face of her patron's determined onslaught. Mrs. Ellsworth looks on Oceola as a kind of refractory material that resists cultivation or refinement. She is in short a missionary. Mrs. Ellsworth embodies that Faustian urge toward total possession of another human being which informs so much of the short fiction of Edgar Allan Poe. This is the urge responsible for slavery and other forms of European empire. Oceola fights with all her strength to fend it off, and to establish her life on an independent footing.

"The Blues I'm Playing" is at once an arraignment of Western culture and an affirmation of Negro folk forms. The classical and jazz idioms, which compete for Oceola's loyalty, give dramatic substance to the theme of cultural dualism which is basic to the Harlem Renaissance. In the sexual sphere, conflicting codes divide the two women. Oceola has a lover she is helping through medical school, and whom she ultimately marries. Mrs. Ellsworth hopes that she will learn to sublimate her sexual desires through art. An irreconcilable conflict thus unfolds between the Platonist and transcendental values of the patron (symbolized by her aspiration toward the stars) and the earthy, down-home folk morality of her protégée.

A sublimated sexuality implies a disembodied art. Through Mrs. Ellsworth, Hughes is satirizing the otherworldly strain in Western art. He decries the separation of art from life, and the transcendental impulse to resolve all human contradictions in the vastness of eternity. Through Oceola's music, on the other hand, Hughes defines his own esthetic. Hers is an art grounded in folk sources, steeped in sensuality, and based on the life-affirming rhythms of the blues. It is a music close to dance, full of movement and expression, vibrant with the joy and pain of living. The blues is an art of paradox and ambiguity, and it is through this form that Langston Hughes has chosen to express his complex sense of life.

In the end, Hughes resorts to a satiric image. The final scene takes place in Mrs. Ellsworth's music room, whose decor is dominated by a row of Persian vases filled with white lilies. As Oceola entertains her patron for the last time, she breaks into a jazz rhythm that shakes the long-stemmed flowers in their rootlessness and artificial isolation: "Mrs. Ellsworth sat very still in her chair looking at the lilies trembling delicately in the priceless Persian vases, while Oceola made the bass notes throb like tomtoms deep in the earth (120)."

"Little Dog" is a prime example of the blues-oriented art of Langston Hughes. It is the story of an old maid who withholds herself from life, and who buys a dog to fill the void at the center of her being. Through her pet she becomes acquainted with, and sexually attracted to, a black janitor who brings the dog his nightly meal of meat and bones. Torn by conflicts over sex and race which she scarcely understands, she moves away in terror of her own emotions. The story is evocative of Sherwood Anderson in its theme of loneliness and lost potential. A delicate tale, it is suffused with a deep compassion which springs perhaps from the author's boyhood loneliness.

"Little Dog" may not seem at first glance to be a satire. But once we notice that Miss Briggs is employed as a bookkeeper, everything falls into place. That vocation, which is not without emotional significance for Hughes, is emblematic of the value system of his father. Business efficiency at the expense of human warmth, an excessively routinized existence, false pride of caste or class, a petty-bourgeois narrowness of soul: these are the targets of Hughes' satire. Miss Briggs, who embodies a sterile way of life, is the butt of a withering irony. The result is a tonality peculiar to the blues.

Pathos and irony mingle here in equal proportions. The point is that Hughes might have focused entirely on the pathetic aspects of the spinster's situation. Or he might have made her the victim of an unalloyed satire. Instead he combines both perspectives into the double vision of the blues. This tragicomic vision prevents the tale from lapsing into sentimentality. At the same time, it requires of us an expansiveness of mind and heart. For the blues specializes in the reconciliation of opposites. It will not permit us to simplify our vision to the detriment of our humanity.

"Red-Headed Baby" is at once the most caustic and the most compelling of Hughes' satires. Written under great compres-

sion, it achieves a depth and resonance unmatched in the
Hughes canon. The story is concerned with a white sailor on
shore leave in a Florida coastal town. He revisits a mulatto girl
whom he deflowered several years ago, but their present
revels are interrupted by a red-headed baby who is bow-
legged, dwarfish, deaf, and dumb. The sailor denies the obvious reality and flees from the situation. Knowledge of paterni-
ty is half-refused by his conscious mind, and yet his sudden
obsession with paying for his drinks bears witness to the surge
of guilt that engulfs him.

The mode of presentation is satiric monologue, consisting
of the sailor's stream of consciousness. An unusual technique
for Hughes, its effectiveness in this story has been ably demonstrated by James Emanuel.[19] Suffice it to observe that the
interior monologue serves to individuate the sailor, and thus
increase audience identification. Dramatic ironies do the rest,
of which one or two examples must suffice. The sailor, longing in his vanity to be distinguished from the girl's casual
lovers, is singled out from the rest in a fashion that destroys
him morally. He calls his son a "runt," but he is the real runt,
who suffers from a stunted or retarded spiritual growth.

The story is a study in damnation. In the opening paragraph, words like *dead* and *hell* and *damned* convey the sailor's
spiritual state. Like the houses of the town, abandoned after
the collapse of the Florida real estate boom, his soul is "half-
built," and "never will be finished." It is symbolic of his in-
capacity for growth that he should sire a retarded child. And a
Negro child at that! To be damned, after all, is to be cast into
outer darkness: "No street lights out here. There never is
where niggers live (122)." But above all, damnation consists of
the conviction that only other men are damned. To preserve
this flattering illusion, a scapegoat is essential. And that is
precisely the fate of the red-headed baby.

The story culminates in a powerful epiphany: "Betsy's red-
headed child stands in the door looking like one of those
goggly-eyed dolls you hit with a ball at the County Fair (126)."

In that obscene American rite of exorcism, all comers are offered three shots for a quarter at their own evil impulses, projected outward and made visibly assailable. The psychodynamics of racial prejudice are here exposed. Like the sailor piling the sins of his youth on the head of his unacknowledged son, white Americans have for generations been tossing baseballs at goggly-eyed dolls. Step right up, ladies and gentlemen: hit the nigger and win a cigar.

From Satire to Celebration

During the winter of 1934-1935, Hughes found himself stranded in Mexico City. He had come by train from Reno, Nevada, after learning of his father's death, only to discover on arrival that he was disinherited. Making the best of a bad situation, he remained in Mexico for several months, until he could make enough money from his writing to afford a return ticket. And being Langston Hughes, which is to say a true *aficionado* of the blues, he managed to enjoy himself in spite of his adversity.

Recounting the episode in his autobiography, Hughes recalls that "For me it was a delightful winter. I have an affinity for Latin Americans, and the Spanish language I have always loved. One of the first things I did when I got to Mexico City was to get a tutor . . . and begin to read *Don Quixote* in the original, a great reading experience that possibly helped me to develop many years later in my own books a character called Simple."[20]

Such were the beginnings of Hughes' faith in the impossible dream. To him it meant primarily the dream of racial equality and confraternity so often desecrated by his white compatriots. Hence the taut dialectic of hope and disillusionment that animates his work and finds its classic statement in the book of poems, *Montage of a Dream Deferred* (1951). When Hughes asks his famous question, "What happens to a dream deferred? / Does it dry up / like a raisin in the sun?" he is not only posing an implicit threat, but also paying an implicit tribute to the power of the dream.[21]

Faith in the invincibility of the dream, no matter how it might be battered in the realm of actuality, was a vital part of the black folk-tradition. Hughes captured this dimension of the folk spirit when he wrote, in a poem called "The Negro Mother," that "God put a dream like steel in my soul."[22] In his bardic role, Hughes wished to honor and commemorate above all else the endurance and tenacity and sheer stamina of black people in the face of white oppression. It was their fidelity to the impossible dream that inspired his mature work and sustained him through his most productive years.

Hughes did not come all at once to his mature vision. The deaths of both parents in the 1930's, and the composition of *The Big Sea* in 1939, prepared the way. The end of his proletarian digression (roughly 1930 to 1939) was likewise a prerequisite to his artistic growth. Relieved of these burdens and preoccupations, his talents reached fruition in the 1940's and early 1950's. The stages of his maturation may be traced in the short fiction written from 1934 to 1952, and collected for the most part in his second book of stories, *Laughing to Keep from Crying*.

In 1933 and 1934, Hughes focused his attention more or less exclusively on the short-story form. Of the stories written during this period, about half were included in *The Ways of White Folks*, while the rest, published at the time in various periodicals, eventually formed the nucleus of *Laughing to Keep from Crying*. The stories written in 1933 were retrospective in nature, looking backward to the 1920's and the heyday of the Harlem Renaissance. The tales composed in 1934 and early 1935, however, were addressed to the issues of the Great Depression, and reflected the politics of Hughes' Marxist phase.

In the spring of 1934, while writing at Carmel, Hughes was frequently a guest of Lincoln Steffens and his wife. According to Milton Meltzer, "He joined with them and many others in the protest movement rising rapidly on the West Coast. They took sides in the battles of the unemployed, of the migratory workers, of the Spanish-Americans and the Negroes for jobs and justice. They wrote leaflets and helped distribute them, they sent letters and signed petitions, they joined picket lines and demonstrations, they went on delegations to relief stations and the state capital."[23]

In the fall of that year, Hughes spent several weeks in Reno, Nevada, where he observed the hardships and sufferings of jobless and rejected men, crossing and recrossing the country in search of work. It must be recalled that from 1929 to 1934 he had been sheltered from the worst effects of the Depression, either by his various patrons or his extended visit to the Soviet Union. What he saw in Reno must have come as something of a shock. Apparently it served to crystallize his Marxist leanings, for among the stories written or revised in Reno are several of his most militant and class-conscious tales.[24]

Eight of Hughes' stories, written from 1934 to 1939, are direct expressions of his revolutionary politics. What is involved from a literary point of view is the creation of a new kind of hero. In *The Ways of White Folks*, heroes were content to establish their psychological or cultural independence of the white world. Now they move from independence to defiance of white power. The new hero may be defined in negative as well as positive terms, and this leads to two distinct types of stories. Some stories seek to discredit the servile or Uncle Tom or renegade black—the class-collaborationist or traitor to his people—while others celebrate the rebellious worker, union organizer, political activist, or incipient revolutionary.

Four of the eight Marxist tales are anti-Uncle Tom. The archetypal figure is the old man of "Little Old Spy"—the former pimp now employed in counterrevolutionary work by one of Cuba's reactionary governments. The metaphor appears again in "Fine Accommodations," where a Southern

Negro educator of accommodationist persuasion is compared in the closing passage to a pimp. "Professor," a companion piece, depicts a black sociologist who sells out to the white power structure. In "Trouble with the Angels," a famous Negro actor playing God in *The Green Pastures* tries to break a strike instigated by the cast to prevent the show from playing to Jim Crow audiences.[25]

These anti-Uncle Tom stories are of course satires. The author's satirical barbs, which formerly were aimed at the ways of white folks, are now directed toward counter-revolutionary elements within the black community. These satires, in short, are intended as a goad. Their implicit norm, which formerly consisted of folk values, now derives from a political ideology, and more precisely from a revolutionary code of appropriately militant attitude or conduct. Often this implicit norm is defined ironically through the derogatory, "red-baiting" remarks of unsympathetic characters. The net result is to heighten or intensify the satirical attack upon the Uncle Tom.

Four of the Marxist tales celebrate the rebel hero. "The Sailor and the Steward" is a pure party-liner, in which a Cuban sailor learns that individual resistance is not as effective as collective bargaining. "Gumption" is the story of an unemployed family whose members combat racial discrimination in the WPA. "Tain't So" depicts a Negro woman faith healer who cures a white Southern lady of her psychosomatic ailments by the simple expedient of contradicting her assertions. "On the Road" is the best of Hughes' Marxist fables. Set in Reno, the story is concerned with a Negro vagrant who tries to destroy a church that has refused him sanctuary in a snowstorm.[26]

Hughes' Marxist tales have an historical importance that transcends their intrinsic worth, for they represent a link between the writings of the Harlem Renaissance and those of the next generation. Their theme of insubordination (or servility turned inside out) is essentially New Negro, but the older concept has been extended to include a new class consciousness. Hughes' satirical attacks on Uncle Tom and his celebration of the rebel hero anticipate Richard Wright's more famous dramatizations of the theme in *Uncle Tom's Children* (1938). Such an observation is not intended to detract from Wright's originality, but rather to stress the continuities of the Afro-American short story.

Even at his most class-conscious, Hughes did not abandon his bardic role. While the surface waves of his art were flowing in a fashionable proletarian direction, the deeper currents were concerned, as always, with the celebration of ethnicity. Throughout his Marxist phase, to change the figure, he was never so intoxicated on red wine as to lose his grasp on black reality. The proof of his sobriety consists of six tales, written from 1934 to 1941, which stress the theme of black identity. These are cautionary tales, in the sense that they constitute a warning to his black readers not to cut their ethnic ties.

These ethnic tales, like their Marxist counterparts, display a negative and positive polarity. At the negative pole, they condemn any loosening of ethnic ties, and especially any denial of one's blackness that is based on a false assumption of superiority. Such negative attacks are again satirical: their target is the racial renegade. They are anti-assimilationist, anti-dickty, or anti-cosmopolitan in thrust. At the positive pole we find stories that affirm the group tradition, prescribe survival tactics, promote fraternal ties, and celebrate communal rituals.

Three of these ethnic tales are satires. "Spanish Blood" depicts a Harlem youth of mixed Puerto Rican and Afro-American parentage who attempts to repudiate his blackness only to have it thrust upon him by some white gangsters. "Slice Him Down" explores the anti-dickty theme: two black buddies who arrive in Reno on the same boxcar get involved in a carving contest over a "hinckty hussy" who holds herself aloof from the common herd. "Who's Passing for Who?" is a satirical attack on the cosmopolitan pretensions of the Harlem

Renaissance. Viewing retrospectively the follies of his youth, Hughes deplores the shallow assimilationism of the black intelligentsia.

Three stories take a more affirmative view of what it means to be black. "Why, You Reckon?" tests the outlaw code of Brer Rabbit against the crisis of the Great Depression, and finds it still a meaningful guide to black survival. "Sailor Ashore" is a tribute to the survival value of the dream. Reflecting Hughes' mature phase, and especially his reading of Cervantes, this tale argues the necessity of having an ideal to live by, even in the most desperate of circumstances. "Big Meeting," one of Hughes' best stories, is a celebration of revivalist religion, and an eloquent defense of its survival value to the black community.

On the formal plane, what can be observed at this stage of Hughes' career is a shift from satire to celebration. Whether writing as revolutionist or bard, in the political or ethnic vein, Hughes is groping toward more affirmative literary modes. Satire persists, but no longer suffices; its objects change, but even that is not enough. Holding the Uncle Tom or racial renegade up to scorn gives way at some point to a more affirmative stance. The satirist, after all, is precise and overt in his antipathies, but vague and indirect in his sympathies. Hughes' desire to be an advocate, proponent, or celebrant thus bursts the seams of the satirical mode.

Hughes was discovering, in short, the basic contradiction between the roles of satirist and bard. While one attacks the enemy without or within, the other strengthens the defenses of the soul. Put another way, his idealistic strain was coming to the fore. His incorrigible optimism, and his stubborn faith in the impossible dream, would not permit him to persist in the jaundiced vision of the satirist. For satire deals with human imperfection, with the limitations of actuality, with the inevitable gap between the actual and the ideal. But Hughes had learned from Cervantes a grudging respect for Perfection, for the limitless and finally invincible power of the dream.

Laughing to Keep from Crying

Hughes' second book of stories is something of a catchall, which gathers up the output of nearly two decades. It is necessarily lacking the thematic unity, tightness of design, and consistency of style of *The Ways of White Folks*, whose fourteen stories were completed in about a year. Despite its diffuseness, however, the book contains some of Hughes' finest work. James Emanuel ranks four of the tales from this collection among the author's best: "Professor," "On the Road," "Big Meeting," and "On the Way Home."[27] I would concur, except in the case of "Professor," which strikes me as too didactic (that is, too explicit and direct) for good satire.

"On the Road" is at bottom an attempt to record certain changes in black consciousness, induced by the desperate circumstances of the Great Depression. The resulting state of mind may be described as prerevolutionary. It is a transitional state in which a black protagonist abandons his former docility and moves in the direction of political revolt. This shift in consciousness necessitates the exorcism or extrusion of certain traits associated with the Christian deity. Before the black man can hope to defend himself against oppression, he must cease to identify with the long-suffering, patiently enduring, dutiful Christ-figure. The Negro's version of Christianity, in short, must be expanded to include the concept of social justice.

The hero of the tale is Sergeant, a Negro vagrant who arrives in Reno in the midst of a snowstorm. Seeking refuge at a parsonage, he is rebuffed by the white minister and directed to a Relief Shelter, where he has already been denied admission on the grounds of race. Half-crazed with hunger and fatigue, he breaks down the doors of the adjoining church. When two policemen try to arrest him, he resists, and is severely beaten. Hallucinating, he imagines that, like Samson, he has pulled the temple down. Surrealistically, a stone Christ descends from the cross and accompanies him to a hobo jungle. When Sergeant awakens in the morning he finds himself in jail, shaking the bars and threatening to break down the door of his cell.

Insofar as the story is a satire, its target is the institutional church, whose moral blindness prevents it from responding with compassion to the plight of the unemployed. The focus of the tale, however, is on Sargeant and his inner transformation. No hero at the outset, he hopes only to accommodate his elemental human needs. Deprived of even these, he grows desperate, violates the law, and emerges in the end as a potential revolutionary. In the course of his rebellion, he takes on the stature of an epic hero. The story, which displays certain features of the tall tale, depicts him as a figure of the folk imagination, like John Henry or Stagolee.

The story is superbly crafted. On the macro-level (structure), realism and fantasy are smoothly joined. Through the device of hallucination, induced by a policeman's club, Hughes prepares us deftly for a supernatural visitation. A dialogue with Christ is a risky business, but he brings it off by means of a terse understatement. On the micro-level (language), the imagery imparts a rich texture to the prose. Images of white-on-black (snowfall at night, or white flakes on a dark skin) sustain the story's racial overtones. Images of light and darkness provide objective correlatives for the moral qualities of vision or blindness. Images of stone are emblematic of an obdurate society and petrified religion.

"Big Meeting" is a moving tribute to the survival value of black religion. The tale depicts a Southern revival meeting as it moves through the successive stages of testimonials, sermon, and invitation to the mourners' bench. The proceedings are observed from an adjoining wood by a double audience: a group of white adults and a pair of Negro youths, all of whom have come to be amused. The teen-age boys, whose mothers are participating in the service, are symbolically positioned between the cynicism of the whites and the religious fervor of their parents. In effect, Hughes invites the younger generation to rise above its skepticism and achieve a sympathetic understanding of its folk tradition.

His strategy consists of disclosing the psychological content of black religion. The worshipers who rise to testify recount their troubles, both personal and racial, and close with the refrain, "But I'm goin' on!" This determination to endure is sustained by the hope of a better future, celebrated in their songs of "de Hallelulian side." The ritual itself, with its rhythmic hand-clapping, body-swaying, and "dancing before the Lord" evokes the ancient African religion and serves to fortify the black identity. The sermon, with its powerful metaphors of slavery and oppression, drawn from Old and New Testament alike, endows their lives with emotional significance and helps them to cope on the interior plane with their oppressed condition.

Much of the story's meaning is conveyed through the impact of events on the double audience. The whites, who have come to enjoy the singing, protect themselves with cynical remarks from the serious implications of the service. At the climax of the sermon they depart with a vague disquiet in their hearts. Meanwhile, under the pressure of the white presence, the boys undergo a drastic change of attitude. Half amused at first, they become increasingly resentful of the white folks' mocking comments. Placed on the defensive, they are forced to vindicate their parents' values. In the end, if not brought to the mourners' bench, they have at least been deeply moved, and thereby reconciled to their religious heritage.

A word should be said about the sermon that comprises half of "Big Meeting." Closely attuned to folk forms, Hughes draws on the emotional power, imaginative vigor, and picturesque language of the folk sermon to carry the main burden of his tale. His masterful representation of the black preacher's oratorical skill bears witness once again to his commitment to the oral tradition. Especially effective is his portrayal of the Crucifixion as a lynching. Unlike the early story

"Home," where he attempts a realistic treatment, here Hughes succeeds in *ritualizing* the lynching theme. Through indirection he gains in power and intensity, and by stressing the divine analogy generates an irony which contains the otherwise intolerable pain.

The last of Hughes' top-notch stories, and the only one to be written after 1935, is "On the Way Home." Begun at Hollow Hills Farm in 1941 and published in *Story Magazine* (May/June 1946), this tale is unique in the Hughes canon for its lack of racial specificity.[28] Since the story is intensely lyrical, depicting the emotions of a man on the occasion of his mother's death, racial designation hardly seems germane. Theme alone, however, does not account for Hughes' departure from his usual ethnicity. We must bear in mind that he had lost his own mother only three years before the story was composed. Like Dunbar, when his subject was too personal for comfort, he "neutralized" it by assuming in effect a white mask.

Carl Anderson is an office worker who has moved to Chicago from his hometown of Sommerville. Lonely, sexually repressed, and something of a mama's boy, he returns once a month to enjoy the old-fashioned pleasures of popcorn and cider with his mother. As the story opens, he receives a telegram informing him that she is gravely ill. A virtual teetotaler, he buys a bottle of wine to fortify himself against disaster, gets drunk, misses his bus, and fails to reach his mother's side before the end. More upset than ever, he rushes to a nearby bar, where a prostitute attempts to entice him to her room. Her frequent reference to "home" destroys his composure, and overcome by grief and remorse he succumbs to a fit of sobbing.

The theme of this story is the indivisibility of freedom and responsibility. Carl looks forward avidly to the new era of sexual freedom that his mother's death will make possible. But he is not prepared to forswear those infantile dependency needs that she has so unstintingly supplied. He wants to grow and to resist growth at the same time. Carl's panic at his impending expulsion from the Garden is the focus of the tale. Like many men, he covets freedom in the abstract, even as he shrinks from its concrete burdens and responsibilities. At the climax of the story, he takes refuge from his fears in drunkenness and passivity, entrusting himself to the false security of a tub of warm water.

James Emanuel perceives the story as a myth of rebirth and renewal: "It is a story . . . of a man whom death brings painfully into the world a second time, in a rebirth made necessary by a superfluity of maternal love."[29] I see it rather as the story of a man's escape from freedom. Carl is barred from manhood by his infantile emotions. An incipient alcoholic, he is far more likely to substitute one form of dependency for another than to achieve a genuine rebirth or liberation. This interpretation would seem to be substantiated by Emanuel's interview with Hughes, in which the author says, "I've known two or three people who in the presence of death go to pieces in a drunken way and think they're having a good time."[30]

If *Laughing to Keep from Crying* represents a falling off from *The Ways of White Folks*, Hughes' third collection carries this decline to the point of mediocrity. *Something in Common* (1963) contains thirty-seven prose pieces, of which nine are mere sketches. Of the twenty-eight stories that remain, twenty are reprints from the first two collections, while only eight are assembled for the first time. Several of the last-mentioned, moreover, were written in 1934-1935, but not included in *Laughing to Keep from Crying*. It is hard to avoid the suspicion that Hughes resorted to his file of rejected stories to pad out the volume.

Of the eight "new" stories, two have been discussed in the context of the author's Marxist phase.[31] As for the remaining six, written from 1944 to 1961, they are uniformly thin and anemic. They are based perhaps on a promising idea, but lacking in a robust development. Instead they display the clever plots and trick endings of the O. Henry tradition. Several of these tales are essentially refurbishings of old material. One or two, like "Rock, Church," are amusing, but lacking in the high seriousness of Hughes' most trenchant comedy. A faltering of the imagination, in short, is everywhere in evidence.[32]

The truth is that *Something in Common* was a commercial rather than imaginative venture. To reissue stories long out of print was, for the aging author, a sort of deferred-income plan. As for the more recent tales, the most that can be said is that they display the weary competence of a jaded professional. From any author who tries to make a living by his craft we must expect a certain amount of inferior work. What matters, however, when the threshing and winnowing is done, is the body of enduring work that remains. In the case of Langston Hughes, no one who has taken the measure of his best work would wish to deny him a secure place in the annals of the Afro-American short story.

Chapter 10

Arna Bontemps

IN the spring of 1970, I attended a conference on black writing at which Arna Bontemps was a guest speaker. Known chiefly as a poet, novelist, and author of children's books, he had also been widely acclaimed for a short story called "A Summer Tragedy." Thinking to spare myself many hours of library research, I asked him in a moment of private conversation whether he had published any other short fiction. His immediate response was negative, but I surmised from a certain hesitation that "no" was not the whole story.

Some months later I received a letter confirming my suspicions:

DEAR ROBERT BONE,

You asked me, when we were at Nassau Community College this year, if I had any short stories other than "A Summer Tragedy." Since returning to my home base in Nashville for the summer I find that I had written more than I remembered and that they had been kept. In fact, there are enough of them to collect, and I now have a plan to put them together forthwith. All are relatively of the same vintage as "Tragedy" and like it had been complimented but not accepted in the few cases when they had been shown to magazines.

Since "Tragedy" is now in print in more than a dozen collections and schoolbooks and pending in almost as many others, I am toying with the idea of showing them to a publisher as a book.

This is just to say that your question rang a bell, and we may get a chance to see what we shall see.

> Best ever,
> (Arna Bontemps)[1]

So much for the Pirandello irony in which criticism conspires in the creation of its own subject matter. We have subsequently had a chance to "see what we shall see" in a posthumous collection called *The Old South: "A Summer Tragedy" and Other Stories of the Thirties* (New York: Dodd, Mead, 1973). The six pieces which comprise the core of this collection were conceived in the summer of 1933, when Bontemps spent a pastoral interlude in northern Alabama. They constitute a kind of spiritual diary of this crucial episode in his young manhood. By a quirk of fate, we cannot close the books on the short fiction of the Harlem Renaissance until 1973, when these stories (save for "A Summer Tragedy") first entered the public domain.

Life and Work

Arna Bontemps (1902-1973) was born of Creole parentage in Alexandria, Louisiana. His father was a bricklayer, stonemason, lay preacher, and sometime trombonist in a New Orleans marching band. A proud man, when two drunken white men ran him off the sidewalk in Alexandria, he moved his family abruptly to Southern California. Bontemps' mother having died in Los Angeles when he was nine or ten, he and his younger sister moved to their grandmother's farm on the outskirts of Watts, which in those days was a semirural area. There, in the midst of the sugar-beet fields, he passed the memorable stages of his boyhood.

When his father took a job on the Owens River Aqueduct,

Bontemps was packed off to a white boarding school. He completed his undergraduate degree at Pacific Union College in 1923, and already dazzled by the literary life, headed for the bright lights of Harlem. Some years later he resumed his formal education at the University of Chicago, where he pursued graduate studies in English and took a masters degree in library science. For twenty-five years, commencing in 1943, he was Head Librarian at Fisk University. During his retirement years, he lectured at the University of Illinois, Chicago Circle, and served as Curator of the James Weldon Johnson Collection of Negro Arts and Letters at Yale.

Bontemps' literary career began in 1924 when he placed a poem in *Crisis*. Throughout the 1920's he continued writing verse, winning several poetry awards and placing his work in a variety of periodicals.[2] In the 1930's he shifted his attention to the novel, publishing *God Sends Sunday* in 1931, *Black Thunder* in 1936, and *Drums at Dusk* in 1939. In 1933, inspired by a brief sojourn in northern Alabama, he tried his hand at short fiction, without much immediate success. At about the same time, having become concerned with the self-image of future generations of Negro youth, he entered the field of children's literature.

The latter half of his career was dominated by children's books and various editorial projects. Among his juveniles were two award-winning volumes, *The Story of the Negro* (1956) and *Free at Last: the Life of Frederick Douglass* (1958). In collaboration with Langston Hughes, he was co-editor of *The Poetry of the Negro: 1746-1949* (1949), and *The Book of Negro Folklore* (1958). His own most notable anthologies have been *American Negro Poetry* (1963) and *Great Slave Narratives* (1969). At the time of his death in 1973, Bontemps was working on a biography of Langston Hughes and an autobiography to be entitled *A Man's Name*.

In the summer of 1933, having joined the ranks of the unemployed in Harlem, Bontemps packed his wife and child into a secondhand Ford and headed South. As he recalls in a prefatory essay to *The Old South,* ". . . the lively and talented young people I had met in Harlem were scurrying into whatever brier patches they could find. I found one in Alabama."[3] Times were hard, to be sure, in rural Alabama, but at least no one starved. Black girls employed in white kitchens brought home leftovers, while the men and boys hunted and fished in woods and streams. Sharecropper families had always raised a few vegetables, kept a few chickens, and gathered nuts or mushrooms in the woods.

Bontemps installed his family in a decaying plantation house, which had the reputation among the countryfolk of being haunted. (This haunted manor house provides the central symbol of his well-known poem, "Southern Mansion"). Later they moved to a small cottage near an abandoned sawmill that proved to be a convenient observation post from which to view Southern Negro peasant life. In these pastoral surroundings, Bontemps undertook his first children's stories, *You Can't Pet a Possum,* and *Sad-Faced Boy.* He also began the series of six pastorals which constitute the structural core of *The Old South.*

The pastoral serenity of rural Alabama, always precarious for black folks, was in special jeopardy during the summer of 1933. For that was the year of the Scottsboro trials, which stirred the passions not only of Alabama, but of the nation and the world. The countryside was permeated by an atmosphere of terror and intimidation, which Bontemps renders graphically in "Saturday Night: Portrait of a Small Southern Town, 1933."[4] Fearful for the safety of his family, Bontemps removed them to Southern California, where he boarded for a time with his father and stepmother. Pausing to assimilate the meaning of his sojourn in the deep South, and enjoying the advantages of hindsight, he soon completed his Alabama tales.

This matter of perspective—or better, retrospective—is

crucial to an understanding of *The Old South*. Black folk-life in Alabama is the thing seen, but the seeing eye is Californian. It was a natural perspective for Bontemps, who grew up in the neighborhood of Watts, and was regaled throughout his boyhood with stories of Louisiana. The structure of *The Old South* reflects this retrospective point of view. Reduced to its essentials (there are some odds and ends that we can safely overlook), the book consists of six Alabama tales, framed by three California pieces best described as personal memoirs. These pieces, which occupy the borderland between fiction and personal reminiscence, control our reading of the Alabama tales.

California Memoirs

"Why I Returned," "The Cure," and "3 Pennies for Luck" serve to establish the California perspective. Written in the 1960's, they look back across a lifetime to the period when Bontemps was a boy of ten or twelve. Their common setting is his grandmother's farm on Alameda Road, with its fine stand of eucalyptus trees, its kitchen garden, barn and pigeon house, horses and heifers. Their central character is Uncle Buddy, Bontemps' great-uncle, his father's *bête noire,* and his grandmother's exasperating brother. Once a young mulatto of extraordinary style and grace, he is presently a broken-down alcoholic, who nonetheless provides a living link between the boy and his Southern folk heritage.

"Why I Returned" is a personal essay claiming for its scope all of Bontemps' life. It is concerned with his family origins in Avoyelles parish, Louisiana, and his decision to return to the South, when he became librarian at Fisk. Loss and recovery is its theme: the loss of a green Eden from which his parents were expelled by the serpent of racism, and the recovery of that lost Paradise, not so much in the green sanctuary of the Nashville campus as in repossession of the self. For what Bontemps came close to losing in Southern California, through the shame and self-hatred of his father, was his black identity. And the curious agent of redemption—the gods working as ever in mysterious ways—was the drunken derelict, his Uncle Buddy.

At the vital center of "Why I Returned" is a vivid contrast between Bontemps' great-uncle and his father. Uncle Buddy was a source of constant mortification to Bontemps *père*, by virtue of his "don't-care" friends and his down-home ways. "To top it all, Buddy was still crazy about the minstrel shows and minstrel talk that had been the joy of his young manhood. He loved dialect stories, preacher stories, ghost stories, slave and master stories. He half believed in signs and charms and mumbo jumbo, and he believed wholeheartedly in ghosts (9)." Buddy, in short, was the living embodiment of Southern Negro folk culture.

Bontemps' father was dedicated to the Booker-T virtues of hard work and success. He was deeply troubled by the possibility that Uncle Buddy, with disastrous consequences to the boy's future, might become a role model for his son. "I took it that my father was still endeavoring to counter Buddy's baneful influence when he sent me away to a white boarding school during my high school years, after my mother had died. 'Now don't go up there acting colored,' he cautioned, and I believe I carried out his wish. . . . But before I finished college, I had begun to feel that in some large and mighty important areas I was being miseducated, that perhaps I should have rebelled (10)."

At issue in this contest for the boy's soul was his sense of roots, and thus his sense of self: "In their opposing attitudes toward roots my father and my great-uncle made me aware of a conflict in which every educated American Negro, and some who are not educated, must somehow take sides. By implication at least, one group advocates embracing the riches of the folk heritage; their opposites demand a clean break with the past and all it represents (11)." The cause of Bontemps' malaise was a father who made him feel ashamed of being black. The cure was the repossession of his folk heritage by learning to love, and even to respect his Uncle Buddy.

"The Cure" is a solidly constructed piece, consisting of a story within a story. The outside plot (or present action) is concerned with a home remedy for alcoholism, prepared by Bontemps' grandmother for her unsuspecting brother. It consists of pouring a bottle of whiskey into a bowl and filling it with tiny fish, then rebottling the tainted liquor and hiding it in a "safe" place. Theoretically, the alcoholic takes a nip and is cured forever. In Uncle Buddy's case, however, the ruse is a dismal failure. "Taste?" he asks. "Don't believe I know. I helt my breath when I drank it. Never did like the *taste* of whiskey (40)."

The inside story, recounted by the old woman in response to her grandson's persistent questioning, tells how Uncle Buddy came to be an alcoholic. Back in Alexandria, Louisiana, in the 1880's, he was courting a beautiful mulatto girl. They were on the verge of marriage when a white businessman took a fancy to the girl. Overwhelming her with gifts, he carried her away to Shreveport and lived with her awhile. When she returned, and tried to effect a reconciliation, Buddy was already a broken man. His relationship with women was permanently damaged: he became a lifelong bachelor, and in fact, a kind of eunuch. The tainted whisky, so to speak, had turned him off forever.

The story ends with a brilliant epiphany. Having absconded with the whiskey, Buddy is seen heading across the beetfields to a nearby swamp. He returns at twilight with his arms full of white flowers and his clothes covered with mud: "When he reached the yard, we could see the mud still clinging to his clothes. He seemed to be weighted down by it. The masses of white flowers were being crushed in his arms, but they grew more and more vivid in the shadows under the trees (39-40)." This striking image of beauty and degradation is an emblem of the Negro past. The two qualities, Bontemps would insist, are inextricable, and must be embraced together if at all.

"3 Pennies for Luck" is a cogent parable of the Harlem Renaissance. It recapitulates the formal history of the age by displaying, in its own structure, the crucial shift from picaresque to pastoral. Like the short fiction of his black contemporaries, that of Arna Bontemps is concerned at bottom with establishing the folk Negro as the moral touchstone of Negro life. To this end, authors of the Harlem Renaissance found it necessary to subdue their impulse toward the picaresque. Foreseeing the possibility of rootlessness, they preserved their sense of roots by enshrining in their hearts some private Arcady. For Bontemps, this green sanctuary was his grandmother's farm on Alameda Road.

The road itself, stretching from the harbor of San Pedro to the center of Los Angeles, functions as a symbol of the picaresque. Like the white shell road in Zora Hurston's "Drenched in Light," it stimulates the boy's imagination and appeals to his spirit of adventure. Even as a boy, the road makes the future artist restless, and impatient to don his travelin' shoes. As a youth, the road becomes his gateway to experience, bearing him away to boarding school, college, and the literary life. But wherever his journey of discovery may take him in the Great World of education, literature, and intellectual achievement, he carries in his pockets a reminder of his folk origins in the form of three lucky pennies acquired on his grandmother's farm.

One day, when Uncle Buddy forgets to fasten the barnyard gate, a heifer escapes into the surrounding beetfields, with Bontemps, his father, and his great-uncle in hot pursuit. In the course of the chase, Bontemps' father loses a rubber tobacco pouch containing the best part of a week's wages. Some months later, the boy discovers the pouch with its contents still intact, save for the coins, which are tarnished to a deep black by their contact with the rubber. Thereafter, through boarding school and college, through the intellectual excitement of the Harlem Renaissance, through his pastoral interlude in Alabama, and into his Chicago years, Bontemps carries three black pennies as a good luck charm.

It is crucial that the pennies are discovered in a field. Though metropolitan centers like New York and Chicago threaten to engulf Bontemps, the tarnished pennies will remind him of the black man's rural past. They will serve, in short, as a touchstone of values. Their black color is equally significant. Lost by his father, recovered by the boy's own efforts, and associated somehow with his Uncle Buddy, the pennies are symbolic of Bontemps' black identity. For despite his many years of miseducation, he ultimately comes to regard his blackness as a form of luck. This conviction—that being black is a piece of good fortune—was an article of faith in the Harlem Renaissance.

Such was the legacy that Bontemps hoped to leave to the next generation. Hence the episode concerning Richard Wright. In Chicago, during the Depression, Bontemps was compelled to part with his good luck charm: "I did it to help another young writer. His name was Richard Wright, and I met him in the Chicago Loop where he was waiting for a street car but didn't have enough money to pay his fare. He needed two more pennies (237)." Wright returned two bright and shiny pennies, "but I never told him how being without my three black pennies had hurt my own chances." Bontemps was passing on the torch to a writer, as he perceived it, of greater promise than himself. It was a courageous gesture, and a fitting epilogue to the Harlem Renaissance.

Alabama Tales

In the light of his California memoirs, we can understand the impulse that took Bontemps to Alabama in the summer of 1933. Ostensibly seeking a refuge from the ravages of the Depression, on a deeper level he was undertaking a journey to his roots—to the rural South of which he knew so much by hearsay but in his adult life had never seen. Like Jean Toomer, he felt compelled to visit the ancestral soil, to stand where slaves had stood, and to dwell for a time in the haunted mansion of the past. Miseducated by his father, no less than white society, he turned to the pastoral tradition as a means of strengthening his black identity.

Bontemps' Alabama tales are scaled and proportioned to the microcosmic world of pastoral. Their setting is the Greenbrier Plantation, which is both a green sanctuary and a brier patch. The best and worst features of the black man's Southern heritage—the flowers and the mud, the beauty and the degradation—are simultaneously on display. The beauty springs not only from the lushness of the countryside, but the spiritual qualities of the black peasantry. The degradation, in this overheated summer of 1933, flows from the legal persecution of the Scottsboro boys. On the formal plane, these tensions are reflected in a counterpoint of pastoral and antipastoral.

The pastoral strain predominates, however, in these stories of the Old South. Despite the antipastoral implications of a piece like "Saturday Night," Bontemps' basic feeling toward his Southern heritage remains affirmative, and he expresses his qualified approval of the Southern scene through the medium of pastoral. The art of Arna Bontemps, despite its superficial resemblances to that of Langston Hughes, is closer in spirit to the transcendental art of Jean Toomer. In the last analysis, what he finds to admire in the black peasantry is its spiritual force. There is some mysterious element in the Negro folk heritage, some transcendent quality that Bontemps strives to capture and commemorate.

The transcendence of everyday reality—including the reality of physical oppression—is Bontemps' essential theme. "The Devil Is a Conjurer," for example, argues the validity of superstition as a means of transforming experience into something rich and strange. "Let the Church Roll On," with its central episode of benchwalking, is a tribute to the folk religion, and especially its capacity for generating miracles. "Hoppergrass Man," which deals with peasant courtship in a comic vein, is concerned with the transcendence of violence through love. In these tales, unfortunately, the theme of transcendence is often overwhelmed by elements of local color. A deeper, fuller, and more compelling statement is achieved in "A Summer Tragedy" and "Boy Blue."

"A Summer Tragedy" is the story of an old couple who have worn out their lives farming for shares on the Greenbrier Plantation. Squeezed dry by the brutal sun, and the no less brutal plantation system, they have reached the end of the road. Jeff has suffered a paralytic stroke which has left him lame, while Jennie is completely blind. Making a sober assessment of their situation, they see no alternative to self-destruction. In fear and trembling, they dress up in their Sunday best, crank up an old battered Ford, drive across the cotton fields which have drained their substance, and turning abruptly down a steep embankment, drown themselves in the river.

The philosophical assumptions of the tale can only be described as pre-existentialist. The old couple, as Jennie's absurd little hat proclaims, are the inhabitants of an absurd universe. Images of mobility and paralysis (or motion-without-progress) suggest that their lives have been spent on a treadmill. Each year finds them deeper in debt to the owners than the year before. Even their reproductive efforts have been futile, for they have lived to see the deaths of five grown children. Yet out of the absurd circumstances of their lives they have wrested a Sisyphean triumph, rolling their heavy stone up the hill again and again, in the face of certain defeat.

The story ends with a powerful epiphany. The car, having dropped out of sight in the river, "lodged in the mud of a shallow place. One wheel of the crushed and upturned little Ford became visible above the rushing water (148)." The *shallow place* is an emblem of the Greenbrier Plantation; the *upturned Ford*, resting on the mudflat, a striking image of the pastoral inversion on which the story turns. For the old couple is morally superior to the environment in which they have passed their lives. By a final act of dignity and courage they have transcended the sordid circumstances of their lives and departed from the scene of their humiliations with their fundamental humanity intact.

"Boy Blue" is the story of a "bad nigger" who becomes a legendary figure by virtue of a deadly standoff with the white sheriff.[5] Confined to the county farm for killing his lover when she attacks him with a cleaver, he breaks jail and takes to the woods in the vicinity of Greenbrier Plantation. Following a brief encounter with a black child whom he terrifies, he is brought to bay near the old haunted mansion. He takes refuge in a shed, and drives off the dogs with a rusted corn knife. The sheriff enters with a gun and shoots the fugitive, but is himself the victim of Blue's "mad artistry" with a knife blade.

The tale is told in two parts, and from two distinct points of view. In Part I we see the action through the eyes of Little Moe, a frightened child to whom events in the adult world seem mysterious, unfathomable. In Part II we relive these events from the viewpoint of the fugitive, whereupon the mystery is dispelled. This shifting point of view underscores the psychological transformation that Blue has undergone from "boy" to man. It also corresponds to a generic shift from the pastoral to epic mode. The tale begins in the diminutive world of pastoral and expands to the epic plane, where events and impressions are heroic, legendary, larger than life.

The narrative mode is not realistic, but folkloristic, with the full range of the Afro-American oral tradition being brought to bear. Behind the "realistic" portraits of sheriff and fugitive are the archetypal figures of Brer Wolf and Brer Rabbit. Blue's desperate flight through the woods draws on the conventions of the slave narrative. When, in the climactic episode, the sheriff's gun goes "root-atoot-toot," we are reminded of the bloody endings of such ballads as "Frankie and Johnny."

"Boy Blue" is in fact something of a tall tale, and its hero is a legendary badman like Stagolee. These accretions from the oral tradition provide a fitting background for Bontemps' apotheosis of the blues hero.

Some such transfiguration is plainly Bontemps' aim. The function of the moonlight, for example, is to dematerialize the landscape, and invest the proceedings with an unearthly aura: "The moon was now directly at his back, touching the earth at the head of the road. For a moment it was as if the bright path led directly from that orb to this, as if Blue had come down that way (183)." Bontemps is groping for a metaphor with which to render the mysterious depths of Afro-American personality. Blacks, he suggests, are moon-people, from an extraterrestrial sphere. Perhaps it is a metaphor for Africa, whose ancient religions he regards as the fountainhead of "soul."

In the shed near the haunted mansion, Boy Blue undergoes his transfiguration. The sheriff is a symbol of what has to be transcended. Blue prepares by calling on the miraculous power of the folk religion, with its capacity for transport and ecstasy: "Here is where ole man Blue gotta get up an' shout (186)." His next resource is the transforming power of the folk imagination. As he slashes at the dogs, he cries, "This here is the nigger what can split a hair with a blade. This is Boy Blue what you reads about (187)." And of course he *is*. For by writing this superb tale, Bontemps has demonstrated for the benefit of skeptics the power of transcendence through art.

From Harlem to Chicago Renaissance

In a little-noticed but important essay which appeared in 1950, Arna Bontemps discusses the demise of the Harlem Renaissance. "The Depression," he asserts, "put an end to the dream world of renaissance Harlem. . . ."[6] Yet even as he laments the passing of those exciting years, he celebrates the advent of a second literary awakening, "less gaudy but closer to realities" than the first. He associates this new development with the Federal Writers Projects of the 1930's, and more precisely with the Illinois Project, whose headquarters were located in the city of Chicago.

Bontemps was himself a firsthand witness of these events. Having left Alabama in the fall of 1933, he spent almost two years with his relatives in Watts before moving on to Chicago. There he enrolled at the university as a graduate student of English in the fall of 1935. Before many months had passed, he made the acquaintance of Richard Wright, and through him, the South Side Writers Group, whose membership included such aspiring authors as poet Margaret Walker and playwright Theodore Ward. Founded by Wright in April of 1936, this group offered mutual criticism and moral support to young black writers within the framework of a Marxist ideology.[7]

Again through Richard Wright, Bontemps came to know the Negro intellectuals employed on the Illinois Writers Project. In addition to Wright and Margaret Walker, these included the novelist Willard Motley, the short-story writer Frank Yerby, the famous dancer Katherine Dunham, and two young social scientists, Horace Cayton and St. Clair Drake. Also part of the Chicago scene, though not of the Writers Project, were novelist William Attaway and poet Gwendolyn Brooks. These are the writers and the cultural milieu that Bontemps has in mind when he insists that "Chicago was definitely the center of the second phase of Negro literary awakening."[8]

Under the influence of these associations, Bontemps' writing took a turn to the left. If we examine his work prior to 1935—his early verse, his first novel, *God Sends Sunday* (1931), and his Alabama tales—we find a sensibility molded by the themes and forms of the Harlem Renaissance. After 1935, however, Bontemps accommodates to the new revolutionary mood. His second novel, *Black Thunder* (1936), depicts the slave rebellion led by Gabriel Prosser, while his third, *Drums at Dusk* (1939), is concerned with the Haitian insurrection whose leader was Toussaint l'Ouverture.

The same shift in sensibility, and much the same timing, can be observed in the career of Langston Hughes. Taken together, the two careers provide us with a reasonable guideline for defining the terminal boundary of the Harlem Renaissance. For up to 1935 or thereabout, Hughes and Bontemps work within the myth of primitivism, while thereafter they incline to what may be described as the myth of Spartacus, or the myth of the revolting slave. It is this myth that animates Richard Wright's first book of stories, *Uncle Tom's Children* (1938), as well as his first novel, *Native Son* (1940).

This alteration in the mythic content of black writing signals the emergence of a new literary generation. From the perspective of 1950, Bontemps tries to define the relationship of the Wright generation to his own: "Obviously the new talents come in schools or waves. Either the writing impulse spreads by a sort of chain reaction or given conditions stimulate all who are exposed to them. One way or the other, Harlem got its renaissance in the middle twenties, centering around the *Opportunity* contests and Fifth Avenue Awards Dinners. Ten years later Chicago reenacted it on WPA without finger bowls but with increased power."[9]

The clear implication is that Chicago, no less than Harlem, was the site of a cultural awakening. If Bontemps is correct, literary historians should be thinking in terms of a Chicago Renaissance. The issues are complex, for variables both of space and time are involved. The torch was passing not only from Harlem to Chicago, but from one generation to the next. Not all of the important work of the Wright generation was accomplished in the city of Chicago, but the new movement clearly had its focus there.

It was no accident in the history of Afro-American letters that Chicago was the graveyard of the pastoral ideal. There is something in that brutal city, physically embodied in its vast

slaughterhouses, that doesn't love a cow. And the
thing in the urgencies and pressures of the Grea.
that spared no leisure for the backward glance. The epitome
of urban and industrial America, Chicago faced resolutely
toward the future rather than the past. It was the prophetic
and visionary Sandburg, after all, who was the city's first
troubador.

Nor was it accidental that Richard Wright played the role of
undertaker. A refugee from Mississippi, he detested the region of his birth with every fiber of his being. This sentiment
was fortified by the ethos of Marxism, whose founder once
delivered a famous dictum on "the idiocy of rural life." Wright
and his Chicago group were to Afro-American letters what
the Ash-Can School had been to an earlier generation of
American painters: they made of urban realism an esthetic
mode. But that, in the American idiom, is another story, and
one that transcends the limits of the present volume.

—Metropolitan New York and Pastoral Nantucket,
1969-1974

Notes

Introduction

1. Frank O'Connor, *The Lonely Voice* (Cleveland and New York: Meridian Books, 1965), p. 83.

2. See *The Lonely Voice*, pp. 13-14.

3. Saunders Redding, "Negro Writing in America," *New Leader, May 16, 1960, p. 8.*

4. *Larry Taylor, Pastoral and Anti-Pastoral Patterns in John Updike's Fiction* (Carbondale: Southern Illinois University Press, 19715, p. 6.

5. I am indebted for the concept of antipastoral to Larry Taylor's *Pastoral and Anti-Pastoral Patterns in John Updike's Fiction.*

6. In an interview with the Washington *Post* (November 16, 1969), Sterling Brown acknowledges the influence of Edwin Arlington Robinson on his own verse. Since Robinson in turn was deeply indebted to George Crabbe, it would be interesting to trace this chain of influence from the eighteenth-century English poet to Sterling Brown's antipastoral, *Southern Road* (1932).

7. See Claudio Guillén, *Literature as System* (Princeton, New Jersey: Princeton University Press, 1971), p. 7.

8. Maya Angelou, *I Know Why the Caged Bird Sings* (New York: Bantam Books, 1971).

Chapter 1

1. William Farrison, *William Wells Brown* (Chicago: University of Chicago Press, 1969), p. 210. Farrison mentions a still earlier prose piece by Brown, published in 1850 (p. 174), but he describes it as only "germinally a short story."

2. William Robinson, ed., *Early Black American Prose* (Dubuque: William C. Brown Co., 1971), Introduction, p. xv.

3. This time frame extends from the publication of Frederick Douglass' *Narrative* in 1845 to the onset of the Civil War.

4. See Albert Stone, "Identity and Art in Frederick Douglass's *Narrative*," *Journal of the College Language Association*, December, 1973, pp. 192-213.

5. See William Wells Brown, "A True Story of Slave Life," *Anti-Slavery Advocate*, December 1852; Frederick Douglass, "The Heroic Slave," *Douglass' Paper*, March 1853; Frances Ellen Watkins Harper, "Two Offers," *Anglo-African Magazine*, September and October 1859, "The Mission of Flowers," in *Moses: a Story of the Nile* (Philadelphia, 1869), and "Shalmanezar, Prince of Cosman," in *Sketches of Southern Life* (Philadelphia, 1872); and Frank Webb, "Two Wolves and a Lamb," *The New Era*, January/February 1870, and "Marvin Hoyle," *ibid.*, March/April 1870 (Moorland Collection, Howard University Library).

6. Charles Chesnutt, *The Life of Frederick Douglass* (Boston: Small, Maynard, & Co., 1899).

7. *The Strength of Gideon* (1900), *In Old Plantation Days* (1903), and *The Heart of Happy Hollow* (1904).

8. Washington was born in 1858; Chesnutt in 1858; DuBois in 1868; Johnson in 1871; and Dunbar in 1872.

9. The notable exception was of course DuBois.

10. Some 150 volumes of local-color stories had appeared by 1900, leaving few regions of the nation without literary representation.

11. Claude Simpson, ed., *The Local Colorists: American Short Stories, 1857-1900* (New York: Harper, 1960), Introduction, p. 5.

12. Louis Rubin, *George Washington Cable: The Life and Times of a Southern Heretic* (New York: Pegasus, 1969), p. 44.

13. Rubin, *op. cit.*, p. 44.

14. See, for example, Dunbar's foreword to his last collection, *The Heart of Happy Hollow.*

15. Chesnutt is indebted in particular to " 'Tite Poulette" and "Madame Delphine," both of which deal with the subject of passing.

16. See Helen Chesnutt, *Charles Waddell Chesnutt: Pioneer of the Color Line* (Chapel Hill: University of North Carolina Press, 1952), pp. 43-60.

17. A useful distinction may be drawn between the Plantation *School,* which flourished in the 1880's and 1890's, and the Plantation *Tradition*, which transcends that time frame, extending from John Pendleton Kennedy's *Swallow Barn* (1832) to Margaret Mitchell's *Gone with the Wind* (1936).

18. "Change the Joke and Slip the Yoke," *Shadow and Act* (New York: Random House, 1963), p. 5.

19. Charles Nichols, "Slave Narratives and the Plantation Legend," *Phylon, 10,* 3 (Third Quarter, 1949), p. 203.

20. In *The Cavaliers of Virginia* (1835), William Caruthers stresses the ties between the aristocratic society of Colonial Virginia and seventeenth-century supporters of the Stuart monarchy.

21. See, for example, Ben Jonson's encomium to the Sidney family and its exemplary way of life, "To Penshurst."

22. Hubbell writes of John Pendleton Kennedy, for example, that "His literary taste was developed mainly from his study of the ancient classics and the English writers of the eighteenth century." Of William Gilmore Simms he remarks that one of his boyhood favorites was *The Vicar of Wakefield.* See *The South in American Literature* (Durham: Duke University Press, 1954), pp. 483-84 and 573.

23. Quoted in Hubbell, *op. cit.,* p. 783.

24. *Ibid.,* p. 784.

25. For an account of Russell's influence on Dunbar's dialect verse see Jean Wagner, *Black Poets of the United States* (Urbana: University of Illinois Press, 1973), pp. 51-59.

Chapter 2

1. William Stanley Braithwaite, "The Negro in American Literature," in Alain Locke (ed.), *The New Negro* (New York: Alfred and Charles Boni, 1925), p. 32.

2. See for example J. Mason Brewer, *American Negro Folklore* (Chicago: Quadrangle Books, 1968), and Richard M. Dorson, *American Negro Folktales* (New York: Fawcett, 1967).

3. Julia Collier Harris, *The Life and Letters of Joel Chandler Harris* (Boston: Houghton Mifflin, 1918), p. 162.

4. Richard Dorson, *American Negro Folktales,* p. 17.

5. Letter from Harris to an unnamed Englishman, June 9, 1883. Quoted in Stella Brewer Brookes, *Joel Chandler Harris, Folklorist* (Athens: University of Georgia Press, 1950), p. 26.

6. For a discussion of the Brer Rabbit tales which places them in this perspective, see Ellen Douglass Leyburn, *Satiric Allegory: Mirror of Man* (New Haven: Yale University Press, 1956), pp. 57-70.

7. Bernard Wolfe, "Uncle Remus and the Malevolent Rabbit," *Commentary,* July 1949, pp. 31-41.

8. Jay Hubbell, *The South in American Literature,* p. 782.

9. Quoted in Hubbell, *op. cit.,* p. 793.

10. Joel Chandler Harris, *Uncle Remus: His Songs and His Sayings* (New York: Appleton, 1880), author's introduction, p. xvii.

11. Joel Chandler Harris, *Uncle Remus: His Songs and His Sayings* (New York: Schocken, 1965), p. 109. Page numbers in parentheses refer to this edition.

12. William Farrison records just such an incident in *William Wells Brown,* p. 33.

13. For a full elaboration of these ideas, see Albert Murray, *The Hero and the Blues* (Columbia: University of Missouri Press, 1973), pp. 35-63.

14. James Weldon Johnson, *Fifty Years and Other Poems* (Boston: The Cornhill Co., 1917), p. 7.

15. James Weldon Johnson, "Brer Rabbit, You's de Cutes' of 'Em All," *op. cit.,* p. 82.

Chapter 3

1. Darwin Turner, "Paul Laurence Dunbar: the Rejected Symbol," *Journal of Negro History, 52,* 1 (January 1967), p. 2.

2. For the facts of Dunbar's life, I am indebted to Virginia Cunningham, *Paul Laurence Dunbar and His Song* (New York: Dodd, Mead, 1947).

3. These stories may be found in *Folks from Dixie* and *The Strength of Gideon.*

4. See W. E. B. DuBois, "Of Mr. Booker T. Washington and Others," *The Souls of Black Folk* (New York: Fawcett, 1961), pp. 42-54.

5. For a convenient reprint of Washington's Atlanta speech, see Arthur Davis and Saunders Redding, *Calvacade: Negro American Writing from 1760 to the Present* (Boston: Houghton Mifflin, 1971), pp. 158-61.

6. See Virginia Cunningham, *op. cit.,* pp. 134-35.

7. Quoted in Benjamin Brawley, *Paul Laurence Dunbar, Poet of His People* (Chapel Hill: University of North Carolina Press, 1936), p. 86.

8. See Cunningham, *op. cit.,* p. 204.

·9. B. Martin Justice was the illustrator of *In Old Plantation Days;* Kemble of the other three collections. The work of both is flagrantly anti-Negro.

10. See Cunningham, *op. cit.,* p. 171.

11. All three stories may be found in *The Strength of Gideon.*

12. From "The Poet," *The Complete Poems of Paul Laurence Dunbar* (New York: Dodd, Mead, 1962), p. 309.

13. William Empson, *Some Versions of Pastoral* (London: Chatto and Windus, 1950), p. 114.

14. For a full-scale treatment of this theme, see his novel, *The Fanatics.*

15. See Hallett Smith, "Elizabethan Pastoral," in *Pastoral and Romance*, edited by Eleanor Terry Lincoln (Englewood Cliffs, New Jersey: Prentice-Hall, 1969), p. 19.

14. For a full statement of this position, see *The Sport of the Gods*, pp. 212-14.

17. Cunningham, *op. cit.*, p. 21.

18. Nathan Huggins, *Harlem Renaissance* (London and New York: Oxford University Press, 1971), pp. 244-301.

19. *Ibid.*, p. 253.

20. *Ibid.*, pp. 263-64.

21. There are several other uncollected Dunbar stories, but these ten represent his significant production beyond the four collections.

22. *Lippincott's Magazine, 68,* 375-81.

23. *Lippincott's Magazine, 68,* 500-8.

24. *The Strength of Gideon*, pp. 341-62.

25. *In Old Plantation Days*, pp. 71-82.

26. Most of these "mordant" tales will be found in Dunbar's third collection, *In Old Plantation Days.*

27. See Davis and Redding, *Cavalcade*, p. 159.

28. See, for example, "Nelse Hatton's Vengeance," *Folks from Dixie*, p. 194.

29. See Thomas Nelson Page, *In Ole Virginia* (New York: Scribner's, 1887).

30. *The Strength of Gideon*, p. 24.

31. *Folks from Dixie*, pp. 29-65.

32. *Ibid.*, p. 64.

33. Prefigurations of this theme may be seen in two vignettes, "The Case of 'Ca'line' " and "The Race Question," where opposing codes of conduct—one white and the other Negro—are juxtaposed.

34. *The Heart of Happy Hollow*, pp. 3-31.

Chapter 4

1. Chesnutt to Cable, June 5, 1890. Quoted in Helen Chesnutt, *Charles Waddell Chesnutt: Pioneer of the Color Line*, pp. 57-58.

2. William Empson, *Some Versions of Pastoral*, p. 196.

³See *The Wife of His Youth*, pp. 168-202.

4. All three stories may be found in *The Wife of His Youth and Other Stories of the Color Line.*

5. Chesnutt's journal for March 17, 1881. Quoted in Helen Chesnutt, *op. cit.*, p. 28.

6. Chesnutt's journal, *circa* 1880. Quoted in Helen Chesnutt, *op. cit.*, p. 19.

7. The stories were "The Goophered Grapevine," August 1887; "Po' Sandy," May 1888; and "Dave's Neckliss," October 1889.

8. Charles Chesnutt, "Superstitions and Folk-lore of the South," *Modern Culture*, May 1901, p. 232.

9. Charles Chesnutt, "Post-Bellum, Pre-Harlem," *Crisis*, June 1931, pp. 193-94.

10. For an explicit statement of these intentions, see Chesnutt's journal for May 29, 1880, quoted in Helen Chesnutt, *op. cit.*, p. 21.

11. "Hot-Foot Hannibal," it seems to me, falls victim to the author's sentimental tendencies.

12. *The Conjure Woman* is available in paperback from the University of Michigan Press. Page numbers in parentheses refer to this edition.

13. Laurence Sterne, *A Sentimental Journey* (New York: E. P. Dutton & Co., 1960), p. 123. Chesnutt has apparently misquoted Sterne, substituting *ram* for *lamb.*

14. *Ibid.*, p. 77.

15. Letter from James Lane Allen to Walter Hines Page, quoted in Helen Chesnutt, *op. cit.*, p. 96.

16. Letter from Charles Chesnutt to Walter Hines Page, quoted in Helen Chesnutt, *op. cit.*, p. 98.

17. Letter from Charles Chesnutt to Houghton Mifflin, August 23, 1899. Quoted in Helen Chesnutt, *op. cit.*, pp. 115-16.

18. I am indebted for a sense of the importance of this story to Gerald Haslam, " 'The Sheriff's Children': Chesnutt's Tragic Racial Parable," *Negro American Literature Forum, 2,* 2 (Summer 1968), pp. 21-25.

19. *The Wife of His Youth* is available in paperback from the University of Michigan Press. Page numbers in parentheses refer to this edition.

20. *Proverbs* 5: 18-20.

21. These three stories may be found respectively in *The Atlantic Monthly,* October 1889; *The Century Magazine,* January 1901; and *The Atlantic Monthly,* June 1904.

22. "Baxter's Procrustes" is most readily available in Abraham Chapman's *Black Voices* (New York: Mentor, 1969). Page numbers in parentheses refer to this edition.

23. Cf. *Black Voices*, p. 53.

24. Cf. *Black Voices*, p. 58.

25. It is the central theme of the episode (Chapters 24-30) in which the two swindlers represent themselves as the English relatives and heirs of the deceased Peter Wilks. Throughout this episode, Huck poses rather unconvincingly as an English servant.

26. Cf. *Black Voices*, p. 61.

27. William Dean Howells, "Mr. Charles W. Chesnutt's Stories," *Atlantic Monthly*, May 1900, pp. 699-701.

Chapter 5

1. A posthumous collection of Bontemps' short fiction appeared in 1973. See Arna Bontemps, *The Old South* (New York: Dodd, Mead, 1973).

2. James Weldon Johnson is a transitional figure whose early dialect verse belongs to the Age of Washington, but whose mature work reflects the impact of the Harlem Renaissance.

3. Jean Toomer was born in 1894; Rudolph Fisher, 1897; Eric Walrond, 1898; Sterling Brown, 1901; Wallace Thurman, 1902; Langston Hughes, 1902; Arna Bontemps, 1902; Zora Hurston, 1903, Countee Cullen, 1903. Claude McKay, a slightly older man, was born in 1889.

4. Among the more provocative recent accounts have been George Kent, "Patterns of the Harlem Renaissance," *Black World*, June 1972; Michael Lomax, "Fantasies of Affirmation: the 1920's Novel of Negro Life," *Journal of the College Language Association*, December 1972; and Nathan Huggins, *Harlem Renaissance* (New York: Oxford, 1971).

5. See Wayne Cooper, ed., *The Passion of Claude McKay: Selected Poetry and Prose, 1912-1948* (New York: Schocken, 1973), p. 7.

6. The color green, as we shall have frequent occasion to observe, is the hallmark of pastoral.

7. Pastoral imagery from the Old and New Testaments is a major influence on the black imagination.

8. The second volume of Hughes' autobiography, *I Wonder as I Wander* (1956) perpetuates the picaresque motif.

9. Alain Locke, "The Negro's Contribution to American Culture," *Journal of Negro Education*, Vol. 8 (1939), pp. 521-29.

10. The fullest development of this metaphor will be found in Zora Hurston's *Moses, Man of the Mountain.*

11. See Paul Kellogg, "The Negro Pioneers," in Alain Locke, ed., *The New Negro* (New York: Albert & Charles Boni, 1925), pp. 271-77.

12. See, for example, "He Who Gets Slapped," by Claude McKay, in Wayne Cooper, *The Passion of Claude McKay,* pp. 70-73.

13. Picaresque novels are frequently advertised as a series of adventures. Thus we have, in eighteenth, nineteenth, and twentieth century examples of the genre, *The Adventures of Joseph Andrews, The Adventures of Huckleberry Finn,* and *The Adventures of Augie March.*

14. I am indebted for this theoretical material to Sara Shumer's unpublished manuscript, "The Privatization of Politics."

15. See Langston Hughes, "The Negro Artist and the Racial Mountain," *Nation,* June 23, 1926.

16. No one managed this feat with greater dexterity than Sterling Brown.

17. William Empson, *Some Versions of Pastoral,* p. 98.

18. The notion of pastoral as moral *touchstone* derives of course from Shakespeare.

19. The magazine she founded in 1925 was called *The Spokesman.*

20. For Bontemps' pastoral interlude in Alabama see his introductory essay to *The Old South.*

21. This, among other factors, may explain why Countee Cullen, who grew up in New York, chose a pastoral setting for his long poem, "The Black Christ."

22. For a full-scale study of this movement, see Bernard Duffey, *The Chicago Renaissance in American Letters* (East Lansing, Michigan: Michigan State University Press, 1954).

23. One thinks especially of *Spoon River Anthology* (1915), *Winesburg, Ohio* (1919), and *Main Street* (1921).

24. It is the same, of course, for Rosalind, who masquerades as a man in order to discover what it means to be a woman.

25. Leo Marx, *The Machine in the Garden* (New York: Oxford, 1964), p. 19.

26. William Empson, *Some Versions of Pastoral,* p. 199.

27. Zora Hurston, "Characteristics of Negro Expression," in Nancy Cunard's anthology, *Negro* (1934), p. 28.

28. Rudolph Fisher's novel, *The Walls of Jericho* (1928), which attempts to reconcile the black elite and the black working-class, is the prime example of this type of pastoral.

29. See especially Rudolph Fisher's *The Walls of Jericho* and Countee Cullen's *One Way to Heaven.*

30. See especially the poetry of Sterling Brown and the "Simple" sketches of Langston Hughes.

31. I have in mind such works as Walter White's *Flight* (1926), Jessie Fauset's *Plum Bun* (1928), and Nella Larsen's *Passing* (1929).

32. This rough hierarchy is based strictly on achievement in the short-story field. Hurston and McKay are major figures in the Harlem Renaissance, by virtue of their work in other genres.

Chapter 6

1. Notable exceptions are certain of Dunbar's dialect poems, and James Weldon Johnson's novel, *The Autobiography of an Ex-Colored Man* (1912).

2. An eloquent statement of linguistic and stylistic qualities unique to Afro-Americans may be found in Hurston's essay, "Characteristics of Negro Expression," which appeared in Nancy Cunard's anthology, *Negro*, in 1934.

3. Zora Hurston, *Dust Tracks on a Road* (Philadelphia and New York: Lippincott, 1942), p. 36.

4. This conflict, recorded in *Dust Tracks on a Road* (1942), also lies at the core of Richard Wright's autobiography, *Black Boy* (1945).

5. *Dust Tracks on a Road*, pp. 71-72.

6. *Ibid.*, p 45.

7. See "Figure and Fancy," *ibid.*, pp. 61-83.

8. Rudolph Fisher, "High Yaller," *Crisis*, October 1925, p. 283.

9. See especially "The Backslider" and "Fire by Night" in *McClure's* of August and December, 1927.

10. Telephone conversation with Pearl Fisher (author's sister), October 15, 1970.

11. These sketches, with one deletion, appeared under the title of "Vestiges" in the Locke anthology.

12. In an effort to keep up with the *Opportunity* literary contests, *Crisis* had inaugurated a series of similar awards.

13. Two juveniles, "Ezekiel" and "Ezekiel Learns," which were published in *The Junior Red Cross News*, have been subtracted from the total.

14. See James Emanuel and Theodore Gross, *Dark Symphony: Negro Literature in America* (New York: The Free Press, 1968), p. 361.

15. See Rudolph Fisher, "The Caucasian Storms Harlem," *American Mercury*, August 1927.

16. "Blades of Steel," *Atlantic Monthly*, August 1927, p. 183.

17. See "Common Meter," *Baltimore Afro-American*, February 1930. The story is more conveniently available in Abraham Chapman's anthology, *Black Voices*.

18. D. H. Lawrence, *The Plumed Serpent* (London, William Heinemann, 1926), p. 443.

19. In his autobiography, *A Long Way from Home* (New York: Lee Furman, 1937), McKay acknowledges that "D. H. Lawrence was the modern writer I preferred above any (p. 247)."

20. *The Plumed Serpent*, p. 444. For a dramatization of these ideas in McKay's fiction, see the contrast between Jake and Ray in *Home to Harlem* and *Banjo*.

21. For a more detailed account of McKay's life and career, see Wayne Cooper (ed.), *The Passion of Claude McKay: Selected Poetry and Prose* (New York: Schocken, 1973), editor's introduction, pp. 1-42.

22. "My Green Hills of Jamaica" (unpublished autobiographical memoir, Schomburg Collection), p. 55.

23. An English edition appeared in 1920 under the title *Spring in New Hampshire*.

24. "Highball" appeared in *Opportunity*, May/June 1927; "Truant" in *Europe* (Paris), 15 Mars, 1928; "Mattie and Her Sweetman" in *This Quarter* (Paris), Fall 1929; and "Near-White" in *Europe*, 15 Juin, 1931.

25. *A Long Way from Home*, p. 304. For the background of McKay's pastoral phase see Part Six of his autobiography, "The Idylls of Africa," pp. 295 ff.

26. See the character of Bita in *Banana Bottom*.

27. W. E. B. DuBois, *The Souls of Black Folk* (New York: Fawcett, 1961), p. 3.

28. *A Long Way from Home*, p. 110.

29. I am indebted for some of these ideas to Sister Mary Conroy, "The Vagabond Motif in the Writings of Claude McKay," *Negro American Literature Forum*, 5, 1 (Spring 1971), pp. 15-23.

30. LeRoi Jones is the chief prophet of extrication in our own time.

31. For McKay's empathy with the Irish and his envy of Irish nationalism, see "How Black Sees Red and Green," *Liberator* (June 1921), pp. 17, 20-21.

32. Page numbers are from Wayne Cooper, ed., *The Passion of Claude McKay*, where this story can most conveniently be found.

Chapter 7

1. See Sterling Brown, *The Negro in American Fiction* (Washington, D.C.: The Associates in Negro Folk Education, 1937), pp. 154-55, and Hugh Gloster, *Negro Voices in American Fiction* (Chapel Hill: University of North Carolina Press, 1948), pp. 180-83.

2. Marquis de Sade, "Idée sur les Romans," *Selected Writings of de Sade*, selected and translated by Leonard de Saint-Yves (London: Peter Owen, Ltd., 1953), p. 287.

3. Walrond's early reading of such serials as "Dick Turpin," "Old Sleuth," and "Dead Wood Dick" is alluded to in his story, "The Voodoo's Revenge," *Opportunity*, July 1925, p. 212.

4. Their migration from Barbados to Panama has been fictionalized in one of Walrond's finest stories, "Tropic Death."

5. See "On Being Black," *New Republic*, November 1, 1922.

6. Eric Walrond, "El Africano," *Crisis*, September 1923, p. 169.

7. See "The Negro Comes North," *New Republic*, July 18, 1923; "The Negro Exodus from the South," *Current History*, September 1923; and "From Cotton, Cane, and Rice Fields," *Independent*, September 24, 1926.

8. See "On Being Black," *New Republic*, November 1, 1922; "Cynthia Goes to the Prom," *Opportunity*, November 1923; and "Vignettes of the Dusk," *Opportunity*, January 1924.

9. See, for example, Baxter of "A Cholo Romance," Alfred of "The Yellow One," and Primus of "City Love."

10. Page numbers in parentheses throughout this chapter refer to the Boni and Liveright edition of *Tropic Death*.

11. See "On Being Black," "On Being a Domestic," "The Stone Rebounds," "Cynthia Goes to the Prom," and "Vignettes of the Dusk."

12. See "Miss Kenny's Marriage" and "City Love."

13. See "A Cholo Romance" and "The Voodoo's Revenge."

14. See especially "On Being Black" and "On Being a Domestic."

15. For Walrond's employment of the neck as a metaphor of race, see "The Stone Rebounds" and "Vignettes of the Dusk."

16. "Vignettes of the Dusk," *Opportunity*, January 1924, p. 20.

17. See especially "Cynthia Goes to the Prom" and "Vignettes of the Dusk."

18. Miss Kenny, for example, is described as the *tar queen*: what the author confers with one hand he retracts with the other.

19. Published some months after *Tropic Death*, this tale should not perhaps be viewed as apprentice work. It is treated here because,

like the pre-fiction and "Miss Kenny's Marriage," it deals with the New York scene.

20. Eric Walrond, "Imperator Africanus," *Independent*, January 1925, p. 8.

21. It is interesting to note, in this connection, that the adolescent heroes of "The Voodoo's Revenge" and "A Cholo Romance" are named respectively *Nestor* Villaine and Enrique *Martin*.

22. Eric Walrond, "El Africano," *Crisis*, September 1923, p. 169.

23. See especially James Huneker, "The Cult of the Nuance: Lafcadio Hearn," Chapter XIII, 240-48 in *Ivory, Apes, and Peacocks* (New York: Scribner, 1915); Albert Mordell, "The Ideas of Lafcadio Hearn," Chapter XVII, 237-43 in *The Erotic Motive in Literature* (New York: Boni and Liveright, 1919); and Herbert Gorman, "Lafcadio Hearn," Chapter VII, 125-35 in *The Procession of Masks* (Boston: B. J. Brimmer, 1923). Walrond is especially likely to have known the latter work, since it was published by a firm whose founder and editor was William Stanley Braithwaite, an American Negro of West Indian descent.

24. For the facts of Hearn's life, I am indebted to Elizabeth Bisland, *The Life and Letters of Lafcadio Hearn* (Boston: Houghton Mifflin, 1906), 2 vols.

25. His marriage to a black woman in Cincinnati had been a source of scandal and social ostracism.

26. See "A New Romantic," "The Most Original of Modern Novelists: Pierre Loti," and "Plot-Formation in Modern Novels," in Albert Mordell, ed., *Essays in European and Oriental Literature by Lafcadio Hearn* (New York: Dodd, Mead, 1923).

27. See especially "Violent Cremation," Cincinnati *Enquirer*, November 9, 1874, and "Gibbeted," Cincinnati *Commercial*, August 26, 1876. These pieces are reprinted in Henry Goodman, ed., *The Selected Writings of Lafcadio Hearn* (New York: The Citadel Press, 1949).

28. For this and the following brief quotations see Lafcadio Hearn, "A New Romantic," in Albert Mordell, *op. cit.*, pp. 129-32.

29. James Huneker, *Ivory, Apes, and Peacocks*, p. 244.

30. See especially "The Last of the Voodoos," *Harper's Weekly*, November 7, 1885, and "New Orleans Superstitions," *ibid.*, December 25, 1886. Both are reprinted in Henry Goodman, ed., *The Selected Writings of Lafcadio Hearn*.

31. Lafcadio Hearn, "The Most Original of Modern Novelists: Pierre Loti," in Albert Mordell, *op. cit.*, p. 137.

32. James Huneker, *Ivory, Apes, and Peacocks*, p. 242.

33. The exception is a sketch called " 'Ti Canotié" (the little canoeists), from which Walrond has borrowed the plot of his own story, "The Wharf Rats." In the Hearn version, two young boys paddle out in a makeshift canoe to dive for coins tossed by tourists from the deck of a steamer. Caught in a tidal current, they drift out to sea, are overtaken by darkness, and in the ordeal that ensues, one perishes. In the Walrond version, the boy is killed by a shark when he dives too deeply in pursuit of a gold sovereign.

34. Lafcadio Hearn, *Two Years in the French West Indies*, p. 14.

35. Lafcadio Hearn, *Two Years in the French West Indies*, p. 90.

36. For this and the following quotation, see Lafcadio Hearn, *Two Years in the French West Indies*, pp. 97-98.

37. Robert Herrick, review of *Tropic Death, New Republic*, November 10, 1926, p. 332.

38. Lafcadio Hearn, *Two Years in the French West Indies*, p. 97.

39. This and the above quotation may be found in Eric Walrond, "Imperator Africanus," *Independent*, January 3, 1925, p. 9.

Chapter 8

1. A notable exception is Darwin Turner's essay on Toomer in his book, *In a Minor Chord* (Carbondale: Southern Illinois University Press, 1971). Turner has absorbed the huge mass of unpublished materials at Fisk and brought them, in convenient summary form, into the public domain.

2. For these quotations see Clifford Mason, "Jean Toomer's Black Authenticity," *Black World*, November 1970, pp. 75-76.

3. *The Crock of Problems*, p. 28. Toomer Collection.

4. *Outline of an Autobiography*, pp. 15-16. Toomer Collection.

5. See especially the long, Whitmanesque poem called "Blue Meridian," in Kreymborg, *et al.*, eds., *The New Caravan* (New York: Macaulay, 1936).

6. Quoted in Darwin Turner, *In a Minor Chord*, p. 34.

7. Darwin Turner, *In a Minor Chord*, p. 35.

8. *Outline of an Autobiography*, pp. 58-59. Toomer Collection.

9. *Outline*, p. 8.

10. It was presumably his four grandparents that Toomer had in mind when he wrote to the editor of *Double Dealer*: "One half of my family is definitely white, the other definitely colored." Jean Toomer to John McClure, June 30, 1922. Toomer Collection.

11. Through Goethe, Toomer discovered "the world of the aristocrat —but not the social aristocrat, the aristocrat of culture, of

spirit and character, of ideas, of true nobility. And for the first time in years and years I breathed the air of my own land." (*Outline*, p. 44).

12. *Outline*, p. 50.

13. *Outline*, p. 51.

14. *Outline*, p. 61.

15. See Lewis Mumford's Introduction to the *Memoirs of Waldo Frank* (Amherst: University of Massachusetts Press, 1973), p. xx.

16. Jean Toomer to Gorham Munson, July 17, 1924. Toomer Collection.

17. These stories, most of which were never published, are in bound volumes in the Toomer Collection under the successive titles, *Lost and Dominant* and *Winter on Earth and Short Stories*.

18. For an exhaustive study of this periodical and its place in American cultural history, see Claire Sacks, *The Seven Arts Critics: A Study of Cultural Nationalism in America, 1910-1930* (Ann Arbor: University Microfilms, 1955).

19. This yearbook of contemporary American writing appeared in 1927, 1928, 1929, 1931, and 1936.

20. See "The Hill," in Waldo Frank, Paul Rosenfeld, and Lewis Mumford, editors, *America and Alfred Stieglitz: a Collective Portrait* (New York: the Literary Guild, 1934), pp. 295-302.

21. The editorial board of S4N consisted of Gorham Munson, Jean Toomer, E. E. Cummings, Thornton Wilder, and John Peale Bishop.

22. Jean Toomer to Sherwood Anderson, December 18, 1922. Toomer Collection.

23. Frank's account of this journey may be found in his *Memoirs*, pp. 102-8. Toomer, on his part, was to write in a letter to the editors of *Liberator* that the visit South with Frank was "the starting point of almost everything of worth that I have done." Quoted in Arna Bontemps' Introduction to the Harper and Row edition of *Cane*.

24. Jean Toomer to Gorham Munson, October 31, 1922. Toomer Collection.

25. Jean Toomer to Waldo Frank, undated. Toomer Collection.

26. See S4N, special issue entitled "Homage to Waldo Frank," September 1923 through January 1924, Special Collections, Columbia University Library.

27. Waldo Frank, *Our America* (New York: Boni and Liveright, 1919), p. 97.

28. Jean Toomer to Waldo Frank, undated letter, which from internal evidence can be assigned to the spring of 1923. Toomer Collection.

29. "Song of the Son," *Cane*, p. 21.

30. *Memoirs of Waldo Frank*, p. 62.

31. See Waldo Frank, "A Prophet in France," *Seven Arts*, April 1917, pp. 639 and 642.

32. Frank's title was inspired by T. S. Eliot's poem, "Preludes."

33. Jean Toomer to Waldo Frank, July 27, 1922. Toomer Collection.

34. "Karintha," for example, was published in *Broom*, January 1922; "Calling Jesus" (then entitled "Nora"), in the *Double Dealer*, September 1922; "Fern," in the *Little Review*, Autumn 1922; and "Kabnis" in *Broom*, September 1923.

35. Among the sketches and vignettes are "Karintha," "Becky," "Carma," "Seventh Street," "Rhobert," and "Calling Jesus."

36. Among the short stories are "Fern," "Esther," "Blood-Burning Moon," "Avey," "Theater," "Box Seat," and "Bona and Paul."

37. Page numbers in parentheses refer to the Harper and Row edition of *Cane*.

38. For references to the Black Madonna, see *Cane*, pp. 31 and 40.

39. *First Corinthians*, 13:12.

40. See "Istil," p. 9 (a sixty-three page prospectus for a novel that was ultimately published as the novella "York Beach"). Toomer Collection.

41. See "Commissioned to Chicago," p. 9. Toomer Collection.

42. *Ibid.*, p. 10.

43. See "Easter," *Little Review*, Spring 1925; "Mr. Costyve Duditch," *Dial*, December 1928; and "Winter on Earth," in Kreymborg, *et al.*, *The Second American Caravan* (New York: Macaulay, 1928).

44. See "Mr. Limph Krok's Famous 'L' Ride," *Lost and Dominant*, p. 121. Toomer Collection.

45. Allen Tate, *The Man of Letters in the Modern World* (Cleveland and New York: Meridian Books, 1955), p. 122.

46. See Alfred Kreymborg, *et al.*, *The Second American Caravan*, pp. 694-715.

47. See "The Hill," *America and Alfred Stieglitz*, p. 297. Italics in the original.

Chapter 9

1. *The Big Sea* (New York: Alfred Knopf, 1940) tells the story of Hughes' life up to 1930. *I Wonder as I Wander* (New York: Rinehart, 1956) brings it up to 1938.

2. *The Weary Blues* (New York: Alfred Knopf, 1926), p. 104.

3. *The Big Sea*, p. 40.

4. *Ibid.*, p. 48.

5. Hughes testified that he had never been a Party member, and I have no doubt of his veracity. From his activities and publications of the 1930's, however, it seems fair to conclude that he was beating the Party out of dues.

6. Sketches and vignettes have not been included in these figures. For the dates of composition of Hughes' stories, I am indebted to James Emanuel's doctoral dissertation.

7. For an autobiographical account of this voyage, see *The Big Sea*, pp. 101-27.

8. See James Emanuel, "The Short Stories of Langston Hughes," unpublished dissertation, Columbia University, 1962.

9. *I Wonder as I Wander*, p. 213.

10. See *The Big Sea*, pp. 326-30.

11. *The Big Sea*, p. 325.

12. See Langston Hughes, "The Negro Artist and the Racial Mountain," *Nation*, June 23, 1926.

13. *The Anatomy of Criticism* (Princeton, New Jersey: Princeton University Press, 1957), p. 225.

14. *Ibid.*, p. 232.

15. See James Emanuel, *Langston Hughes* (New York: Twayne, 1971), p. 175.

16. Page numbers in parentheses refer to the original Knopf edition.

17. *The Ways of White Folks*, pp. 6, 8, and 13.

18. Richard Kostelanetz, "The Politics of Passing: the Fiction of James Weldon Johnson," *Negro American Literature Forum, 3*, 1 (Spring 1969), p. 24.

19. See "The Literary Experiments of Langston Hughes," in Therman O'Daniel's collection of critical essays, *Langston Hughes: Black Genius* (New York: William Morrow, 1971), pp. 171-82.

20. *I Wonder as I Wander*, p. 291.

21. Langston Hughes, *Montage of a Dream Deferred* (New York: Henry Holt, 1951), p. 71.

22. Langston Hughes, *The Negro Mother* (New York: Golden Stair Press, 1931), p. 16.

23. Milton Meltzer, *Langston Hughes* (New York: Thomas Crowell Co., 1968), p. 184.

24. The Reno tales include "Slice Him Down," "On the Road," "Fine Accommodations," "Gumption," "The Sailor and the Steward," and "Professor."

25. Unless otherwise specified, these tales will be found in *Laughing to Keep from Crying* (New York: Henry Holt and Company, 1952). "Fine Accommodations" may be found in *Something in Common and Other Stories* (New York: Hill and Wang, 1963).

26. "The Sailor and the Steward" may be found in *Anvil*, July/August 1935. "Gumption" may be found in *Something in Common*.

27. James Emanuel, *Langston Hughes*, p. 175.

28. So troublesome was this feature to Whit Burnett, the editor of *Story*, that he wrote to Hughes urging him to resubmit a "colored" version! For full details of this revealing incident, see James Emanuel, *Langston Hughes*, p. 136.

29. James Emanuel, *Langston Hughes*, p. 136.

30. *Ibid.*, p. 134.

31. "Gumption" and "Fine Accommodations," written in 1935, were collected for the first time in 1963.

32. The following stories are the subjects of this judgment: "Thank You, M'am," "Rock, Church," "His Last Affair," "The Gun," "Patron of the Arts," and "Blessed Assurance."

Chapter 10

1. Arna Bontemps to Robert Bone, July 19, 1970.

2. These poems were eventually collected in a book of verse entitled *Personals* (1964).

3. *The Old South*, p. 15.

4. See *The Old South*, pp. 157-69.

5. The title of the story appears as "Boy Blue" in the Table of Contents, but as "Blue Boy" in the text. Since the main character is consistently referred to as "Boy Blue," I take that to be the story's proper title.

6. Arna Bontemps, "Famous WPA Authors," *Negro Digest*, June 1950, p. 43.

7. While Bontemps never joined the South Side Writers Group,

he speaks warmly in *The Old South* of "the heartiness of a writing clan that adopted me and bolstered my courage (18)."

8. Arna Bontemps, "Famous WPA Authors," *Negro Digest*, June 1950, p. 46.

9. *Ibid.*, p. 47.

A Note on Bibliography

SHORT-STORY collections by black Americans constitute the backbone of the present study. Some seventeen collections, published from 1895 to 1935, are listed in the Bibliography, Part A. Part B contains a list, compiled here for the first time, of the *uncollected stories* by major figures, including some like Rudolph Fisher and Zora Hurston, who made their mark in the genre without having published a collection.

Langston Hughes and Arna Bontemps present a special case. Certain of their stories, written in 1934 and 1935, were not collected, or in some cases even published, until a much later date. Notwithstanding, they belong to the pastoral phase with which this study is concerned, and I have felt free to include them in my argument.

By "Afro-American Short Fiction" I have meant primarily the short-story form. Short fiction constitutes a continuum ranging from the sketch or vignette through the short story proper to the novella or short novel. But I have tried to keep for the most part to the middle ground. Prose sketches with very slender narrative development have been eliminated, for example, from lists of stories by Jean Toomer or Langston Hughes. I have tried to feature, in short, the black writer's most substantial achievement in a well-established literary genre.

Bibliography

A. SHORT-STORY COLLECTIONS BY AFRO-AMERICAN
AUTHORS, 1895-1935:

1895: Alice Moore, *Violets and Other Tales*, Boston, by the author
(Miscellany).

1898: Paul Dunbar, *Folks from Dixie*, New York, Dodd Mead.

1899: Alice Dunbar (formerly Alice Moore), *The Goodness of St.
Rocque and Other Stories*, New York, Dodd Mead.

1899: Charles Chesnutt, *The Conjure Woman*, Boston, Houghton
Mifflin.

1899: Charles Chesnutt, *The Wife of His Youth, and Other Stories of
the Color Line*, Boston, Houghton Mifflin.

1900: Paul Dunbar, *The Strength of Gideon*, New York, Dodd Mead.

1903: Paul Dunbar, *In Old Plantation Days*, New York, Dodd Mead.

1904: Paul Dunbar, *The Heart of Happy Hollow*, New York, Dodd
Mead.

1906: George McClellan, *Old Greenbottom Inn and Other Stories*,
Louisville, by the author.

1907: James McGirt, *The Triumphs of Ephraim*, Philadelphia, by the
author.

1912: Joseph Cotter, *Negro Tales*, New York, Cosmopolitan Press.

1920: Fenton Johnson, *Tales of Darkest America*, Chicago, *The Favorite Magazine*.

1922: William Pickens, *The Vengeance of the Gods*, Philadelphia, A.
M. E. Book Concern.

1923: Jean Toomer, *Cane*, New York, Boni and Liveright (Miscellany).

1926: Eric Walrond, *Tropic Death*, New York, Boni and Liveright.

1932: Claude McKay, *Gingertown*, New York, Harper and Brothers.

1934: Langston Hughes, *The Ways of White Folks*, New York, Knopf.

B. INDIVIDUAL AUTHORS (a Selection)

I. PAUL DUNBAR
   a. Collections
      1. *Folks from Dixie* (1898).   (12 stories)
      2. *The Strength of Gideon* (1900).   (20 stories)
      3. *In Old Plantation Days* (1903).   (25 stories)
      4. *The Heart of Happy Hollow* (1904).   (16 stories)

   b. Uncollected Stories

      1. "The Gambler's Wife," Dayton *Tattler*, December 13, 20, 27, 1890. Anonymous.
      2. "His Bride of the Tombs," Dayton *Tattler*, December 13, 20, 27, 1890. Signed Philip Louis Denterley.
      3. "His Failure in Arithmetic," Dayton *Tattler*, December 20, 1890. Anonymous.
      4. "The Tenderfoot," A. N. Kellogg Newspaper Co., *circa* 1891.
      5. "Little Billy," A. N. Kellogg Newspaper Co., *circa* 1891.
      6. "Lafe Halloway's Two Fights," New York *Independent*, September 7, 1899.
      7. "The Emancipation of Evalina Jones," *People's Monthly*, April 1900.
      8. "The Lion Tamer," *Smart Set*, January 1901.
      9. "The Mortification of the Flesh," *Lippincott's*, August 1901.
      10. "The Independence of Silas Bollender," *Lippincott's*, September 1901.
      11. "The White Counterpane," *Lippincott's*, October 1901.
      12. "In a Circle," *Metropolitan Magazine*, October 1901.
      13. "The Minority Committee," *Lippincott's*, November 1901.
      14. "The Visiting of Mother Danbury," *Lippincott's*, December 1901.
      15. "Jethro's Garden," *The Literary Era*, July 1902.
      16. "The Vindication of Jared Hargot," *Lippincott's*, March 1904.
      17. "The Way of Love," *Lippincott's*, January 1905.
      18. "The Churching of Grandma Pleasant," *Lippincott's*, March 1905.

II. CHARLES CHESNUTT
  a. Collections
    1. *The Conjure Woman* (1899).   (6 stories)
    2. *The Wife of His Youth, and Other Stories of the Color Line* (1899).   (9 stories)
  b. Uncollected Stories
    1. "Uncle Peter's House," *The Cleveland News and Herald,* December 1885.
    2. "A Tight Boot," *The Cleveland News and Herald,* January 30, 1886.
    3. "A Bad Night," *The Cleveland News and Herald,* July 22, 1886.
    4. "Cartwright's Mistake," *The Cleveland News and Herald,* September 19, 1886.
    5. "Tom's Warm Welcome," *Family Fiction: The Great International Weekly Story Paper,* November 27, 1886.
    6. "The Fall of Adam," *Family Fiction,* December 25, 1886.
    7. "A Busy Day in a Lawyer's Office," *Tid Bits,* January 15, 1887.
    8. "McDugald's Mule," *Family Fiction,* January 15, 1887.
    9. "How Dasdy Came Through," *Family Fiction,* February 12, 1887.
    10. "A Soulless Corporation," *Tid Bits,* April 16, 1887.
    11. "Aunt Lucy's Search," *Family Fiction,* April 16, 1887.
    12. "Wine and Water," *Family Fiction,* April 23, 1887.
    13. "A Grass Widow," *Family Fiction,* May 14, 1887.
    14. "The Doctor's Wife," *Chicago Ledger,* June 1, 1887.
    15. "A Metropolitan Experience," *Chicago Ledger,* June 15, 1887.
    16. "A Virginia Chicken," *Household Realm,* August 1887.
    17. "A Midnight Adventure," *Register,* New Haven, Conn., December 6, 1887.
    18. "A Secret Ally," *Register,* New Haven, Conn., December 6, 1887.
    19. "A Doubtful Success," *The Cleveland News and Herald,* February 17, 1888.
    20. "An Eloquent Appeal," *Puck,* June 6, 1888.
    21. "A Fool's Paradise," *Family Fiction,* November 24, 1888.
    22. "How A Good Man Went Wrong," *Puck,* November 28, 1888.

23. "Gratitude," *Puck*, December 1888.
24. "The Origin of the Hatchet Story," *Puck*, April 24, 1889.
25. "Roman Antique," *Puck*, July 17, 1889.
26. "Dave's Neckliss," *Atlantic Monthly*, October 1889.
27. "A *Cause Célèbre*," *Puck*, January 14, 1891.
28. "A Deep Sleeper," *Two Tales*, March 11, 1893.
29. "Aunt Mimy's Son," *The Youth's Companion*, March 1, 1900.
30. "Lonesome Ben," *The Southern Workman*, March 1900.
31. "The Sway-Backed House," *The Outlook*, November 1900.
32. "Tobe's Tribulations," *The Southern Workman*, November 1900.
33. "The March of Progress," *Century*, January 1901.
34. "The Partners," *The Southern Workman*, January 1901.
35. "Baxter's Procrustes," *Atlantic Monthly*, June 1904.
36. "The Prophet Peter," *Hathaway Brown Magazine*, April 1, 1906.
37. "The Doll," *Crisis*, April 1912.
38. "Mr. Taylor's Funeral," *Crisis*, April 1915.

III. ZORA HURSTON
   a. Collections
       None
   b. Uncollected Stories
       1. "Drenched in Light," *Opportunity*, December 1924.
       2. "Spunk," *Opportunity*, June 1925.
       3. "Magnolia Flower," *The Spokesman*, July 1925.
       4. "John Redding Goes to Sea," *Opportunity*, January 1926.
       5. "Muttsy," *Opportunity*, August 1926.
       6. "Sweat," *Fire*, November 1926.
       7. "The Gilded Six-Bits," *Story Magazine*, August 1933.
       8. "The Conscience of the Court," *Saturday Evening Post*, March 18, 1950.

IV. RUDOLPH FISHER
   a. Collections
       None
   b. Uncollected Stories
       1. "The City of Refuge," *Atlantic Monthly*, February 1925.

2. "Ringtail," *Atlantic Monthly*, May 1925.
3. "High Yaller," *Crisis*, October/ November 1925.
4. "The Promised Land," *Atlantic Monthly*, January 1927.
5. "Blades of Steel," *Atlantic Monthly*, August 1927.
6. "The Backslider," *McClure's Magazine*, August 1927.
7. "Fire by Night," *McClure's Magazine*, December 1927.
8. "Common Meter," *Negro News Syndicate*, February 1930.
9. "Dust," *Opportunity*, February 1931.
10. "Ezekiel," *American Junior Red Cross News*, March 1932 (juvenile).
11. "Ezekiel Learns," *American Junior Red Cross News*, February 1933 (juvenile).
12. "Guardian of the Law," *Opportunity*, March 1933.
13. "Miss Cynthie," *Story Magazine*, June 1933.
14. "John Archer's Nose," *Metropolitan Magazine*, January 1935 (detective story).

V.   CLAUDE MCKAY
   a.   Collections
       1. *Gingertown* (1932)   (12 stories)
   b.   Uncollected Stories
       1. "Little Lincoln," *The Liberator*, February 1922.
       2. "A Little Lamb to Lead Them," *The African*, May/June 1938.

VI.   ERIC WALROND
   a.   Collections
       1. *Tropic Death* (1926)   (10 stories)
   b.   Uncollected Stories
       1. "On Being a Domestic," *Opportunity*, August 1923.
       2. "Miss Kenny's Marriage," *Smart Set*, September 1923.
       3. "The Stone Rebounds," *Opportunity*, September 1923.
       4. "Cynthia Goes to the Prom," *Opportunity*, November 1923.
       5. "Vignettes of the Dusk," *Opportunity*, January 1924.
       6. "A Cholo Romance," *Opportunity*, June 1924.
       7. "The Adventures of Kit Skyhead and Mistah Beauty," *Vanity Fair*, March 1925.
       8. "The Voodoo's Revenge," *Opportunity*, July 1925.
       9. "City Love," *The American Caravan* (1927), ed. by Alfred Kreymborg, *et al.*

VII. JEAN TOOMER
    a. Collections
        1. *Cane* (Miscellany, 1923).   (7 stories)
    b. Uncollected Stories
        1. "Easter," *Little Review*, Spring 1925.
        2. "Mr. Costyve Duditch," *Dial*, December 1928.
        3. "Winter on Earth," *The Second American Caravan* (1928), ed. by Alfred Kreymborg, *et al.*
        4. "Of a Certain November," *Dubuque Dial*, November 1, 1935.

VIII. LANGSTON HUGHES
    a. Collections
        1. *The Ways of White Folks* (1934).   (14 stories)
        2. *Laughing to Keep from Crying* (1952).   (19 stories)*
        3. *Something in Common* (1963).   (8 stories)**
    b. Uncollected Stories
        1. "Bodies in the Moonlight," *Messenger*, April 1927.
        2. "The Young Glory of Him," *Messenger*, June 1927.
        3. "The Little Virgin," *Messenger*, November 1927.
        4. "Luani of the Jungle," *Harlem*, November 1928.
        5. "The Sailor and the Steward," *Anvil*, July/August 1935.
        6. "Two at the Bar," *Negro Story*, August/September 1945.

IX. ARNA BONTEMPS
    a. Collections
        1. *The Old South: "A Summer Tragedy" and Other Stories of the Thirties* (1973).   (12 stories)

*Exclusive of prose sketches.
**Exclusive of sketches and reprints.

Index